# Praise for *Discovering Wisdom in Proverbs*

"There's no women's Bible study I recommend more than those in this series! Each time a new one comes out, I'm excited to share it with others, and *Discovering Wisdom in Proverbs* is no exception. The balance of accessibility and depth makes these studies a perfect fit for anyone who wants to learn more about God's Word."

—**Natasha Crain**, speaker, podcaster, and author of four books, including *Faithfully Different*

"As a culture, we are saturated in information but starving for wisdom. This creative and meaningful Bible study holds the cure—helping us dive into the ultimate wisdom found in the book of Proverbs. This talented team has discovered how to combine rich Bible study with beautiful art and stories. Pam, Jean, and Karla have done it again!"

—**Arlene Pellicane,** author of *31 Days to Becoming a Happy Wife* and host of the *Happy Home* podcast

"What do you get when you combine the artistic talent of Karla Dornacher, the in-depth expository teaching of Jean Jones, and the practical application steps of Pam Farrell into one Bible study? A fun and unique dive into Scripture that is neither stuffy nor fluffy. This study will help you have the godly wisdom you have always longed for."

—**Sharon Jaynes,** conference speaker and author of 25 books, including *When You Don't Like Your Story* and *The Power of a Woman's Words.*

"As a church prayer coordinator, I often receive prayer requests to send out to our prayer team that ask for wisdom for decisions or complicated relationship issues. God's Word is filled with wisdom that can guide our hearts, minds, and souls. So I was delighted to see that the newest Bible study in the Discovering the Bible series is *Discovering Wisdom in Proverbs*. I love everything about this book and this whole series—the strong teaching, the questions that make me dig into Scripture, the personal reflections, and the varied opportunities to express myself creatively. As with the earlier Bible studies in this series, this new one truly teaches the book of Proverbs, and readers will grow in faith and understanding as they dig into its richness. I recommend it highly!"

—**Janet Holm McHenry,** author of 25 books, including the bestselling *PrayerWalk* and *The Complete Guide to the Prayers of Jesus*

"I have always been magnetically attracted to the book of Proverbs in the Old Testament. It sets forth ancient wisdom that was meant to be passed from generation to generation. One of the most refreshing approaches to study Proverbs in our generation is this new volume by Farrel, Jones, and Dornacher. Not only do they distill and explain the wisdom of Proverbs, but they also present their study with style and beauty that enhances the whole experience. If your church or Bible study group is looking for a study that will generate measurable results in people's lives, then *Discovering Wisdom in Proverbs* is the perfect choice."

—**Craig J. Hazen, PhD,** professor of apologetics, Talbot School of Theology, Biola University

"*Discovering Wisdom in Proverbs* is not your average Bible study. It provides historical background, cultural context, and a deep dive into the meanings of words and phrases based on the original language. All of this, combined with teachings about how to apply the insights learned and creative ways to remember them, guarantees another winner from this amazing writing trio."

—**Grace Fox,** podcaster, Bible teacher, and author of *Fresh Hope for Today*

# DISCOVERING WISDOM IN PROVERBS

## PAM FARREL & JEAN E. JONES
### author & KARLA DORNACHER
illustrator

HARVEST HOUSE PUBLISHERS
EUGENE, OREGON

Cover design by Bryce Williamson

Cover illustrations by Karla Dornacher

Cover photo © tomograf, (RF) royalty free, Andrea Colarieti / Getty Images

Interior design by Janelle Coury

The artist grants permission for the artwork and coloring pages to be reproduced for personal and small group use. Duplication or distribution for other purposes must be approved by Harvest House Publishers.

For bulk, special sales, or ministry purchases, please call 1-800-547-8979. Email: Customerservice@hhpbooks.com

 This logo is a federally registered trademark of the Hawkins Children's LLC. Harvest House Publishers, Inc., is the exclusive licensee of this trademark.

# Discovering Wisdom in Proverbs

Copyright © 2023 by Pam Farrel's devotion text © Pam Farrel, Creative Connection Text © Karla Dornacher, All other text © Jean E. Jones, Illustrations © Karla Dornacher
Published by Harvest House Publishers
Eugene, Oregon 97408
www.harvesthousepublishers.com

ISBN 978-0-7369-8147-7 (pbk)

**Printed in the United States of America**

23 24 25 26 27 28 29 30 31 / CM / 10 9 8 7 6 5 4 3 2 1

## Dedication

To all those joining us in this journey to discover wisdom:

Welcome! May your journey through Proverbs be richly rewarded as you grow in wisdom and lean ever more on your heavenly Father. May your relationships thrive, and may God's blessings on your life be abundant.

~ All of us

To our *Immanuel,* God with us, giving your power, provision, and peace when I most need it (Matthew 1:23). To ministering angels who watch over me (Hebrews 1:14). To the medical team of Los Robles: you are life-giving. To my faithful friends for your prayers and tangible support. To my beloved husband: your love carries me when in good times and hard times (1 John 4:19). To the *Harvest House* team for ministry opportunities. To my mom and all my mentors for pouring godly wisdom into my heart, mind, and life (2 Timothy 2:2). Thank you!

~ Pam

To Gloria Thompson, who first invited me to be part of women's ministry and who imparted so much wisdom to me: Thank you! To Clay, your love, help, and wisdom made this book possible.

~ Jean E.

To Cindy Nellis, who invited me to my very first Bible study, and the dear woman who hosted it in her home. I may have forgotten your name, but I will never forget how God used you to introduce me to Jesus and the Wisdom of his Word that forever changed the course of my life.

~ Karla

# Contents

## Do You Want to Find Wisdom in Proverbs?

In high school, I read a chapter of Proverbs each day for a year. There's something beneficial about reading advice on a dozen or so unrelated topics—one is sure to address whatever is going on in life at that moment. But reading Proverbs topically also helps because it allows us to meditate on a topic more broadly and observe the nuances that are part of wisdom.

So in this journey through the book of Proverbs, we'll do both. Proverbs begins and ends with long poems we'll examine verse by verse. Between those long poems are miscellaneous proverbs. For these, each chapter's Day 1 lesson will guide us into reading several chapters straight through, and the Day 2 to Day 5 lessons will pick up one or more themes from the reading and develop them topically, bringing in related proverbs.

I've chosen *The New International Version* as the primary Bible translation for this study because for Proverbs, "the one who" often captures the meaning better than "the man who."

We're glad you're joining us for this journey of discovering wisdom in Proverbs. It's packed full of life-changing insights and down-to-earth counsel. Expect your relationships with God, family, friends, and colleagues to flourish.

### Why We Wrote This Discovery Book for You

Pam, Karla, and I (Jean), with our different paths and gifts, have connected over our love for interacting with God's Word and encouraging others to experience the hope of his promises and faithfulness.

With love,

Jean F., Pam, Karla

## The Treasures in Each Chapter

We collaborated on this book to inspire *you*. Here's what you'll find in every chapter.

### Daily Lessons—Jean

You'll hear from me throughout this journey. In each chapter, I share an introduction to our main topic and five daily lessons that will take 20 to 25 minutes to finish. Each Day 1 lesson will guide you through reading approximately three chapters in Proverbs. The Day 2 to Day 5 lessons take an in-depth look at topics from the reading. Each Day 5 lesson concludes by guiding you in a private time of worship and prayer. The lessons use these icons:

> ♥ This personal question is designed to help you apply what you're learning and to spark a rich discussion if you're engaging in the study with friends.

> ☁ This activity guides you in prayer and worship.

> 🖥 This is an activity with further instructions on DiscoveringTheBibleSeries.com.

### The Little Details—Jean

Along the way you'll see sidebars titled The Little Details. These are extra insights for seasoned Christians and those who thrive on details.

### Pam's Simply Beautiful Wisdom—Pam

Pam's devotionals invite you to rest in God's strength and love. She shares some of her go-to ways for remembering and holding on to the wisdom of Proverbs. She'll take you forward with faith and hope.

### Karla's Creative Connection—Karla

You'll hear from Karla at the end of each chapter. She'll encourage you to connect creatively with God and others as you delight in his eternal wisdom throughout this study.

### Illustrations—Karla

The bookmarks and coloring pages will help you connect with God's Word as you spend time coloring and meditating on each verse. You can also slip designs under a page in your Bible, sketchbook, or journal for tracing.

### Creative Ideas—All of Us

I've listed creative ideas at the end of each Day 1 lesson. Additionally, the Creative Ideas appendix offers more ways to express, experience, and meditate on Scripture passages. Discover your favorites! Use them to etch God's eternal wisdom on your heart.

## Discover More on DiscoveringTheBibleSeries.com

🖥 Here are the extras you'll find on our website.

- Instructions for how to use this discovery book for both small groups and individual study
- A small group leaders guide
- Links to worship music
- Links to articles that go deeper into chapter topics

## Chapter 1

# Proverbs 1:1–3:35
## The First Step to Wisdom

How do we pursue wisdom?

## Day 1

### Discover Proverbs' Blessings

My then boyfriend and now husband, Clay, gave me (Jean) a white faux leather Bible for my seventeenth birthday—my first Bible that included the Old Testament. Then he suggested we read a chapter of Proverbs each day according to the day of the month along with whatever else we were reading in our Bibles. That was easy because Proverbs contains 31 chapters.

Proverbs changed our lives.

Clay accepted Jesus as Lord just two days before he turned 13. I did likewise around my fifteenth birthday. But neither of us had been raised in a Christian home, and we discovered we had numerous habits that godly wisdom exhorted us to change.

Being teenagers, the instructions on sexual temptation jumped out as relevant. The relationship advice compelled both of us to alter how we treated people, especially each other. And the guidance about conversations transformed our speech.

I pray Proverbs will do the same for you.

**What Is a Proverb?**

As a child, I loved *Aesop's Fables*. The delightful animal tales concluded with a life lesson in the form of a proverb. For example, "The Fox & the Grapes" ended with "There are many who pretend to despise and belittle that which is beyond their reach."[1] And who can forget the moral of "The Hare & the Tortoise": "The race is not always to the swift" (which, incidentally, comes from Ecclesiastes 9:11)?[2]

Additionally, we've all heard proverbs like "The early bird catches the worm" and "A penny saved is a penny earned." These short, memorable sayings make it easy to recall important principles.

1. ♥ What's a saying you heard growing up? Or what was your favorite story in *Aesop's Fables*? *"The best laid plans of mice and men are sure to go astray."*

The book of Proverbs contains pithy adages like those above. They, too, teach valuable lessons. Unlike folk wisdom, however, the love of God and his truth undergird the proverbs in the Bible.

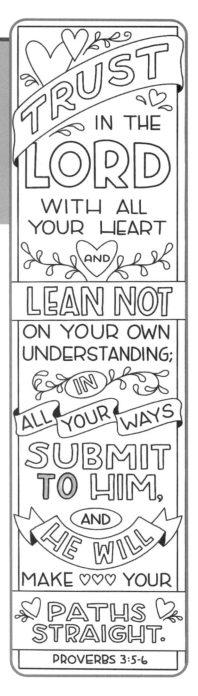

TRUST IN THE LORD WITH ALL YOUR HEART AND LEAN NOT ON YOUR OWN UNDERSTANDING; IN ALL YOUR WAYS SUBMIT TO HIM, AND HE WILL MAKE YOUR PATHS STRAIGHT. PROVERBS 3:5-6

## The Little Details
### The Wisdom Books

*Job* examines why bad things sometimes happen to people who love God, obey his commands, and repent when they sin. It begins and ends with prose, while the rest of the book is poetry.

*Psalms* is entirely poetry with optional titles. It contains a dozen or so wisdom psalms, such as Psalms 1; 19; 32; 34; 37; 49; 73; 112; 119; 127; 128; and 133.

*Proverbs* consists of pithy statements that offer practical advice for life. Discourses bookmark miscellaneous advice.

*Ecclesiastes* reflects poetically on the meaning of life.

*Song of Songs* is not technically wisdom but rather love poems. Some interpret it allegorically as reflecting Christ's love for the church.

## How Should We Read Proverbs?

When I first read Proverbs as a teenager, I was confused. I knew some of the proverbs in *Aesop's Fables* were general truisms. For instance, "A kindness is never wasted" from "The Lion & the Mouse" is often but not always true—at least from a solely human perspective. In other words, they're not promises.

But what about the book of Proverbs? Since Jesus called the Bible "the word of God," should I interpret all the proverbs as promises?[3]

The answer is no, we can't treat all the proverbs as promises, because proverbs by nature are general truisms. For example, many biblical proverbs communicate the benefits of living God's way and the hazards of not doing so. These wise sayings accurately reflect real-life consequences, but we all experience exceptions. In fact, the book of Job examines those exceptions and asks why bad things sometimes happen to those who love and obey God.

Additionally, a short proverb on a subject like finances won't tell us all there is to know about the topic. Other proverbs provide nuance and perspective.

Nonetheless, some proverbs read like promises because they *are* promises. Promises in other Bible books anchor these proverbs as promises.

## Who Wrote Proverbs?

When we want wisdom, we need to know whether the person from whom we're seeking advice is wise, right? So let's check out the author of Proverbs. It's easy to do because the book begins with a title that includes the author's name. In this study book, we'll circle blessings and box names and categories of people. That will make it easy to glance through pages to find blessings and to whom they're given.

2. In Proverbs 1:1 below, circle what the book contains and box the author's name.

1:1 The proverbs of Solomon son of David, king of Israel.

Titles show that Solomon wrote three of the seven collections in the book and may have collected the proverbs in two others. Others authored the final two collections.

Solomon was the son of King David and Bathsheba. At God's command, David bypassed his older sons and crowned young Solomon to co-reign with him.

After David died, God appeared to Solomon in a dream and told him to ask for whatever he wanted.

3. For what two blessings did Solomon ask in 2 Chronicles 1:10?

wisdom & knowledge

God was pleased with Solomon's request. Here's his reply in 2 Chronicles 1:11-12:

> Since this is your heart's desire and you have not asked for wealth, possessions or honor, nor for the death of your enemies, and since you have not asked for a long life but for wisdom and knowledge to govern my people over whom I have made you king, therefore wisdom and knowledge will be given you. And I will also give you wealth, possessions and honor, such as no king who was before you ever had and none after you will have.

That tells us something important: Asking God for wisdom pleases him.

4. (a) According to James 1:5, what should you do if you lack wisdom? (b) Will God find fault with that? (c) What will he do?

ask Him

God granted Solomon so much wisdom that the queen of Sheba heard about it and traveled many miles to test him. So yes, Solomon is a worthy wisdom teacher.

## How Is Proverbs Arranged?

Proverbs contains seven collections of proverbs, each with an introductory title.

I. Preamble and Prologue (1:1–9:18)

II. Proverbs of Solomon (10:1–22:16)

III. Thirty Sayings of the Wise (22:17–24:22)

IV. Further Sayings of the Wise (24:23-34)

V. More Proverbs of Solomon (25:1–29:27)

VI. Sayings of Agur (30:1-35)

VII. Sayings of King Lemuel and His Mother (31:1-31)[5]

The first collection is a lengthy, nine-chapter discourse that introduces us to wisdom. We'll read the first third of that introduction today, so let's jump in!

## God's Word to Us in Proverbs

Take a moment to pray for insight as you read God's Word.

5. ♥ Read chapters 1–3 in Proverbs. (a) What stood out to you in your reading? Why? (b) How can you apply that insight to your life this week?

That's it for today. In this lesson we discovered what a proverb is, how to read Proverbs, who wrote Proverbs, and how Proverbs is arranged. In our next lesson we'll learn the book of Proverbs' purpose and which verse is its motto.

💻 Go to DiscoveringTheBibleSeries.com for extras that accompany the chapters in this discovery book.

## The Little Details
### For Budding Poets

For those of you who love to write, I provide tips on engaging with Scripture through writing poetry, proverbs, and psalms in a sidebar with the Day 1 lessons. I also provide examples at the end of those lessons.

You'll find a poem at the end of this Day 1 lesson. It's a **quatrain**, meaning it uses a rhyming pattern of *abab cdcd*, and so on. The poem's lines are **anapestic trimeter**. *Anapest* means the meter has two light stresses followed by a heavy stress. *Trimeter* means there are three metrical feet (that is, three groups of two light and one heavy stresses). Here's the first line with stressed syllables in bold and a bar between metrical feet:

In the **Lord** | trust with **all** | of your **heart**.

### Types of Metrical Feet

To write your own poem, choose from any of these:

*Iamb*: light stress followed by heavy stress

*Trochee*: heavy stress followed by light stress

*Dactyl*: heavy stress followed by two light stresses

*Anapest*: two light stresses followed by a heavy stress

*Spondee*: two equal stresses[4]

# Pam's Simply Beautiful Wisdom

*The one who gets wisdom loves life; the one who cherishes understanding will soon prosper.*

Proverbs 19:8

My husband, Bill, and I have teamed for ministry during our entire married life—42 years at the writing of this book. Our ministry is Love-Wise, and we like to say we park ourselves at the corner of God's love and God's wisdom. Proverbs 19:8 is our theme verse, and if you looked it up in the original Hebrew (and added in the definitions of key words), it would read something like this: "He who acquires [procures to own] wisdom loves [has affection for] himself [own soul, life, and desires]. The one who safeguards [puts a hedge around, a guard of protection] understanding [intelligence, caprice or the impulsive change of mind or action] will find [attain, acquire, meet up with] success [the pleasant, agreeable, and good].

Now, this word *good* is first seen in Genesis when God created everything and pronounced it was *tob*. After studying *tob* throughout the Old Testament, I like to summarize its meaning as "good: beautiful, best, bountiful, and blessed." Isn't that the kind of life we all long for?[6]

Wisdom in this verse is the center of a person, the place where the heart, feelings, and intellect are stored. In Psalm 111:10, we're reminded that "the fear of the Lord is the beginning of wisdom." So when we plant an awe of the Creator in our center, like a seed, wisdom can grow and blossom.

How, then, can we gain godly wisdom? James 1:5 says, "If any of you lacks wisdom, you should ask God, who gives generously to all without finding fault, and it will be given to you." I call this verse "cupcake theology," because when we lack [fall behind or fall short] in our wisdom [skill, insight, or intelligence], we can ask, request, or petition wisdom from God, and he gives it *generously, bountifully, liberally,* and *graciously* in a simple, understandable, uncomplicated way—holding nothing back! So the way God gives wisdom reminds me of that thick, sweet, delicious frosting on top of our favorite cupcake. Even when we ask of him over and over, God's voice is sweet, and he gives wisdom without reproach, meaning he doesn't curse, insult, mock, blame, or punish us—even if we didn't apply or handle his wisdom well the times we asked before.

This week, make or buy a cupcake and enjoy thanking God for his wisdom as you enjoy this Bible study.

We can be thankful that God lavishes us with his wisdom, because we need it. While doing research for my book *7 Simple Skills for Every Woman: Success in Keeping Everything Together*, I learned that the average person has to make from five thousand to twenty-five thousand decisions a day! While some choices are simple (eat this or that, park here or there), many are complicated. So Bill and I have spent most of our ministry years helping people not just learn the verses in God's Word but also how to apply them to their daily lives.

In our *Simple Skills* teaching, we share decision-making tests, the first being the ***Obvious Test***.

Ask yourself, *Is this decision so obvious that I'm wasting time thinking about it?* Some decisions are obvious because either God has clearly spoken to the area in question or they're generally accepted as best practices. If you overthink these decisions, you become needlessly sidetracked and train yourself to stall when you ought to push forward.

Consider these obvious decision examples based on the best practices in life:

- Get out of bed. Get dressed. Brush your teeth.
- If a police car's lights start flashing behind you, pull over.
- Regularly get a good night's sleep.

- If someone does something nice, say "Thank you."

Here are a few of the most obvious decisions clearly directed by the One who made us:

- Put God's Word into your mind in some way every day (Romans 12:2; Psalm 1:1-3).
- Choose what's good over what's evil (Romans 12:9).
- When faced with sexual temptation, run away from it (1 Thessalonians 4:3-8).
- When you're inclined to worry, pray instead (Philippians 4:6-7).
- In the midst of every situation, find a way to give thanks (1 Thessalonians 5:16-18).
- Confess sin as soon as you're aware of it (1 John 1:9).
- Choose your friends wisely (1 Corinthians 15:33).[7]

When you train yourself to do the obvious, you develop healthy habits that become automatic. These habits make you more efficient as they conserve your energy for more complex choices. They also raise your confidence level as success in simple tasks builds a positive track record for the decisions that aren't as obvious.

Elisabeth Elliot was a young woman when her missionary husband, Jim, was martyred in the jungles of Ecuador, leaving her with an infant daughter. Elisabeth made a "do the obvious" statement when she adopted this simple decision-making principle: "Do the next thing."[8] Love the next person. Care for the next need. Answer the next call. She moved from a life that was unraveling to a strong, vibrant life and ministry by simply doing the next thing.

I often remind myself to *Just do the next thing!*—especially when waiting for a door of opportunity to open or wishing for more details on the path God has led me.

*Pam*

## Experiencing Scripture Creatively (Optional)

Experiencing Scripture through multiple means helps plant its messages in us so we better remember its truths. It also gives us more ways to draw near to God in worship.

The Creative Ideas appendix lists many ways you can engage with Scripture creatively. Peruse them for inspiration when you have a little extra time. In addition, I (Jean) suggest ideas tailored to each chapter at the end of the Day 1 lessons, like these:

- Color Karla's full-page illustration at the end of this chapter while repeating the words of the verse aloud. (Bonus: This is an easy and fun way to memorize Scripture!)

- Color the sidebar toppers using distinct color schemes. Use your favorite on the bookmark on this chapter's opening page.

- Choose a verse that stood out to you from what you read today, then follow Karla's instructions at the end of the chapter to creatively connect with it.

- Write a poem concerning one or more proverbs from this chapter. Add a title that identifies the contents and includes your name, similar to Proverbs 1:1. Here's an example:

  *A poem of Jean concerning Proverbs 3:5-6.*
  In the Lord trust with all of your heart.
  On your own understanding lean not.
  From his ways let your steps not depart,
  and your paths he will straighten as ought.

## The Little Details

**The Queen of Sheba's Assessment of Solomon in 2 Chronicles 9:5-8:**

She said to the king, "The report I heard in my own country about your achievements and your wisdom is true. But I did not believe what they said until I came and saw with my own eyes. Indeed, not even half the greatness of your wisdom was told me; you have far exceeded the report I heard. How happy your people must be! How happy your officials, who continually stand before you and hear your wisdom! Praise be to the LORD your God, who has delighted in you and placed you on his throne as king to rule for the LORD your God. Because of the love of your God for Israel and his desire to uphold them forever, he has made you king over them, to maintain justice and righteousness."

---

*Day 2*

# Discover Proverbs' Purpose

Another thing that initially confused me about Proverbs was the repetition. Since most verses have two parts, were the people in the two parts the same people or different people? My problem was I didn't understand Hebrew poetry!

Let's take a quick look at how Hebrew poetry works.

## Understand Hebrew Poetry

Except for the titles that introduce the seven collections, the proverbs are poetry. Hebrew poetry doesn't rhyme, but it does order words in a way that emphasizes the poet's point. Most poetic lines have two segments with parallel elements. Proverbs 1:2 below is an example of a single poetic line with two segments. Here, I've labeled the line segments *a* and *b*:

a     For gaining wisdom and instruction;
b          for understanding words of insight

Notice that the phrase *for gaining* is parallel to *for understanding*, and the phrase *wisdom and instruction* is parallel to *words of insights*. Hebrew poetry invites us to compare and contrast elements. In this case, segment *b* expands on segment *a*. Most Bible translations indent all but the first segment of a poetic line, as I have above.

## Get to Know Proverbs

Chapters 1–9 are the first collection of proverbs and introduce the entire book. The collection contains speeches, each of which is a poem.

### The Preamble: How Will Proverbs Help Us?

I've printed some verses so you can practice working with line segments without worrying about differences in translations. Let's examine Proverbs' preamble in verses 2-7 of chapter 1. There, Solomon tells us why he produced the book.

> **6.** In Proverbs 1:2a below, circle the two things you can gain from Proverbs. Circle the one additional thing you can gain in 2b.
>
> 1:2     For gaining wisdom and instruction;
>              for understanding words of insight.

We sometimes need wisdom to understand insightful words, don't we?

> **7.** In Proverbs 1:3 below, circle what you can receive from Proverbs (3a) and what you will then be able to do (3b).
>
> 1:3     For receiving instruction in prudent behavior,
>              doing what is right and just and fair.

The Bible's commands tell us the big picture of what God wants us to do. The proverbs teach us how to wisely act in areas the commands may not cover.

Solomon next tells us about two types of people his book will help.

8. In Proverbs 1:4 below, circle three things the book of Proverbs gives. Box the two words describing those who need Proverbs.

> 1:4 For giving <u>prudence</u> to those who are simple,
> <u>knowledge</u> and <u>discretion</u> to the young—

Remember how initially I was confused when a proverb used two descriptions of people? If the descriptions are parallel and not contrasted, then they're usually the same person. In verse 4, *simple* and *young* are parallel and do indeed describe the same person. All youths start out naive, not knowing right from wrong or good from bad. In fact, the first collection of proverbs is addressed to youths in need of parental guidance. It has plenty of gems to help adults of all ages, though, as we'll see in the next verse.

9. Read Proverbs 1:5. (a) For what two types of people did Solomon write? (b) What can they gain from Proverbs? *the wise, those with understanding — more wisdom, guidance*

Solomon also wrote Proverbs for the wise. Throughout the book, he uses several terms to describe the wise, including *discerning, prudent, righteous, upright, generous,* and *diligent.* Whether you're simple or wise, Proverbs can help you.

10. Read Proverbs 1:6. What four things does Proverbs help people understand? *explore the meaning*

Next Solomon imparts his first word of wisdom and names a third people category. We'll underline wise actions and wavy-underline foolish actions.

11. In Proverbs 1:7 below, underline what is the beginning of knowledge. Box the name in 7a and the people in 7b. Wavy-underline what fools do.

> 1:7 The fear of the LORD is the beginning of knowledge,
> but fools despise wisdom and instruction.

This third category is the *fool*—the person who is no longer simple but has rejected wisdom's ways. Other names that describe a fool are *wicked, lazy,* and *stingy.* Solomon did not write Proverbs for fools.

Why? Because *the fear of the LORD is the beginning of knowledge.* Fools don't fear the Lord, and so they can't receive the benefits Proverbs offers. This verse is the book's motto.

In her book *The Right Kind of Confident,* author Mary Kassian defines fear as "a strong or overwhelming sense that someone or something is greater than I am, and that it exerts a force beyond my control."[9] *The fear of the Lord* is reverence and awe that recognizes subservience to Almighty God, trembles before his power, and dares not turn grace into a license for sin.[10]

C.S. Lewis illustrates such respect to children in *The Lion, the Witch and the Wardrobe* when Mr. Beaver describes Aslan, the great Lion who is King of Beasts and Son of the Emperor-Beyond-the-Sea: "'Safe?...Who said anything about safe? 'Course he isn't safe.

**The Little Details**
*The Wise: Deborah*
During the years after the Israelites came to the promised land but before they had kings, the people mainly did what was right in their own eyes. The book of Judges describes a cycle: The people abandon God, God gives them over to their enemies, the people cry out for God's help, God sends them a deliverer, and the people follow God until the deliverer dies.

Judges 4 describes one of the wise leaders of Israel, Deborah. She was a prophetess who helped decide between disputes.

One day the Lord told her to tell military commander Barak to lead troops against their enemy, but he wouldn't go unless Deborah accompanied him. She agreed but told him his hesitancy would cost him the honor of capturing the commander of the enemy's army.

The Lord was with Deborah and Barak, and Barak defeated the enemy. But the enemy's commander escaped and hid in a tent. There, a woman named Jael struck him down as he slept.

The land had peace for 40 years.

Not all the deliverers had Deborah's wisdom, though. Coming sidebars will show foolish and simple leaders.

The Lord miraculously delivered Israel from its enemies through the deliverer Gideon. But after Gideon's death, the Israelites worshiped idols again.

Gideon had 70 sons. One of them, Abimelek, went to his mother's family in Shechem and enticed them with these words: "Which is better for you: to have all seventy of [Gideon's] sons rule over you, or just one man?" (Judges 9:2). They gave him money he then used to hire wicked men who helped him murder his brothers.

Abimelek ruled from Shechem for three years. Then the citizens plotted against him, and he laid an ambush for the city's army and struck them down. The remaining citizens locked themselves in a tower in an idol's temple. Abimelek set the tower on fire, killing everyone.

He then attacked another city and captured it. When its citizens took refuge in a tower, he attempted to set it on fire, too, but a woman dropped a millstone on his head. "Thus God repaid the wickedness" of Abimelek and the people of Shechem (9:56-57).

But he's good. He's the King, I tell you.'"[11] To fear God is to respect his power and authority and therefore to obey. Yet we also have confidence before him because we know "his mercy extends to those who fear him" and he "accepts from every nation the one who fears him and does what is right."[12]

12. ♥ Look back at the items you circled. Which benefit from reading Proverbs do you crave most? Why?

### Listen to the Right People

In the first nine chapters of Proverbs, Solomon teaches a son how to pursue wisdom. He's preparing the lad for government work. Old Testament professor Bruce K. Waltke writes, "Solomon intended to transmit his wisdom to Israel's youths by putting his proverbs in the mouths of godly parents (1:8-9)."[13] Solomon realized, of course, that not everyone would have godly parents. So he wrote his lessons not just for his own adolescent offspring but for everyone who wants to pursue wisdom.

That's fabulous news for those who, like me, weren't raised in a Christian home. We have access to wise teaching too!

In Proverbs 1:8-19, Solomon explains that many voices claim to offer the best way to happiness. He clarifies which to heed and which to reject.

13. Read Proverbs 1:8-10. List to whom the son should listen and not listen.

| Listen To | Don't Listen To |
|---|---|
|  |  |

The instruction of godly parents is like jewelry. It adorns. Sinful men also call out. Their voices can be enticing, persuasive, and manipulative. Solomon warns about the kinds of enticements they'll offer.

14. Use Proverbs 1:11-14 to fill in the blanks below with what sinful people say.

Let's lie in wait for _____ .
Let's ambush _____ .
We will get all sorts of _____ things
and fill our houses with _____ .

The sinful see stealing as a get-rich-quick scheme.

15. Read Proverbs 1:15-16. (a) What is Solomon's exhortation (15)? (b) What reason does he give (16)?

So don't even go to watch!

**16.** Read Proverbs 1:17-19. (a) When sinful people ambush the innocent, whom are they truly ambushing (18)? (b) What does ill-gotten gain do to a person (19)?

*themselves*

Those who plunder and steal fail to see that the trap they set for others entraps them. Their quest for riches will cost their lives. A millennium after Solomon wrote this, the apostle Paul wrote similar words in 1 Timothy 6:9-10:

> Those who want to get rich fall into temptation and a trap and into many foolish and harmful desires that plunge people into ruin and destruction. For the love of money is a root of all kinds of evil. Some people, eager for money, have wandered from the faith and pierced themselves with many griefs.

Loving money rather than God is not the way to eternal life.

In this lesson we discovered that Proverbs' purpose is to teach wisdom. We saw that the book places people in three categories: simple, wise/righteous, and fool/wicked. By fearing the Lord, the simple start to become wise. But if they reject the fear of the Lord, they start to become fools. We also found that godly and sinful people compete for our allegiance. In our next lesson we'll discover how to pursue wisdom.

## *Day 3*

# Pursue Wisdom

Peers pressure us. The media beckon us. Bosses may threaten us. Wherever we turn, voices call us to abandon God's ways for something they promise will be better.

### Pursue Wisdom Early
We've heard both the voice of Solomon as a godly parent and the voice of sinful men. Now Solomon gives us a third voice: the voice of wisdom personified as Lady Wisdom. *Personification* gives human characteristics to something not human. We're covering a lot of material today, so I've provided most verses and passages for you.

**17.** Read Proverbs 1:20-21. Is wisdom hard to find? ☐ Yes ☒ No

That's good news. We'll underline wise actions.

**18.** In Proverbs 1:22-23 below, box those whom Lady Wisdom calls (22abc). Underline what she tells them to do (23a). Circle what she will then do for them (23bc).

1:22 How long will you who are ⬚simple⬚ love your simple ways?
How long will ⬚mockers⬚ delight in mockery
and fools hate knowledge?
23 <u>Repent</u> at my rebuke!
Then ⟨I will pour out my thoughts to you,⟩
⟨I will make known to you my teachings.⟩

## The Little Details
### *Duane A. Garrett on Proverbs 1:17-19:*
Verse 17 is confusing as translated in the NIV and most versions. Even if one is willing to admit that a bird is intelligent enough to recognize the purpose of a trap when it sees it (which is doubtful), the proverb has no point in context. In addition, the Hebrew cannot sustain the translation "spread a net." The line is best rendered, "In the eyes of a bird, the net is strewn [with grain] for no reason." In other words, the bird does not see any connection between the net and what is scattered on it; he just sees food that is free for the taking. In the process he is trapped and killed. In the same way, the gang cannot see the connection between their acts of robbery and the fate that entraps them.

In vv. 18–19 the teacher brings his point home: the gang members are really ambushing themselves. The very reverse of their proposal in v. 11 has come about. Also, v. 19 concludes, it will ever be that way.[14]

## The Little Details
### The Simple: Jephthah

Judges 10–11 describes the consequences of remaining simple. The Israelites had again abandoned God, so he allowed the Ammonites to oppress Israel. The Ammonites practiced child sacrifice, which God forbade.[15]

Jephthah was a mighty warrior whose family in Gilead had driven him away. When the Ammonites threatened, Gilead's elders went to Jephthah and promised him he would be their head if he saved them.

Jephthah didn't know God's laws, and when the Spirit of the Lord came on him, he didn't consider that to be an adequate sign of God's help. So he tried to manipulate God by vowing to sacrifice whatever first came out of his house's door if he returned from battle triumphant. Houses had courtyards for animals, and he likely expected an animal to exit.

But the vow was rash because a human might emerge. Indeed, when he returned victorious, his only child greeted him.

Jephthah didn't seek a priest's advice. If he had, he would have learned that he could redeem his daughter.[16] Instead, he fulfilled his outrageous vow, and his ignorance brought tragedy.

*Mockers* are fools who laugh at those who follow God's ways. The good news here is that the simple and foolish can repent and seek wisdom.

Up to now, we've boxed people, circled blessings, underlined wise actions, and wavy-underlined foolish actions. Now we'll also wavy-circle penalties.

> **19.** In Proverbs 1:24-27 below, wavy-underline foolish actions (24-25). Wavy-circle what will happen to the fool because of it (26-27).
>
> 1:24    But since you refuse to listen when I call
>             and no one pays attention when I stretch out my hand,
> 25    since you disregard all my advice
>             and do not accept my rebuke,
> 26    I in turn will laugh when disaster strikes you;
>             I will mock when calamity overtakes you—
> 27    when calamity overtakes you like a storm,
>             when disaster sweeps over you like a whirlwind,
>             when distress and trouble overwhelm you.

The mockery of fools comes back on them.

> **20.** How does wisdom respond to those who hate knowledge and don't fear the Lord (1:28-29)?

Wisdom will not get them out of the consequences of spurning her.

> **21.** In Proverbs 1:30-31 below, wavy-underline foolish actions (30). Wavy-circle the penalties of those actions (31).
>
> 1:30    Since they would not accept my advice
>             and spurned my rebuke,
> 31    they will eat the fruit of their ways
>             and be filled with the fruit of their schemes.

The earlier in life we learn to pursue wisdom, the better.

> **22.** In Proverbs 1:32-33 below, box the three people mentioned. Wavy-circle what happens to the first two types of people. Circle what happens to the third.
>
> 1:32    For the waywardness of the simple will kill them,
>             and the complacency of fools will destroy them;
> 33    but whoever listens to me will live in safety
>             and be at ease, without fear of harm.

Jesus spoke similarly of the wise and the foolish in Matthew 7:24-27:

> Therefore everyone who hears these words of mine and puts them into practice is like a wise man who built his house on the rock. The rain came down, the streams rose, and the winds blew and beat against that house; yet it did not

fall, because it had its foundation on the rock. But everyone who hears these words of mine and does not put them into practice is like a foolish man who built his house on sand. The rain came down, the streams rose, and the winds blew and beat against that house, and it fell with a great crash.

## Pursue Wisdom Diligently

Solomon addresses his offspring again, explaining how to receive the Lord's blessings.

> 23. In Proverbs 2:1-4 below, underline what Solomon says to do.
>
> 2:1 My son, if you accept my words
>      and store up my commands within you,
> 2 turning your ear to wisdom
>      and applying your heart to understanding—
> 3 indeed, if you call out for insight
>      and cry aloud for understanding,
> 4 and if you look for it as for silver
>      and search for it as for hidden treasure…

Solomon equates wisdom's value to hidden treasure's value.

> 24. In Proverbs 2:5 below, circle the two things that will happen if you do all the things in verses 1-4.
>
> 2:5 Then you will understand the fear of the LORD
>      and find the knowledge of God.

Search wholeheartedly for wisdom, and you will know God.

> 25. What blessings does the Lord give those who seek wisdom (2:6-8)?
>
> wisdom, Knowledge, understanding
> common sence, integrity.
> guards and protects

God looks out for the wise.

> 26. In Proverbs 2:9-11 below, circle the benefits wisdom offers.
>
> 2:9 Then you will understand what is right and just
>      and fair—every good path.
> 10 For wisdom will enter your heart,
>      and knowledge will be pleasant to your soul.
> 11 Discretion will protect you,
>      and understanding will guard you.

Next Solomon explains why we need wisdom's protection.

## The Little Details
### "LORD" versus "Lord"

Many English-language Bibles use small caps when translating the Hebrew word *yᵉhōwāh*, which is God's name for himself (Exodus 6:2). It's usually translated "LORD" but occasionally "GOD." Some Bible versions translate a similar word, *yᵉhōwih*, as "GOD" while others tend to translate both "LORD."

A word translated "God" is *ᵉlōhiym*, and a word translated "Lord" is *ᵃdōnāy*. The word *ᵃdôn* is translated "Lord" or "lord," depending on whether it refers to God or a person.[17]

*accept*
*store up*
*listen*
*apply*

Search wholeheartedly for wisdom, and you will know God.

**The Little Details**
*Israel's Exiles*

The kingdom of Israel over which Solomon ruled split in two after his death: Israel to the north and Judah to the south.

The northern kingdom of Israel immediately broke their covenant with God. Although he sent prophets to call them back to proper relationship with him, they continued to pursue other gods. The Lord sent Assyria to exile Israel in 722 BC. Many people fled south to Judah, where they could learn to have relationship with God.

The southern kingdom of Judah eventually broke their covenant with God too. God sent Babylon to exile the people there in three stages, the final one in 586 BC. Babylon burned the temple Solomon built.

But God promised he would one day bring the people back. In 539 BC, Cyrus conquered Babylon and gave the Jews funds and supplies to return to the land and build a new temple. A small remnant returned. They built homes and a temple but remained under foreign rule.

In Jesus's day, Rome ruled the provinces that covered approximately where Israel and Judah had formerly existed. After a Jewish revolt in AD 70, Rome burned the temple.

27. Read Proverbs 2:12-15. (a) From whom will wisdom save you (12a)? (b) Which of the descriptions of such people most stands out to you (12b-15)?

*evil wisdom*
*those who turn from the right way*

Wicked people's words are *perverse,* causing harm rather than good. Taking *straight paths* is living according to God's commands. Taking *crooked paths* is living in a way that disregards God's commands. *Dark ways* refers to hiding sin and evil intentions.

About those who live in darkness, Jesus said, "Everyone who does evil hates the light, and will not come into the light for fear that their deeds will be exposed. But whoever lives by the truth comes into the light, so that it may be seen plainly that what they have done has been done in the sight of God" (John 3:20-21).

28. Read Proverbs 2:16-19. (a) From whom else will wisdom save you (16a)? (b) What has she done with the marriage vows she made before God (17b)? (c) To where does her house lead (18a)?

The adulterous woman uses *seductive words* to seduce men into affairs. Though *her house* appears to be a pleasure palace, it is the doorway to *death* (at the time this was written, a convicted adulterer could receive a death sentence).[18] But the *paths to the spirits of the dead* speaks of the place where spirits go after physical death to await the resurrection and final judgment. Those who enter her house leave the *paths of life.*

Solomon writes that wisdom saves from wicked men and adulterous women. Remember, he writes to his son, but gals can likewise beware wicked women and adulterous men.

Next Solomon summarizes wisdom's benefits.

29. In Proverbs 2:20-22 below, underline wise actions (20). Box the six descriptions of people (20-22). Circle blessings the upright and blameless will have (21). Wavy-circle penalties the wicked and unfaithful will face (22).

2:20 Thus you will walk in the ways of the good
        and keep to the paths of the righteous.
21    For the upright will live in the land,
        and the blameless will remain in it;
22    but the wicked will be cut off from the land,
        and the unfaithful will be torn from it.

God's covenant with Israel stated that if they lived as his people and obeyed his commandments, he would allow them to live in his land. But if they broke his covenant with them, he would expel them from the land. This foreshadowed what will happen after the final judgment: Those who love God will abide with him forever in the new heavens and earth, but the wicked will be cut off from that land.[19]

**30.** ♥ Describe a time you asked God for wisdom and he gave it to you.

In this lesson we learned that we should pursue wisdom extravagantly, early, actively, and earnestly. We must refuse wicked people's enticements and adulterers' seductions. Next we'll see how to be wise in our relationship with God.

## *Day 4*

## Live a Life God Blesses

When Clay and I discovered our two tween foster girls couldn't read well, we offered them a deal. If they each read *The Lion, the Witch and the Wardrobe* and *The Magician's Nephew* aloud, we'd take them to Disneyland. One of them read to Clay while the other read to me. When the younger girl wanted to back out, the older one reminded her not to forget Disneyland. With that encouragement, they both succeeded! Working out the words in these children's tales (steeped in spiritual symbolism) improved their skill.

Just as we promised to reward reading, so God promises to reward certain actions. Just as the action we rewarded developed a necessary life skill, so the actions God rewards develop necessary kingdom skills. Today we'll see how to live a life God blesses.

### Trust God Wholeheartedly
Solomon has written about relationships with parents and companions. Now he addresses people's relationships with God.

**31.** In Proverbs 3:1-2 below, underline commands (1ab). Circle their benefits (2ab).

> 3:1 My son, do not forget my teaching,
>    but keep my commands in your heart,
> 2 for they will prolong your life many years
>    and bring you peace and prosperity.

Of course, keeping our heavenly Father's commands brings us peace and prosperity as well. One way to keep his commands *in your heart* is to memorize them. As to prolonged life, God sent his Son, Jesus, to bring us eternal life: "God so loved the world that he gave his one and only Son, that whoever believes in him shall not perish but have eternal life" (John 3:16).

**32.** Read Proverbs 3:3-4. (a) What qualities should never leave you (3)? (b) What blessings will they win you (4)?

Picture love and faithfulness as a necklace adorning your neck for all to see. Then imagine them as part of your heart, shaping your character.

The actions God rewards develop necessary kingdom skills.

## The Little Details
### New Testament Wisdom

***Romans 16:19:*** Everyone has heard about your obedience, so I rejoice because of you; but I want you to be wise about what is good, and innocent about what is evil.

***Ephesians 5:15-17:*** Be very careful, then, how you live—not as unwise but as wise, making the most of every opportunity, because the days are evil. Therefore do not be foolish, but understand what the Lord's will is.

***2 Timothy 3:15-17:*** From infancy you have known the Holy Scriptures, which are able to make you wise for salvation through faith in Christ Jesus. All Scripture is God-breathed and is useful for teaching, rebuking, correcting and training in righteousness, so that the servant of God may be thoroughly equipped for every good work.

***James 3:13:*** Who is wise and understanding among you? Let them show it by their good life, by deeds done in the humility that comes from wisdom.

33. ♥ How can you show love and faithfulness to someone this week?

Now we come to my favorite pair of verses in Proverbs. It's one of the first passages of Scripture I memorized.

34. Write out Proverbs 3:5-6 below. Circle the benefit in verse 6.

> *He will show you which path to take.*

We *trust* the Lord when we believe his words, depend on him, and obey him. When we *submit* our will to God's, we *lean not on* our *own understanding*.

A girlfriend who was raised in church but had not yet become a Christian told me the Bible was written by a bunch of old men who knew nothing about modern times. Therefore, she reasoned, she could decide which commands to obey and which to ignore. One day, though, her conscience wouldn't let her excuse her actions. She knew she needed forgiveness. She asked God to forgive her, believed in Jesus as Lord, and started searching the Bible to see what it said about right and wrong. She was no longer leaning on her own understanding.

As you *trust in the Lord*, he will *make your paths straight*. He'll mold your character and cause you to bear godly fruit. Jesus put it this way: "I am the vine; you are the branches. If you remain in me and I in you, you will bear much fruit; apart from me you can do nothing...If you keep my commands, you will remain in my love" (John 15:5, 10).

35. Use Proverbs 3:7-8 to fill in the blanks below.

| | | |
|---|---|---|
| Do not be | *impressed with your own wisdom* | . |
| Instead | 1) *fear the LORD* | . |
| | 2) *turn away from evil* | . |
| This will bring | 1) *healing* | to your body. |
| | 2) *strength* | to your bones. |

Now that I've been a Christian for many years, I've seen the results of both obeying and ignoring God's commands—in my life and in others' lives. The first few years I didn't understand the reason behind many instructions, such as not letting the sun go down on your anger.[20] But over time I saw both obedience's good fruit and the hardships of thinking we know better than God how the world ought to act.

Some skeptics judge God's commands and actions as amoral. For example, atheist Mark Twain wrote to his wife, "The [Deity] that I want to keep out of the reach of, is the caricature of him which one finds in the Bible. We (that one and I) could never respect each other, never get along together. I have met his superior a hundred times—In fact I amount to that myself."[21] This is an example of being *wise in your own eyes*.

While verses 5 and 7 in Proverbs 3 warn against intellectual arrogance, neither is anti-intellectual. As we've read, Proverbs repeatedly urges us to pursue knowledge and understanding.

> **36.** Read Proverbs 3:9-10. (a) With what should we honor the Lord (9)? (b) Summarize what God does for those who honor him this way (10).

To *honor the Lord with your wealth*, give first to him when you receive income. *Firstfruits* are the first crops to appear in a season. Jews brought the first of their grain harvest to the temple. They could not eat any of the harvest until they offered the first of it to the Lord in celebration and thanksgiving.[25]

The New Testament has something similar: "Remember this: Whoever sows sparingly will also reap sparingly, and whoever sows generously will also reap generously...And God is able to bless you abundantly, so that in all things at all times, having all that you need, you will abound in every good work" (2 Corinthians 9:6, 8).

> **37.** ❤ What are some ways you can help the poor, support your church, care for missionaries, and aid other ministries?

If you want to know more about helping persecuted Christians, the Voice of the Martyrs has resources at persecution.com.

> **38.** Fill in the blanks from Proverbs 3:11-12.
>
> 3:11 Don't _____reject_____ the Lord's discipline,
> Don't ____be upset at____ his rebuke,
> 12 Because the Lord disciplines those he ___loves___,
> as a father the son he ___delights in.___ in.

Hebrews 12:5-6 quotes this passage and tells us not to forget its word of encouragement. Verses 7 and 11 read:

> Endure hardship as discipline; God is treating you as his children. For what children are not disciplined by their father?...No discipline seems pleasant at the time, but painful. Later on, however, it produces a harvest of righteousness and peace for those who have been trained by it.

Part of trusting God wholeheartedly requires accepting God's discipline.

> **39.** ❤ Think of a current hardship in your life. How does seeing hardship as God's loving way of producing fruit in you help you endure it?

In this lesson we discovered that we live a life God blesses when we adorn ourselves with

**The Little Details**
*The Festivals of Firstfruits and Weeks*

The *Festival of Firstfruits* was part of three celebrations connected to Passover. On the day after the first Sabbath after Passover, Jews brought a sheaf of the first ripe barley stalks to the temple and offered it to the Lord along with other sacrifices. They couldn't eat any of the new barley crop until they made this offering. This showed their gratitude for the new harvest and their expectation of a greater harvest to come.[22]

Seven weeks later, Jews returned to the temple for the *Festival of Weeks* (also known as *Pentecost*). This celebrated the wheat harvest. They brought wheat grains and bread loaves along with other offerings for a day of celebration.[23]

What's significant about these two celebrations? Jesus rose from the dead during the Festival of Firstfruits as "the firstfruits of those who have fallen asleep" (1 Corinthians 15:20). He baptized his followers with the Holy Spirit on the Festival of Weeks in celebration of the harvest of souls he was reaping.[24]

**The Little Details**
*Revelation 22:1-2 on the Tree of Life:*

Then the angel showed me the river of the water of life, as clear as crystal, flowing from the throne of God and of the Lamb down the middle of the great street of the city. On each side of the river stood the tree of life, bearing twelve crops of fruit, yielding its fruit every month. And the leaves of the tree are for the healing of the nations.

unfailing love and faithfulness, trust the Lord wholeheartedly, submit to him in all ways, and honor him with our wealth. Those whom the Lord loves he disciplines to mold their character and produce spiritual fruit. Our next lesson will explore even more of wisdom's blessings.

## Day 5

# Seek Wisdom's Blessings

Once during a challenging work season, two programmers on a different team from mine decided to sabotage our company-wide project and show they could produce better results. One of them stole project notes from a legally blind team member. When she alerted me, I confronted the man, who laughed over being caught. He returned the materials, apparently having made copies. They tried other shenanigans, including shutting down my team's access to mainframes after hours. But the Lord helped us overcome obstacles, the saboteurs gave up trying to produce a better platform, and we successfully finished.

Years later the man who had taken the notes needed work and asked me for a reference. I told him I couldn't give him one because his actions had showed him to be untrustworthy. By forsaking "love and faithfulness," he'd forfeited "favor and a good name in the sight of God and man" (Proverbs 3:3-4).

The passages we'll read today compare how the wise and foolish seek prosperity and prestige and what end results they achieve.

### Discover the Way to Great Blessings

Do you want to be blessed? Solomon is about to tell us how.

> **40.** Read Proverbs 3:13-15. Check the people who are more blessed:
>
> ☐ Those who find wisdom ☐ Those who find great wealth

Solomon next explains why this is so.

> **41.** Read Proverbs 3:16-18 below. Circle wisdom's blessings.
>
> 3:16 Long life is in her right hand;
> in her left hand are riches and honor.
> 17 Her ways are pleasant ways,
> and all her paths are peace.
> 18 She is a tree of life to those who take hold of her;
> those who hold her fast will be blessed.

That's quite a list! Notice that wisdom brings *riches*. *Tree of life* refers to eternal life.

> **42.** Read Proverbs 3:19-20. What three things did the Lord use when he created the heavens and the earth?

If the Lord created with wisdom, ought we not value wisdom too?

> **43.** In Proverbs 3:21-24 below, underline commands. Circle benefits.
>
> 3:21 My son, do not let wisdom and understanding out of your sight,
> preserve sound judgment and discretion;
> 22 they will be life for you,
> an ornament to grace your neck.
> 23 Then you will go on your way in safety,
> and your foot will not stumble.
> 24 When you lie down, you will not be afraid;
> when you lie down, your sleep will be sweet.

Wisdom shows you the way to eternal life. It protects you and removes anxiety.

> **44.** Read Proverbs 3:25-26. If you have godly wisdom that begins with the fear of the Lord, why do you not need to fear the kinds of troubles that befall the godless?

The wise trust the Lord and submit to him. He in turn showers blessings on them.

## Discover the Way to Honor

Now Solomon turns to practical wisdom.

> **45.** Use Proverbs 3:27-28 to fill in the blanks below.
>
> Don't withhold _____ from those who deserve it.
> Don't delay giving what's due when _____ .

I concentrate well and dislike interruptions, so these two verses have helped me better balance life and prioritize people over tasks.

> **46.** Use Proverbs 3:29-30 to fill in the blanks below.
>
> Don't_____ against your neighbor.
> Don't accuse anyone for _____ .

This is one area where the aforementioned scheming programmer acted foolishly. When he asked me to give him a reference for another company, I explained why I couldn't. I was surprised when he teared up, yet they weren't tears of repentance. When I encountered him again at another company, he was still plotting against others to promote himself.

Envy causes people to choose devious ways. They crave the power, prestige, popularity, and prosperity others have, but they don't think they can achieve them without underhanded methods.

**The Little Details**
*Allen P. Ross on the New Testament's Use of Proverbs:*
The book of Proverbs appears in the Jewish lists of the books of the canon...and is commonly cited as authoritative scripture in the *Mishnah*. The NT quotes Proverbs various times (Mt 16:27 [Pr 24:12]; Ro 3:15 [Pr 1:16]; 12:16 [Pr 3:7], 20 [Pr 25:21-22]; Heb 12:5-6 [Pr 3:11-12]; Jas 4:6 [Pr 3:34], 13 [Pr 27:1]; 1Pe 2:17 [Pr 24:21]; 4:8 [Pr 10:12], 18 [Pr 11:31]; 5:5 [Pr 3:34]; 2Pe 2:22 [Pr 26:11]). So the book is unquestionably an integral part of the Holy Scriptures.[26]

## The Little Details
### Psalm 119

Psalm 119 is an acrostic poem. In Hebrew, each of the eight lines in its stanzas start with the same letter of the alphabet. It contains a stanza for every letter of the Hebrew alphabet.

**47.** In Proverbs 3:31-35 below, box the people. Underline commands. Circle the blessings befalling the wise. Wavy-circle the penalties facing the wicked and fools.

> ³:³¹ Do not envy the violent
> or choose any of their ways.
> ³² For the LORD detests the perverse
> but takes the upright into his confidence.
> ³³ The LORD's curse is on the house of the wicked,
> but he blesses the home of the righteous.
> ³⁴ He mocks proud mockers
> but shows favor to the humble and oppressed.
> ³⁵ The wise inherit honor,
> but fools get only shame.

While the Lord actively works in the world today, the final judgment will display the ultimate bestowal of honor or shame, as Daniel 12:2-3 describes:

> Multitudes who sleep in the dust of the earth will awake: some to everlasting life, others to shame and everlasting contempt. Those who are wise will shine like the brightness of the heavens, and those who lead many to righteousness, like the stars for ever and ever.

In this lesson we found the way to blessings and honor.

### Wisdom's Worth

**48.** ♥ In what way did you apply wisdom from Proverbs to your life this week?

This chapter showed us that the purpose of Proverbs is to teach wisdom. It categorizes people as either simple, wise/righteous, or fool/wicked. Because we encounter many voices claiming to offer prosperity and happiness, we must judge them correctly and heed wisdom's call. Wisdom brings lasting blessings and shows us how to live a life God blesses. The wise trust the Lord wholeheartedly and submit to him, knowing he loves and molds us. In our next chapter, we'll see why the wise embrace sexual purity.

### Wisdom Worship

Find a quiet place and prepare your heart for grateful worship.

Psalms is the Bible's prayer book. Several of the psalms are wisdom psalms; that is, they instruct us in God's ways. They give us the opportunity to thank God for supplying wisdom and to, in prayer, commit to pursuing wisdom. Let's conclude our time in this chapter by worshiping with one of the wisdom psalms. Find a quiet place and prepare your heart for worship.

 Turn to Psalm 119:1-16 in your Bible and pray the passage aloud.

## Karla's Creative Connection

*Trust in the LORD with all your heart, and do not lean on your own understanding.*
*In all your ways acknowledge him, and he will make straight your paths.*

Proverbs 3:5-6 ESV

I'm so glad you're here and longing to creatively connect with God throughout this Bible study. I've loved illustrating the key verses for each chapter, and I do hope you'll get out your crayons or colored pencils and add your own colorful personality to each illustration. But coloring is just one way to express your God-given creativity when seeking a closer relationship with the Lord. As we explore God's wisdom in Proverbs, I encourage you to also explore a different creative exercise each week, designed to open your eyes and your heart to the beauty and blessings of our amazing God.

As I pondered this week's key verse, I thought about how impossible it is to trust someone we don't know. How can we if we don't know whether they're trustworthy or reliable? And the same is true about our ability to trust God. Only to the degree we know him are we willing and able to trust him, to acknowledge him, and to invite him into our everyday lives.

So how do we get to know anyone? By spending time with them. Getting to know who they really are through having a relationship with them. And the same is true of our knowledge of God. God loves us and wants us to know who he is and to know him in a personal way. We can say we know God, but if we're not reading and engaging with the Scriptures, our knowledge of him can too easily be distorted by our own thinking and emotions.

The Bible is God's story about who he is in all his glory and majesty. And he directed its writing as a love letter to you and me so we could know not just about who he is but about his heart. About how much he loves us and desires a personal relationship with each one of us.

To creatively connect with God this week, try reading your Bible as his love letter to you. Don't just read it as words on a page. Use your imagination—your creativity—to connect with him, to hear him speaking personally and intimately to your heart. If a verse says, "my son," insert your own name. Listen to God's voice as he calls you to seek wisdom in Proverbs. Hear the desire of his Fatherly heart as he longs for you to follow him and live a life of beauty, bounty, and blessing.

*Karla*

TRUST IN THE LORD WITH ALL YOUR HEART ·AND· LEAN NOT ON YOUR OWN UNDERSTANDING; IN ALL YOUR WAYS SUBMIT TO HIM, AND HE WILL MAKE YOUR PATHS STRAIGHT.

PROVERBS 3:5-6

FOR YOUR WAYS ARE IN FULL VIEW OF THE LORD, AND HE EXAMINES ALL YOUR PATHS.

PROVERBS 5:21

## Chapter 2

# Proverbs 4:1–6:35
## Sexual Sanity

Why do the wise embrace sexual purity?

## Day 1

## God's Word on Sex

Chloe and Megan's[1] lives were upended just months apart.

Ever since she'd caught him watching hard-core porn, Chloe had suspected her husband, Daniel, might be unfaithful. She began to wonder if his weekly cooking classes were about more than just getting to know a business in which he wanted to invest.

One evening she followed Daniel to class, parked where she could see his Porsche, and then watched as he and a young woman emerged from the building, laughing, and got into his car. Chloe walked over and knocked on Daniel's window. It turned out the "investment" he'd been talking about was launching this gal's start as a restaurateur.

Megan, on the other hand, never suspected a thing. Her husband, Andrew, was active at church. Yes, he traveled a lot for work, but she trusted him completely—until she discovered he'd been sleeping with someone at one of his regular destinations and was addicted to porn.

The kicker? The women Daniel and Andrew had affairs with knew the men were married.

### Do We Want to Know What God Says About Sex?

Talking about a biblical perspective of sex has become challenging because so many people view the Bible as irrelevant and constraining. So let's start with an important question.

1. ♥ If God has something to say about sex, do you want to know what it is? Explain.

### What Jesus Taught About Sex

Since the chapters we'll read today address adultery, let's look at what Jesus taught about it. What we now call the Old Testament, Jesus called Scripture or the Law, the Prophets, and the Psalms. Jesus said Scripture is "the word of God" and "cannot be set aside" (John 10:35). So when he taught on sexual morality, he assumed his Jewish listeners knew the commandments in the law of Moses.

By Jesus's day, some religious leaders disagreed over how to interpret laws about divorce (see sidebar on the next page). Read how he responded when asked about the disagreement.

The Pharisees had many rules they called *the tradition of the elders* (Mark 7:5). They intended these to be a hedge around the law of Moses. Two Pharisees influential in developing these traditions were Hillel and Shammai, both of whom headed schools. They taught in the late first century BC and early first century AD. Neither is named in the Bible, but the apostle Paul's teacher Gamaliel was Hillel's grandson (Acts 22:3).[2]

Hillel and Shammai differed in their views on divorce. "Shammai required divorce (and permitted remarriage) only for sexual infidelity; Hillel permitted divorce for 'any good cause.'"[3] Jesus did not require divorce after marital unfaithfulness as Shammai and Hillel did. And he disagreed with Hillel's broad view on what constitutes grounds for divorce.

2. Read Matthew 19:3-9. (a) How did the Creator make us (4)? (b) What does Jesus say about marriage in verse 6? (c) What does he say about a man who divorces his wife for reasons other than sexual immorality and then remarries (9)?

In Matthew 5:27-32, Jesus says more on the subject and quotes the Old Testament:

> You have heard that it was said, "You shall not commit adultery." But I tell you that anyone who looks at a woman lustfully has already committed adultery with her in his heart. If your right eye causes you to stumble, gouge it out and throw it away. It is better for you to lose one part of your body than for your whole body to be thrown into hell. And if your right hand causes you to stumble, cut it off and throw it away. It is better for you to lose one part of your body than for your whole body to go into hell.
>
> It has been said, 'Anyone who divorces his wife must give her a certificate of divorce.' But I tell you that anyone who divorces his wife, except for sexual immorality, makes her the victim of adultery, and anyone who marries a divorced woman commits adultery.

Jesus was stricter than the Pharisees. But he was also more merciful. Unlike the Pharisees, he offered the repentant forgiveness. Indeed, Jesus died on the cross to cleanse us from sin. We'll cover both God's design and mercy in this chapter.

## God's Word to Us in Proverbs

As you read our text in Proverbs, remember that Solomon writes to single young men. Still, the principles behind his advice apply to all.

Take a moment to pray for insight as you read God's Word.

3. ♥ Read chapters 4–6 in Proverbs. (a) What stood out to you in your reading? Why? (b) How can you apply that insight to your life this week?

Solomon has a lot to say about adultery, doesn't he? And no wonder: His parents were David and Bathsheba, the most famous adulterers in history. Even though the Bible doesn't cast Bathsheba in the role of a wanton woman (see upcoming sidebar), the consequences that played out from their sin illustrate Proverbs' warnings well. So we'll read parts of their story in our lessons.

Today's lesson examines Jesus's teaching about marriage, lust, and adultery. In the next lesson we'll discover what David taught Solomon about wisdom.

# Pam's Simply Beautiful Wisdom

*Keep your heart with all vigilance, for from it flow the springs of life.*

Proverbs 4:23 ESV

My husband, Bill, and a friend were traveling on the Autobahn in Germany, which has no speed limit. As they were zipping down this freeway in a Mini Cooper, a Porsche whizzed by them. Bill thought, *It sure would be fun to be in that powerful car!* Minutes later he drove by the Porsche, now engulfed in flames. The driver had forgotten to respect the power of the engine.

Sex is like a sports car. It can carry a marriage to exciting places, but when you disrespect God's design before an "I do," it can burn you. The word picture in Proverbs 4:23 is of guarding your heart like a diligent soldier. (To gain a vital overview on God's principles, read through Proverbs with a red pen, and with a heart, mark all the verses on love, sex, and relationship.)

*"God is love"* (1 John 4:8, 16)! The entire Bible is one long love letter, and God intended sex as a loving bond between a husband and a wife: "They become one flesh" (Genesis 2:24). In the New Testament, the apostle Paul tells us God connects a loving marriage to how Christ loves the church: "'For this reason a man will leave his father and mother and be united to his wife, and the two will become one flesh.' This is a profound mystery—but I am talking about Christ and the church" (Ephesians 5:31-32).

The method God most uses in my life to introduce his love to others is the authentic love Bill and I share. We don't even have to say anything about our marriage or intimacy; people just see it!

## Your Love Is a Light!

To have love that radiates *out*, you have to let God's love permeate *in*. The choice to love comes down to two key questions:

### #1: Do you believe God loves you?

"God so loved the world that He gave His only begotten Son, that whoever believes in Him should not perish but have everlasting life" (John 3:16 NKJV).

God *proved* his love when he died to pay the price for our sins and selfishness.

### #2: Do you love God?[4]

"If you keep my commandments, you will abide in my love, just as I have kept my Father's commandments and abide in his love. These things I have spoken to you, that my joy may be in you, and that your joy may be full" (John 15:10-11 ESV).

As you read the Bible, note that God gives freedom in an intimate relationship (check out Song of Songs), yet he also gives guidelines that protect the heart, health, and well-being of individuals. In our book *Red-Hot Monogamy*, Bill and I share that you can say "Y.E.S.!" to sex if it meets all three of these criteria:

*Y*ield to God and to each other. To gain the benefits of the gift of sex, we must embrace God's guidelines. The number one indicator of sexual fulfillment is *trust* built by intimacy with a committed, faithful *spouse*.

"God wants you to be holy and completely free from sexual immorality" (1 Thessalonians 4:3 GNT).

*Holy* means devoted and set apart as valuable. *Sexual immorality* is any sex outside the parameters of marriage. God reminds married couples of healthy boundaries too:

"Let marriage be kept honorable in every way, and the marriage bed undefiled" (Hebrews 13:4 ISV).

*E*xtended in love. No one should feel forced, coerced, controlled, demeaned, or intimidated. In the Old Testament, the word most often used for sexual relations is *know*. Aim to know your mate by expressing commitment, appreciation, value, and desire, and then intimacy will thrill, protect, and create a safe environment where love can blossom.

"Above all, be loving. This ties everything together perfectly" (Colossians 3:14 GW).

*S*ecured with privacy. Your sex life is a sacred, intimate relationship between you and your spouse. Kick out pornography and all counterfeits.

"If sinners entice you, do not consent" (Proverbs 1:10 ESV).[5]

When our vertical relationship with God is healthy, our horizontal relationships with others will be healthier too.[6] When we allow God to love us, we gain the ability to love more like him.

When we first began our relationship, Bill and I decided we would do our best to love each other according to God's guidelines. We were two imperfect individuals that God was working to redeem—me from the pain of being raised by an erratic, alcoholic father, and Bill from the impact of a childhood dominated by a mother racked with emotional chaos. And we knew we would find it easier to obey God's plan to wait for sexual intimacy until marriage if we took a step away from temptation. So we chose to not kiss until the commitment of engagement. We listened attentively to God and made decisions intently, marrying within a year of our first date—at age twenty.

God whispers his love into our own love stories.

On our honeymoon, I stepped out of the shower, and as I looked in the mirror all the old messages began to play in my mind: *unworthy*, *unlovable*, and *unwanted*. I began to criticize myself aloud.

Bill was sitting on the bed and thought, *Oh dear! She's going to get all depressed, and it will take the rest of our honeymoon to coax her out of this negative spiral! Lord, will you please help a guy out?*

Then a thought he knew was heaven-sent crossed his mind: *Bill, you can do a better job than that mirror.*

My husband came over and gently wrapped me in his arms, looked into my eyes, and said, "Pam, let me be your mirror. If you need to know what a beautiful, godly, amazing woman you are, come see me. Let me be your mirror."[7] I immediately changed. The outpouring of God's love through Bill revived my soul and my ability to receive and give love.

Let God pour his love into you, and then be a mirror reflecting his love to others.

P.S.: Listen to the song "Let Me Be Your Mirror" and music video *Mirror* about this moment in the extras of this lesson.[8]

### Experiencing Scripture Creatively (Optional)

If you have extra time, consider these suggestions for creatively engaging with verses from this week's reading. The appendix has even more ideas.

- Visit a park with paths and examine them for items that don't belong there, such as trash or large rocks. Remove them from the paths while repeating the key verse. Meditate on how God removes what doesn't belong in your life.

- Follow Karla's instructions at the end of this chapter for creatively imagining your path as it relates to this verse.

- Color Karla's full-page illustration at the end of the chapter while repeating the words of the verse aloud. When you're finished, check to see if the activity enabled you to memorize the verse.

- Color the sidebar toppers using distinct color schemes. Choose your favorite to use on the bookmark on this chapter's opening page.

- Create a poem from one or more proverbs. Here's an example:

  *A couplet of Jean concerning Proverbs 4:23.*
  Above all else, do guard your heart
   for all your actions from it start.

**The Little Details**
*For Budding Poets*

The example poem is a **couplet**, meaning its rhyming pattern is *aa bb*, and so on. Its lines are **iambic tetrameter**. *Iamb* means the rhythm uses a light stress followed by a heavy stress. *Tetrameter* means there are four groups of light and heavy stresses per line. Here's the first line with stressed syllables in bold and a bar between metrical feet:

A**bove** | all **else,** | do **guard** | your **heart**

## The Little Details
### *What the Story Omits*

The tale of David and Bathsheba spurs much speculation. The 1951 film *David and Bathsheba* paints her as a temptress, while more recent writings condemn him as a rapist. But what conclusions does the text warrant?

In ancient days, flat roofs were fenced and treated like patios. David probably walked the palace roof often, so why was Bathsheba bathing where she could be seen from there? Was she trying to seduce the king? The text doesn't say but nowhere condemns her directly.

Was Bathsheba overwhelmed by the king's authority and afraid to refuse him? The text doesn't say.

Did David foolishly think *We'll just talk*, but then the two succumbed to mutual attraction? Again, the text doesn't say.

We can, however, be sure this was not rape, because the Bible doesn't hold back when describing such atrocities. Also, 1 Kings 15:5 says David's sin was against Uriah, Bathsheba's husband. Additionally, David and Bathsheba appear to have had a close relationship afterward: She bore David four more sons and held considerable court influence.

*Day 2*

# Why Wisdom?

The Lord God called David a man after his own heart (1 Samuel 13:14; Acts 13:22). Nonetheless, David wasn't sinless. He sinned spectacularly and suffered gut-splitting consequences. In middle age, he stayed behind while his troops went out to fight, perhaps because his men forbade him to go with them to battle after he'd nearly died.[9]

> **4.** Read 2 Samuel 11:1-5. What word did Bathsheba send to David in verse 5?

What David did in secret was about to be exposed by a child born before Solomon.

> **5.** ♥ What emotions do you imagine David and Bathsheba each felt when she discovered her pregnancy?

### Get Wisdom

Before we continue this saga, let's jump to Proverbs.

> **6.** Read Proverbs 4:1-4a below. Box the people (1a, 3ab). Underline the commands (1ab). Circle the benefit (1b). Write "David" by 3a and "Bathsheba" by 3b.
>
> 4:1 Listen, my sons, to a father's instruction;
>     pay attention and gain understanding.
> 2 I give you sound learning,
>     so do not forsake my teaching.
> 3 For I too was a son to my father,
>     still tender, and cherished by my mother.
> 4 Then he taught me, and he said to me…

When Solomon was young and simple, David taught him these life lessons.

> **7.** In Proverbs 4:4b-9 below, underline commands. Circle benefits (4b, 6ab, 8ab, 9ab).
>
> 4:4 "Take hold of my words with all your heart;
>     keep my commands, and you will live.
> 5 Get wisdom, get understanding;
>     do not forget my words or turn away from them.
> 6 Do not forsake wisdom, and she will protect you;
>     love her, and she will watch over you.
> 7 The beginning of wisdom is this: Get wisdom.
>     Though it cost all you have, get understanding.
> 8 Cherish her, and she will exalt you;
>     embrace her, and she will honor you.

> 9     She will give you a garland to grace your head
> and present you with a glorious crown."

Verse 7 is the key: "The beginning of wisdom is this: Get wisdom. Though it cost all you have, get understanding." Why get wisdom even if it costs everything? David learned the hard way when he foolishly forsook the sixth, seventh, and tenth of the Ten Commandments God gave the people through Moses. The results wrenched David's heart and nearly wrecked a kingdom.

## Listen Up!

**8.** List the commands and the benefits following them brings (4:10-13).

| Commands | Benefits That Come from Obeying |
| --- | --- |
|  |  |
|  |  |
|  |  |

David's sin nearly cost him his life. It did cost the lives of some dear to him and brought him to wish he had died instead.[10] But that's getting ahead of the story.

**9.** In Proverbs 4:14-17 below, box people (14ab). Underline commands (14ab, 15ab). Wavy-underline evildoers' actions (16ab, 17ab).

> 4:14    Do not set foot on the path of the wicked
> or walk in the way of evildoers.
> 15      Avoid it, do not travel on it;
> turn from it and go on your way.
> 16      For they cannot rest until they do evil;
> they are robbed of sleep till they make someone stumble.
> 17      They eat the bread of wickedness
> and drink the wine of violence.

In California, you can enter and exit toll roads only at specified spots. Areas of heavy traffic have barricades between the toll lanes and the regular lanes so no cars can enter or exit for long stretches. The first time I got stuck in a barricaded toll lane, I couldn't exit for miles beyond my destination, costing me more in tolls and time than I intended.

Stepping into sin can be like entering a barricaded toll lane. You often can't exit when you want to, and it costs more than you expect.

When David asked his men to bring Bathsheba to him, he *set foot on the path of the wicked.* When he learned she was pregnant, he walked further on that path. He sent for her husband, Uriah, to bring him battle news. Then he told the man to go home, expecting him to sleep with his wife so he would assume the child was his. But Uriah chose not to go. The next night David got him drunk and again told him to go home, but once more, Uriah refused. So then David sent a sealed message to his army's commander: Put Uriah where the fighting is heaviest and then pull back so he'll be killed.

Once we start on the wrong path, it's hard not to *walk in the way of evildoers,* desperately hiding sins. Some are so far on those paths that *they cannot rest until they do evil.*

**The Little Details**
***The Commands David Broke***

The sixth commandment is "You shall not murder" (Exodus 20:13). The seventh is "You shall not commit adultery" (verse 14). And the tenth includes, "You shall not covet your neighbor's wife" (verse 17).

Leviticus 18 expands commands about sexual relations and includes this: "Do not have sexual relations with your neighbor's wife and defile yourself with her" (Leviticus 18:20). Sin defiled people and separated them from God. They had to offer sacrifices to cleanse themselves before they could fellowship with God again. But there was no sacrifice for most intentional sins, like murder and adultery.

The New Testament says this about adultery: "The commandments, 'You shall not commit adultery,' 'You shall not murder,' 'You shall not steal,' 'You shall not covet,' and whatever other command there may be, are summed up in this one command: 'Love your neighbor as yourself'" (Romans 13:9).

## The Little Details
### Hillary Morgan Ferrer on Pornography:

In 2019, the world's largest porn conglomerate reported *42 billion visits*. So basically the entire earth's population times six visited their site. That's double what they had a mere two years prior. And the amount of *new* content added to the site? Enough to watch porn all day, every day… for 165 years. And remember that is just *one* porn site in *one* year. That doesn't even include the approximate 26 million other sites that exist, several of which *also* boast visits in the billions per year…

We would all like to think that porn is a "them" problem. Not *us*. Not *our* husbands. Not *our* kids…According to Covenant Eyes, more than half of pastors have struggled with porn, and 57 percent of youth pastors "live in constant fear of being discovered" for their porn addiction. When it comes to our kids' conception of porn, 90 percent of teens and 96 percent of young adults are *neutral, accepting, or encouraging* of porn consumption. Yep, you read that right. Nearly every kid at school has no problem watching porn and will happily text their favorite videos to their friends so they can join in the fun.[11]

Solomon summarizes David's teaching in the next passage.

> **10.** Use Proverbs 4:18-19 to fill in the blanks.
>
> The path of the righteous is like_____ .
> The way of the wicked is like _____ .

When Clay and I travel, we take a nightlight for hotel bathrooms. That way, when we need to get up in the middle of the night, we don't trip on a bench, stub a toe on a dresser, or knock over a suitcase. Experience teaches these things!

Following God's commands is like walking in *the full light of day*—you can see clearly so nothing trips you. But rejecting God's commands is like walking in *deep darkness*—you stumble repeatedly over things you cannot see.

### Guard Your Heart

Solomon next turns to the heart and what it receives through our senses.

> **11.** To the left of each body part below, write the letter of the relation it has to the father's words (Proverbs 4:20-22). Each body part has one unique match.

| Body Part | Relation to Father's Words |
|---|---|
| Ears | A. Should always watch |
| Eyes | B. Should store |
| Heart | C. Should turn to |
| Whole body | D. Will receive health from |

The heart receives knowledge through the ears and eyes, so we must be careful what we take in from them.

> **12.** To the left of each body part, write the letter of what to do with it (Proverbs 4:23-27). Each body part has one unique match. Verse 24 has two body parts; the rest have one.

| Body Part | What to Do with It |
|---|---|
| Eyes | A. Consider paths carefully |
| Foot | B. Don't allow corrupt talk near |
| Heart | C. Guard above all else |
| Lips | D. Keep free from perversity |
| Mouth | E. Keep from evil |
| Thought/Mind | F. Look straight ahead |

In the introduction to this chapter, we saw that neither Daniel nor Andrew took care to guard his *heart*. Their ears and *eyes* took in porn, flooding their thoughts with an insatiable desire for more.

In Mark 7:20-23, Jesus explains that food isn't what defiles us:

> What comes out of a person is what defiles them. For it is from within, out of a person's heart, that evil thoughts come—sexual immorality, theft, murder, adultery, greed, malice, deceit, lewdness, envy, slander, arrogance and folly. All these evils come from inside and defile a person.

**13.** ♥ What are some practical ways to guard your heart by controlling what it receives from your eyes and ears?

In this lesson we read that the beginning of wisdom is "Get wisdom"! Don't step onto a sinful path even for a moment. We won't stumble on the path of the righteous, but we'll trip repeatedly on the way of the wicked. We must guard what we see and hear, because what goes into our hearts drives our actions. In our next lesson we'll read of the bitterness of adultery and the sweetness of marriage.

## *Day 3*

## Bitter Gall or Refreshing Water?

In today's lesson Solomon warns of adultery's dire consequences. He should know.

After Bathsheba mourned the death of her husband, David married her, and she gave birth to a baby boy. David might have gotten away with sin except for this: "The thing David had done displeased the LORD" (2 Samuel 11:27). The Lord sent the prophet Nathan to rebuke David.

**14.** Read 2 Samuel 12:9-14. (a) How did David treat the word of the Lord (9)? (b) What would now not depart from David's house (10)? (c) What would someone do with David's wives (11)? (d) How did David respond to the rebuke (13)? (e) What consequence would David not face (13)? (f) What further consequence would he face (14)?

All happened as Nathan prophesied. First, David's oldest son raped his half-sister. Next, her brother Absalom killed his rapist half-brother. Then Bathsheba's grandfather[12] Ahithophel—David's most trusted advisor—conspired with Absalom to overthrow David. Ahithophel told Absalom to sleep with ten of David's wives to prove he'd taken the throne. He did this in a rooftop tent "in the sight of all Israel" (2 Samuel 16:22). But David's men defeated Absalom's forces and killed Absalom despite David's orders to spare the young man. Ahithophel then killed himself.

Tragedy after tragedy can come from one wicked decision.

Still, God granted grace. When David repented, God took away his sin and said David would not die. Bathsheba bore David four more sons, including Solomon. And Solomon, having seen adultery's folly, makes it the subject of his next lecture.

Tragedy after tragedy can come from one wicked decision.

## The Little Details

### *Two New Testament Passages on Sexual Immorality:*

***1 Corinthians 6:18-20:*** Flee from sexual immorality. All other sins a person commits are outside the body, but whoever sins sexually, sins against their own body. Do you not know that your bodies are temples of the Holy Spirit, who is in you, whom you have received from God? You are not your own; you were bought at a price. Therefore honor God with your bodies.

***1 Thessalonians 4:3-7:*** It is God's will that you should be sanctified: that you should avoid sexual immorality; that each of you should learn to control your own body in a way that is holy and honorable, not in passionate lust like the pagans, who do not know God; and that in this matter no one should wrong or take advantage of a brother or sister. The Lord will punish all those who commit such sins, as we told you and warned you before. For God did not call us to be impure, but to live a holy life.

## Beware the Adulterer's Allure

Solomon warns his young charge against the seductive speech of the temptress.

> **15.** In Proverbs 5:1-6 below, box the people (1a, 3a). Underline commands (1ab). Circle wisdom's blessings (2ab). Wavy-circle adultery's penalties (4ab, 5ab).
>
> 5:1 My son, pay attention to my wisdom,
>       turn your ear to my words of insight,
> 2 that you may maintain discretion
>       and your lips may preserve knowledge.
> 3 For the lips of the adulterous woman drip honey,
>       and her speech is smoother than oil;
> 4 but in the end she is bitter as gall,
>       sharp as a double-edged sword.
> 5 Her feet go down to death;
>       her steps lead straight to the grave.
> 6 She gives no thought to the way of life;
>       her paths wander aimlessly, but she does not know it.

Listen to the father, not the temptress. No matter how enticing, alluring, and sugary her words, giving in ends in bitterness.

### *Beware Adultery's Consequences*

Solomon next explains the reasons for his warnings.

> **16.** Read Proverbs 5:7-10. In the first column below, summarize the commands (7-8). In the second column, list what people stand to lose if they ignore these commands (9-10).
>
> | Commands | What People Stand to Lose |
> |---|---|
> |  |  |

David had lived as a man after God's own heart. But when his adultery was exposed, he lost his *honor*, *dignity*, and moral authority to correct his sons. He caused foreigners to despise God. And the consequences were severe.

Today adultery still destroys reputations and devastates families. *Wealth* vanishes as wage earners support two households and *enrich* lawyers.

> **17.** ♥ Describe the consequences of adultery that have affected someone you know.

## Embrace Your Wife

There's a God-sanctioned alternative: faithful marriage. This is the New Testament's solution to sexual temptations as well: "If anyone is worried that he might not be acting honorably toward the virgin he is engaged to, and if his passions are too strong and he feels he ought to marry, he should do as he wants. He is not sinning. They should get married" (1 Corinthians 7:36).

> **18.** Read Proverbs 5:15-20. (a) From whose well should the young man drink (15)? (b) With whom should he be intoxicated (18-19)? (c) With whom should he not be intoxicated (20)?

Old Testament professor David A. Hubbard explains the metaphors:

> Fidelity is the opening theme (v. 15). *"Cistern"* and *"well"* were prized possessions in a climate where rainfall was scarce and a time when the techniques of drilling deep wells were not yet discovered. The cistern collected rain water and could store any overflow of a well fed by a spring (*"running water"*). The two nouns describe the wife, and the *"water,"* fresh from a spring, pictures the refreshment of love making (see also Song 4:12, 15). The contrast between the harlot's honey that goes bitter (vv. 3-4) and the wife's water that stays sweet ("running") is the point of the whole chapter.[13]

A wife's lovemaking satisfies her husband's desires like fresh water. Marriage is God's gift to people. Some make comments that suggest God is against pleasure, like "This is so good, it must be sinful!" But as you can see from Proverbs, God's not against sex. After all, he made the pleasures. He's only against the misuse of them.

C.S. Lewis explains this well in *The Screwtape Letters*, where a senior devil counsels a junior devil on how to make a Christian stumble.

> Never forget that when we are dealing with any pleasure in its healthy and normal and satisfying form, we are, in a sense, on the Enemy's ground. I know we have won many a soul through pleasure. All the same, it is His invention, not ours. He made the pleasures: all our research so far has not enabled us to produce one. All we can do is to encourage the humans to take the pleasures which our Enemy has produced, at times, or in ways, or in degrees, which He has forbidden. Hence we always try to work away from the natural condition of any pleasure to that in which it is least natural, least redolent of its Maker, and least pleasurable.[14]

---

Marriage is God's gift to people.

---

## The Little Details
### *Bruce K. Waltke on Gazelle and Fowler:*

[Gazelles in Canaan] cannot be bred as domesticated animals because they are adapted to quick flight, and they panic when confined. *From the hand* probably refers to the principal method of hunting gazelles by the use of large, natural stone corrals ("kites") in the shape of triangles open at one end into which gazelles would be driven. Though the walls of these corrals were far too low to serve as a barrier, gazelles would not jump them. Trapped here, and often injured, they would be slaughtered en masse...*And as a bird*...shifts the imagery from an equid [horse] to a bird to emphasize the need for deliverance and to clarify the manner...Both the gazelle and the bird, once aware that they are caught in a trap, give all their attention to escaping the hunter's hand. So also the surety by alertness and swift action may escape the trap that his words have gotten him into...As he got into the trap by shaking hands, now he must escape that hand.[15]

### *Remember That the Lord Watches*
Solomon has another reason his son should avoid adultery.

> **19.** Check the boxes of the three reasons Proverbs 5:21-23 gives for avoiding adultery.
>
> ☐ Angry spouse will seek revenge ☐ Health will fail
>
> ☐ Dishonor will cover ☐ Lack of discipline will bring death
>
> ☐ Evil deeds will ensnare ☐ The LORD sees all

Just as David discovered, our deeds are never hidden from God. Sins ensnare. Sexual sins can break families, abolish peace, and threaten health.

The good news for David—and for us—is that God offers grace and forgiveness. David wrote Psalm 51 in response to Nathan's rebuke. He still suffered the consequences of his wrongdoing. Nonetheless, God forgave him. First John 1:9 tells us, "If we confess our sins, he is faithful and just and will forgive us our sins and purify us from all unrighteousness."

In this lesson we learned why adultery is foolish and how enjoying marriage fully is God's gift. We should beware adultery's consequences, embrace our spouse, and remember that the Lord sees all. Next we'll discover more that affects the family.

## *Day 4*

# Preserve the Family

Proverbs 5 named financial depletion as one reason to avoid adultery. Chapter 6 continues the theme of damaging finances through outside connections.

## Protect Family Finances

The first five verses of Proverbs 6 deal with the foolishness of getting into binding legal agreements when you have no control over the circumstances. For example, a gullible son might cosign a loan (put up security) for someone even though he can't afford to repay the loan if necessary, putting himself in the lender's power.

> **20.** Read Proverbs 6:1-5. (a) What foolish actions are traps and snares (1-2)? (b) What must one who has been so trapped do (3-5)?

Here, either the neighbor is the outsider ("stranger") for whom the lad cosigned, or he cosigned for a stranger who owes his neighbor.[16]

A similar entanglement can happen when parents decide to help their children financially beyond what the parents can afford. For example, some moms and dads aren't aware that personally taking out loans to pay for their children's college education lacks the safeguards that student loans have and can eat up what would otherwise be their retirement funds.[17]

## Work Diligently

Naivety is not the only flaw that threatens a family's finances. So can laziness. I consider myself blessed that my parents insisted we finish chores and homework before playing or calling friends. It was a great motivator and taught us not to be lazy. So when my husband and I fostered children who weren't accustomed to completing homework or even attending school, we set down the same rule.

> **21.** ♥ How did your parents try to combat laziness? Or how do you or did you discourage laziness in your children?

Here's what Solomon tells the slothful.

> **22.** In Proverbs 6:6-11 (ESV) below, box the people (6, 9, 11). Underline commands (6). Circle blessings (6, 8). Wavy-underline foolish actions (9, 10). Wavy-circle penalties (11).
>
> 6:6  Go to the ant, O sluggard;
>           consider her ways, and be wise.
>
> 7  Without having any chief,
>           officer, or ruler,
>
> 8  she prepares her bread in summer
>           and gathers her food in harvest.
>
> 9  How long will you lie there, O sluggard?
>           When will you arise from your sleep?
>
> 10  A little sleep, a little slumber,
>           a little folding of the hands to rest,
>
> 11  and poverty will come upon you like a robber,
>           and want like an armed man.

The *ant* can *harvest* in *summer* because she worked ahead of time without being forced. The Bible commands that we take care of the poor but not the lazy: "We gave you this rule: 'The one who is unwilling to work shall not eat'" (2 Thessalonians 3:10).

## Beware the Wicked

When I worked as a computer consultant, a client asked me to meet with him and one of the VPs. I was glad to hear from him, because I'd turned in the project months earlier and was waiting for him to test and approve it so we could schedule the final steps. But when we met, he told the VP I'd been busy and unable to work on it. Confused, I started to correct him, but he winked at me several times and gestured for me to be silent with his fingers. His untrustworthiness was obvious. Once my invoice was paid, that job was over.

Next, we'll double underline character qualities and double-wavy-underline character flaws.

**23.** In Proverbs 6:12-15 (ESV) below, box people (12a). Wavy-underline bad actions (12b, 13ab, 14ab). Double-wavy-underline flaws (14a). Wavy-circle penalties (15ab).

> 6:12 A worthless person, a wicked man,
>      goes about with crooked speech,
> 13 winks with his eyes, signals with his feet,
>      points with his finger,
> 14 with perverted heart devises evil,
>      continually sowing discord;
> 15 therefore calamity will come upon him suddenly;
>      in a moment he will be broken beyond healing.

The Hebrew word translated *worthless* is used in Judges 20:13 to describe rapists. *Crooked speech* is lies and deceptions. The troublemaker gestures to his conspirators as he *devises evil*. He is *continually sowing discord*, like social media trolls. Recognize and avoid them, but also take heart that their judgment—*calamity*—will come.

### Avoid the Seven Things the Lord Hates

Proverbs has a numbered list of actions the Lord hates. Such lists often begin with a number that's one fewer than the total number.

**24.** What are the seven things the Lord hates (6:16-19)?

| | |
|---|---|
| 1 | 5 |
| 2 | 6 |
| 3 | 7 |
| 4 | |

Those who love the Lord certainly want to know what things he hates so they can avoid them or repent from them. Thankfully, God offers grace.

## Protect Marriage

Now Solomon returns to sexual purity. If you've lived long enough, you know people whose marriages dissolved after adultery. Sometimes the unfaithful spouse repents, begs for forgiveness, and makes the necessary changes to begin the slow process of rebuilding trust. But often the family breaks apart, the children feel abandoned, and holidays are never the same.

**25.** Use Proverbs 6:20-24 to fill in the blanks below.

Keep, don't forsake, bind to your heart, fasten around your neck: _____
_____ .
They will
1) _____ you when you walk.
2) _____ you when you sleep.
3) _____ you when you awake.
They are
1) a _____ .
2) a _____ .
3) the _____ .
They will keep you from: _____ .

**The Little Details**
***The Billy Graham Rule***
Billy Graham brainstormed with friends over how to maintain integrity as traveling evangelists, and they came up with four rules to help avoid temptations evangelists face: greed, sexual immorality, criticizing churches, and exaggeration. One of the rules was not traveling, meeting, or even eating alone with women who weren't their wives.[18] The Bible doesn't command this rule, but they decided it would be best to avoid not only temptation but even the appearance of impropriety.

Young women need to beware the *smooth talk of* male adulterers, especially when they promise that divorce from their wives is coming.

## Flee Seducers

Some men and women pursue affairs with married people because making someone break their wedding vows makes them feel valuable and strong. Single serial seducers brag about conquests. But any who fall for the guiles of these people are not held innocent.

**26.** In Proverbs 6:25-29 (ESV) below, underline commands (25ab). Box people (26ab, 27a, 29ab). Wavy-circle penalties (27b, 28b, 29b).

6:25 Do not desire her beauty in your heart,
and do not let her capture you with her eyelashes;
26 for the price of a prostitute is only a loaf of bread,
but a married woman hunts down a precious life.
27 Can a man carry fire next to his chest
and his clothes not be burned?
28 Or can one walk on hot coals
and his feet not be scorched?
29 So is he who goes in to his neighbor's wife;
none who touches her will go unpunished.

*Carrying fire next to his chest* means embracing the adulteress. *Walk on hot coals* and *touches her* are euphemisms for sex with her. Adulterers usually think they won't be found out and therefore won't face consequences.

Andrew and Daniel discovered this passage's scorching truth. When Andrew told his mistress he wanted to break up, she threatened to call Megan and tell her everything. When he returned home, he confessed. Daniel told Chloe that the woman he was seeing broke things off after Chloe caught them. Chloe gave him another chance.

*Consider Adultery's Consequences*

**27.** Use Proverbs 6:30-33 to fill in the blanks below.

Thieves pay _____ if caught.
Adulterers
    1) have no _____ ,
    2) _____ themselves,
    3) get _____ ,
    4) their _____ will never be wiped away.

If you've never known someone who's committed *adultery*, you may not know how much it harms them. But if you have seen the anguish and pain it causes, Proverbs 6:32 makes total sense. Andrew got metaphorical *blows* and literal *disgrace*, lost his ministry, and suffered *shame*. Daniel assumed Chloe would keep silent and he'd escape consequences. Initially, his wife did bear her pain in silence. We'll return to her story.

In this lesson we found ways to preserve the family, including shunning rash financial pledges, working diligently, recognizing the wicked, and avoiding things the Lord hates. We also looked at ways to protect ourselves from seducers and saw the consequences of sexual immorality. In the next lesson we'll find hope for the hurting.

## Day 5

# Hope for the Hurting

Chloe's and Megan's lives became surreal as they tried to process a situation they never dreamed could happen to them as Christians married to Christians.

Although Chloe gave Daniel another chance and stayed silent, he kept disappearing. She hired a private detective. One day Daniel saw an envelope from the detective and knew he'd been caught. He confessed to adultery with more women, and he and Chloe separated.

Chloe told Clay and me what was happening. Clay and the men in their discipleship group urged Daniel to take steps showing repentance, including telling his children the reason he and Chloe were separated. He refused. He wanted to be Fun Dad. He was sorry he got caught, not sorry for what he'd done. Chloe filed for divorce. Clay disfellowshipped him from the group.

Andrew begged Megan's forgiveness. He started seeing a counselor and attending meetings for sex addiction. She needed time to think and finally said she'd give him another chance if he changed jobs to one that didn't require travel. But Andrew didn't want to change jobs. Though his repentance seemed real, it didn't go far enough for Megan to feel safe.

Shortly, we'll look at the hope of forgiveness when you've wronged someone and the hope of recovery when you've been wronged. For now, let's look at two passages beyond the prologue.

**28.** Do adulterers usually admit wrong (Proverbs 30:20)?

    ☐ Yes    ☐ No

In Proverbs 30:20, eating is a euphemism for sexual activity. Both satisfy an appetite.

> **29.** Read Proverbs 23:26-28. (a) What does the father want from the son (26a)? (b) What does the father want the son to observe (26b)? (c) What dangerous three things are wayward women like (27ab, 28a)? (d) What do wayward women increase among people (28b)?

The son mustn't give his *heart* to these women, for they are like three dangerous things. If he shuns this advice, he'll be a traitor to God and family. Like Daniel and Andrew were.

Earlier we read that Jesus said, "If your right eye causes you to sin, tear it out and throw it away. For it is better that you lose one of your members than that your whole body be thrown into hell" (Matthew 5:29 ESV). The fact is we don't need to tear out an eye, but we do need to radically tear out the obstacles that trip us up, whether porn, erotic novels, or fashion magazines. We can engage parental controls and filters for televisions, smartphones, and computers and enlist the help of accountability partners.

> **30.** ❤ What safeguards do you take against sexual temptation?

## The Hope of Forgiveness

While Chloe's and Megan's marriages did not survive their husbands' affairs, some marriages do survive affairs—with hard work, true repentance, and grace. I have relatives and friends who've been able to rebuild trust and recover. In her book *Messy Beautiful Love: Hope and Redemption for Real-Life Marriages*, Darlene Schact writes of how her husband forgave her after she had an affair:

> Loving his wife as Christ loves the church, Michael reached down to me with a hand of grace when I needed it most. When every thought told me that I was unworthy of love, something miraculous happened that changed the way that I look at marriage and the way that I look at our Savior. It was the realization that I am saved by nothing but the power of grace.
>
> Perhaps that's how the woman who was caught in adultery felt when she was brought to Jesus. Face-to-face with her Savior, she was left with nothing but His hand of grace. What did Jesus write in the sand with His finger that day? Some say He was listing sins—and perhaps He was. But a part of me will always wonder whether it was an invitation that beckoned her to come home to a place where sin is washed away by the blood of an incomparable Savior.[20]

Even if a wronged spouse decides not to stay in a marriage, for the truly repentant there remains hope for forgiveness.

## The Little Details

### Helpful Verses for Recovering from Abandonment

**Hebrews 13:5-6 (ESV):** He has said, "I will never leave you nor forsake you." So we can confidently say, "The Lord is my helper; I will not fear; what can man do to me?"

**Romans 12:19 (ESV):** Beloved, never avenge yourselves, but leave it to the wrath of God, for it is written, "Vengeance is mine, I will repay, says the Lord."

**Romans 2:1, 22 (ESV):** In passing judgment on another you condemn yourself, because you, the judge, practice the very same things... You who say that one must not commit adultery, do you commit adultery?

 *Optional*: If you need forgiveness now, turn to Psalm 51 in your Bible and pray it aloud. Then write 1 John 1:9 below.

## The Hope of Recovery

Adulterers harm not just themselves but their families. If your spouse has been unfaithful, I'm truly sorry for your pain. I hurt for you. In the hope of helping, here are lessons I learned from men and women in your situation.

***Remember God will never leave or forsake you.*** When a partner declares us unworthy of love, it's easy to wonder if God will do likewise. Don't let that happen. Memorize Hebrews 13:5-6 (see sidebar).

***If you seek counsel, find a counselor who fears the Lord.*** Since the fear of the Lord is the beginning of wisdom, this is essential. You need godly advice.

***Don't take revenge.*** Don't set your spouse's clothes on fire or drag a key along the side of a treasured vehicle. Don't slander. When you share your story, do so without exaggeration (see Romans 12:19 in sidebar).

***Don't have an affair.*** Trying to prove you're still attractive via an affair or one-night stands won't make you feel better. It will make you culpable (see Romans 2:1, 22 in sidebar).

***Don't equate divorce with unforgiveness.*** Manipulators may claim divorce means you haven't forgiven and that's worse than adultery. Don't believe that lie. You can forgive and still require right consequences. Get wise counsel on how to move forward with a truly repentant spouse or without an unrepentant one. Don't worry when getting through the emotions takes time even though you've forgiven. Work through it prayerfully.

***Don't take underserved blame.*** Your spouse's infidelity is not your fault. Apologize for anything you've done wrong that you haven't already made right, but don't accept responsibility for another's actions.

***Don't hide.*** You need the body of Christ. Find godly, insightful, supportive friends. Briefly explain what's happened: "My spouse had an affair, and we're separated."

***Remember your worth and praise come from God.*** Human judgments don't count. Seek God's praise. Memorize 1 Corinthians 4:1-5.

### Help Kids Recover

***Don't bad mouth your spouse to your kids.*** Be truthful but brief. Don't try to get them to correct your spouse; that's not their job.

***Assure your kids of your love and God's love.*** When a parent abandons a family, children wonder why that parent didn't love them enough to stay. They act out frustrations, confusion, and anger. Give extra patience. Memorize Hebrews 13:5-6 together.

***Make your faith obvious to your kids.*** When children realize that the wayward parent didn't believe in God's ways as much as claimed, they naturally question their own faith. Read the Bible with them. Let them see you depending on God's love.

***Enlist the help of godly adults.*** Try to have godly relatives and friends around to help kids process what's happened.

**31.** ♥ What advice would you give someone with an unfaithful spouse?

In this lesson we saw that adulterers often don't admit they've done wrong. For those who do, there's hope for forgiveness. For those who've been wronged, there's hope for recovery.

## Wisdom's Worth

**32.** ♥ In what way did you apply wisdom from Proverbs to your life this week?

This chapter examined Jesus's teaching about marriage, lust, and adultery. We discovered that what we take in through our senses goes into our hearts and comes out in actions. We absorbed reasons to avoid adultery and enjoy marriage. We looked at ways to preserve the family finances. Finally, we found hope for the wrongdoers and the wronged. In our next chapter we'll look at how to defeat temptation.

### *Wisdom Worship*

Find a quiet place and prepare your heart for grateful worship.

 Turn to Psalm 119:17-40 in your Bible and pray the passage aloud.

## Karla's Creative Connection

*For your ways are in full view of the LORD, and he examines all your paths.*

Proverbs 5:21

Have you heard or seen the quote that encourages us to "dance like no one is watching"? I love to dance, so this resonates with my heart. I want the freedom to creatively expressive myself as my body moves to the music, not caring what other people think of me. But the reality is that someone *is* always watching, and this week's key verse reminds us of this truth. That someone is God, and I do very much care what he thinks of me.

We love that God has promised to never leave us or forsake us, but that also means we can't hide from his sight. He's always watching over us as a loving Father keeping a watchful eye over his child. No secrets are hidden between us.

Sometimes when I've stepped out in faith or been obedient to do what's right, I've imagined Jesus smiling at me with a twinkle in his eye, pleased with my willingness to trust him. On more than one occasion I've also imagined him shaking his head in dismay as he watched me lose my wallet...again! Yes. I've not only lost my own wallet multiple times, but I also managed to lose my husband's once! Amazing that each one was found and returned—a true testimony to God's grace and watchful eye for sure!

And then, of course, the Lord has seen me at my worst. He's watched me struggle with anger and hurt the people I love the most. He's watched me turn my back on him during a time of pain and suffering and walk down a dark path that almost destroyed my relationship with him. He's watched me make poor choices over and over. But instead of turning his back on me, like the loving Father he is, he's called to me in the darkness and never given up on me. I am so thankful that he disciplines those he loves, leading us to a place of repentance and putting our feet back on the right path.

Your ways are in full view of the Lord—the good and the not so good. As you take time this week to examine the path you're on with him, imagine seeing it through his eyes and not yours. When you see something that's not pleasing to him, repent. Ask for and receive his forgiveness, and be thankful for his grace. I also hope you'll take some time to creatively connect with your heavenly Father by allowing yourself to imagine him smiling at you—because he does! Whenever you're afraid he might be shaking his head in dismay because you've "done it again," know he still loves you and is always interceding for you.

*Karla*

THE FEAR OF THE LORD IS THE BEGINNING OF WISDOM, AND KNOWLEDGE OF THE HOLY ONE IS UNDERSTANDING.

PROVERBS 9:10

## Chapter 3

# Proverbs 7:1–9:18
## Three Calls

Why does godly wisdom surpass worldly wisdom?

### Day 1

## "Come Here!"

According to Greek mythology, the Sirens were beautiful, winged enchantresses. In Homer's *The Odyssey*, the ship captain Odysseus learns he must sail by them with great care lest the Sirens' "piercing songs" lure his men into turning the ship toward their shores, where all would perish.[1]

Odysseus takes heed and instructs his men on what to do for safe passage. As his ship nears the Sirens, the wind suddenly dies. The men take down the sails, and Odysseus plugs their ears with wax. Then they tie Odysseus to the mast so he can safely hear the seductive singers. They begin to row, and soon Odysseus hears melodic singing: "Odysseus! Come here!"[2]

### God's Word to Us in Proverbs

Today we'll read poems describing women who call "Come here!" to passersby. They try to convince people they need what they offer.

> 🧠 Take a moment to pray for insight as you read God's Word.

> 1. ♥ Read chapters 7–9 in Proverbs. (a) What stood out to you in your reading? Why? (b) How can you apply that insight to your life this week?

### The First Step Toward Defeating Temptation

Proverbs 7 continues what Proverbs 5–6 began. Here, the father describes seeing a gullible youth fall for a wayward woman's wiles. He uses what he's seen as a lesson in recognizing temptation and thwarting the temptress's tactics. While he's warning his son about adultery in particular, his advice helps us defeat all temptations. We'll look at his first step in defeating temptation in this lesson and the rest in the next.

*Keep God's Word Always in Your Consciousness*
The father tells his son to listen carefully.

## The Little Details
### For Budding Poets

The example poem is a *tercet*, meaning the rhyming scheme is *aaa bbb* and so on. The lines are ***iambic pentameter***. *Iamb* means a light stress followed by a heavy stress. *Pentameter* means lines have five metrical feet (five pairs of light and heavy stresses). Here's the first line with heavy stresses in bold and bars between feet:

The **word** | of **God** | im**plant** | in **heart** | and **mind**

To write tercets, first write the thoughts you want to express, using the number of syllables you'll need per line (it's easier to rhyme longer lines). Then use a rhyming dictionary or rhyming website to find words that fit your thoughts. Rewrite the thoughts so the lines rhyme and the rhythm is consistent. Use a thesaurus to improve word choices.

2. Read Proverbs 7:1-5 (ESV) below. Box people (1a, 5ab) and body parts (2b, 3ab). Underline commands (1ab, 2ab, 3ab, 4ab). Circle blessings (2a, 5a).

> 7:1 My son, keep my words
> and treasure up my commandments with you;
> 2 keep my commandments and live;
> keep my teaching as the apple of your eye;
> 3 bind them on your fingers;
> write them on the tablet of your heart.
> 4 Say to wisdom, "You are my sister,"
> and call insight your intimate friend,
> 5 to keep you from the forbidden woman,
> from the adulteress with her smooth words.

Note the passage contrasts the father's *words* with the adulteress's *smooth words*. The *apple of your eye* is the delicate pupil that needs protection. Old Testament scholar Allen P. Ross writes:

> The expression "the apple of your eye" (...v.2) is literally "the little man in your eye," having reference to the pupil, where the object focused on is reflected. The point is that this teaching is so precious it must be guarded that closely. Verse 3 strengthens the admonition by alluding to the instruction for heeding the law given in Deuteronomy 6:8. The images used stress the memorization and retention of the teachings.[3]

*Write them on...your heart* means memorize these commands. This is the foremost rule of avoiding sexual sin.

3. ♥ What verse have you memorized to help you avoid any type of temptation?

That's it for today. In this lesson we looked at Solomon's first step toward defeating temptation. In our next lesson we'll discover five more.

# Pam's Simply Beautiful Wisdom

*Watch the path of your feet, and all your ways will be established.*

Proverbs 4:26 NASB

"How do I discern the will of God in my life?" is one of the questions I'm most often asked. I have a series of messages on *How to Cultivate a Simply Beautiful Life*, and there I share the 4 C's I use to discern God's will for my life.

## Seek Counsel

"Many are the plans in a person's heart, but it is the LORD's purpose that prevails" (Proverbs 19:21).

You can investigate what the Bible has to say on most any subject. Ask God for direction, and when he gives you a verse or passage, record it. Then if things get tough, you can go back and see that God gave you clear counsel.

"In abundance of counselors there is victory" (Proverbs 11:14 NASB).

Spend time with those who love you, love God's Word, and love helping you find God's will. Christian mentors, counselors, parents, grandparents, teachers, professors, Bible study leaders, and clergy are all people who would easily be comfortable helping you discern God's will.

## Listen for the Spirit's Conviction

When you attend a Bible-based college and learn how to rightly interpret God's Word, you discover he often repeats himself. That's especially true if what he has to say is significantly important at the time. I've found that to be the case in my life. When God is trying to get my attention, I hear the same message from him through several different sources: during my quiet time while reading the Bible, or from a sermon, a book, a magazine, a blog, song lyrics, or the lips of a friend. On a radio program or podcast.

I also look for the fruit of the Spirit as I go forward. Sometimes God commands us to take a step in the direction he's leading and then opens the path of provision. In Joshua 3, the priests are carrying the ark of the covenant over the Jordan River into the promised land. The Bible says the water stopped flowing as soon as their feet touched the river.

Sometimes you must step out in faith and look for the fruit of the Spirit. If you're stepping into God's plan, you'll experience "love, joy, peace, patience, kindness, goodness, faithfulness, gentleness, self-control" (Galatians 5:22-23 ESV).

## Ask for Confirmation

You may have heard "Put out a fleece and ask for a sign" based on the story of Gideon. We can learn a lot from the timid leader Gideon. God had assured him that if he went into battle for the noble cause he'd directed, Gideon would win the battle. But Gideon was afraid, so he asked God to make himself very clear:

> Then Gideon said to God, "You say that you have decided to use me to rescue Israel. Well, I am putting some wool on the ground where we thresh the wheat. If in the morning there is dew only on the wool but not on the ground, then I will know that you are going to use me to rescue Israel." That is exactly what happened. When Gideon got up early the next morning, he squeezed the wool and wrung enough dew out of it to fill a bowl with water. Then Gideon said to God, "Don't be angry with me; let me speak just once more. Please let me make one more test with the wool. This time let the wool be dry, and the ground be wet." That night God did that very thing. The next morning the wool was dry, but the ground was wet with dew (Judges 6:36-40 GNT).

Our patient God knows we sometimes need extra encouragement. When Bill and I moved into the pastorate in Southern California, housing prices had escalated so much that there was no way we'd qualify for a loan to buy an already-built home. Our only shot was to secure the funds to build one ourselves.

Bill had experience working as an architectural draftsman, and he was handy at the remodel on our first home, so we both believed he had the skill. But he just couldn't see how he'd be able to build a house, our family, and a church family all at the same time. So we asked for a sign. Bill prayed, "Lord, if building a home is your will, make it obvious at church this Sunday."

Without any announcement or prompting from the pulpit, as people exited after the service, a plumber, a cement worker, a roofer, a cabinetmaker, and a contractor all offered to donate time to build a home—and a parishioner offered to help with the down payment on the construction loan we'd need!

## Look at the *C*ircumstances

Sometimes all doors appear to be closed. But Jesus told us this: "Ask and it will be given to you; seek and you will find; knock and the door will be opened to you. For everyone who asks receives; the one who seeks finds; and to the one who knocks, the door will be opened" (Luke 11:9-10).

When God wants us to knock on a door for a length of time, it's to build passion in our hearts that will carry us forward once he opens the door. Eventually, if it's his will, the doors *will* open, and the pieces of the puzzle will form a beautiful picture of your future![4]

### Experiencing Scripture Creatively (Optional)

If you have extra time, consider these suggestions for creatively engaging with verses from this week's reading. The appendix has even more ideas.

- Follow Karla's instructions at the end of this chapter for creating a sacred space.
- Color Karla's full-page illustration at the end of the chapter while repeating the words of the verse aloud.
- Color the sidebar toppers using distinct color schemes. Choose your favorite for the bookmark on this chapter's opening page.
- Write a poem based on something in the chapter that stood out to you. Here's one on the six ways to defeat temptation found in Day 1 to Day 3.

  *A poem of Jean concerning Proverbs 7:1–8:21.*
  The Word of God implant in heart and mind;
  Provision do not make for flesh inclined.
  Seductions' tactics know and be not blind.
  Refuse temptation's call to come draw near.
  Control your heart so harms cannot adhere.
  To nobler song of Christ incline your ear.

# More Steps Toward Defeating Temptation

The Sirens' seductive song offers Odysseus glorious praise, unending pleasure, ceaseless joy, and all the knowledge for which he longs.[5] He orders his men to release him, but they can't hear because of the wax in their ears and merely tie him to the mast tighter.

The woman we'll read about in Proverbs 7 offers a young man praise, pleasure, and joy as well—but for a single night.

## Make No Provision for the Flesh

In the previous lesson, we saw that Solomon offered advice for defeating temptation: Keep God's Word always in mind. Now he'll continue advising, beginning with an illustration.

> 4. In Proverbs 7:6-9 (ESV) below, box people (7abc). Wavy-underline risky actions (8ab).
>
> 7:6  For at the window of my house
>        I have looked out through my lattice,
>  7  and I have seen among the simple,
>        I have perceived among the youths,
>        a young man lacking sense,
>  8  passing along the street near her corner,
>        taking the road to her house
>  9  in the twilight, in the evening,
>        at the time of night and darkness.

Solomon looks through *the lattice* that shields his open window and sees a young man leaving friends as *twilight* turns to night. The youth thinks *darkness* gives him cover, but the teacher sees him take *the road* toward temptation instead of away from it.

Perhaps the lad thought, *I'm not going to commit adultery. I'm just going to see if she's outside. I just want to see her and maybe talk to her. That's all.* But he did the opposite of what Paul later counsels: "Make no provision for the flesh, to gratify its desires" (Romans 13:14 ESV). Instead of avoiding temptation, he walks right into it.

## Recognize Seduction

The seductress is recognizable by her dress, attitude, manner, and place.

> 5. Read Proverbs 7:10-12 (ESV) below. Box the person (10a). Wavy-underline descriptions of her.
>
> 7:10  And behold, the woman meets him,
>         dressed as a prostitute, wily of heart.
>  11  She is loud and wayward;
>         her feet do not stay at home;
>  12  now in the street, now in the market,
>         and at every corner she lies in wait.

*Lies in wait* is ominous. Let's read what she does.

## The Little Details
### Bruce K. Waltke on Israelite Homes:

*At the window* refers to an opening in the wall of a house for light and air...[I]t was about 50 cm. [20 in.] square...An Israelite house... typically consisted of one or two stories, with the upper story of the domestic domain set aside for living and light storage and the lower story the economic domain for stabling and/or for storage and tools. Only the ground plan of the lower story is known; it typically had three or four rooms. During the period of the monarchy [the years Israelite kings ruled Israel and Judah], the entry was in the center of the front wall, leading into a courtyard floored with beaten earth...The lower story of an Israelite house lacked windows as a precaution against theft.[6]

## The Little Details

### *Bruce K. Waltke on Proverbs 7:17's Perfumes:*

She now stimulates him with aphrodisiac smells; all three names for perfumes in this verse are also found in Song 4:14 as odiferous images of sexual love...The bed consisted of a frame placed on four legs and was covered to the extent that cushions and blankets could be laid on it. Only the rich owned furniture in the ancient orient. The fragrances also contribute to the luxurious setting... *Myrrh*...is a fragrant gum-resin, used in both solid and liquid forms, manufactured by tapping south Arabian or African balsam trees...Myrrh was also pulverized into a fine powder and placed in a sachet worn between a woman's breasts (Song 1:13). *Lignaloes* ["aloes" ESV]...is a precious spice from the southeast Asian and north Indian eaglewood tree...In the Bible it always occurs with myrrh (Song 4:14). *Cinnamon*...is obtained from the bark of the cinnamon tree... The bark was peeled off, and from it light, flowing oil was gained, or the bark was dried and traded in the form of bars...Only kings and the very wealthy could afford to use [these perfumes] lavishly (Ps. 45:7-8[8-9]; Song 3:6-7).[9]

6. In Proverbs 7:13-20 (ESV) below, wavy-underline the adulteress's actions (13) and invitations (18).

> 7:13 She seizes him and kisses him,
> and with bold face she says to him,
> 14 "I had to offer sacrifices,
> and today I have paid my vows;
> 15 so now I have come out to meet you,
> to seek you eagerly, and I have found you.
> 16 I have spread my couch with coverings,
> colored linens from Egyptian linen;
> 17 I have perfumed my bed with myrrh,
> aloes, and cinnamon.
> 18 Come, let us take our fill of love till morning;
> let us delight ourselves with love.
> 19 For my husband is not at home;
> he has gone on a long journey;
> 20 he took a bag of money with him;
> at full moon he will come home."

The seductress appeals to all the young man's senses. The *sacrifices* that accompany *vows* would be in thanks for an answered prayer, though it's unclear whether she's Israelite or Canaanite. For both, worshipers had to eat the meat from the offering by the following day. If she's Canaanite, she needs a sexual partner as well.[7] She flatters the youth, saying, *I have come out to meet you, to seek you eagerly*, just what a lad who may not feel valued wants to hear. She offers, "We'll sit down to eat and lie down to play." Her bed adorned with expensive *linens* and spices shows wealth and desire; it may be an allurement he has yet to experience. She offers *love*—but only *till morning*. She assures him they will not be caught, for her *husband* is away for some time.[8]

### Refuse to Give In

This is the time for the young man to refuse her just as Joseph refused Potiphar's wife: "How then could I do such a wicked thing and sin against God?" (Genesis 39:9).

7. In Proverbs 7:21-23 (ESV) below, wavy-underline how the adulteress seduces the youth (21ab) and his foolish action (22a). Wavy-circle what it will cost him (23c).

> 7:21 With much seductive speech she persuades him;
> with her smooth talk she compels him.
> 22 All at once he follows her,
> as an ox goes to the slaughter,
> or as a stag is caught fast
> 23 till an arrow pierces its liver;
> as a bird rushes into a snare;
> he does not know that it will cost him his life.

Just as a cow on the way to a Golden Arches factory doesn't know its end is near, so the young man doesn't know he's on the way to eternal death.

## Control Your Heart

A 22-year-old gal told my husband, "You know, I really like this guy, but he's not a Christian, so I'm not letting my heart love him." That's profound. And controlling our hearts is something we all can do.

> 8. In Proverbs 7:24-25 (ESV) below, box people and body parts (24ab, 25a). Underline commands.
>
> 7:24   And now, O sons, listen to me,
>             and be attentive to the words of my mouth.
> 25      Let not your heart turn aside to her ways;
>             do not stray into her paths…

## Remember the Consequences

Here's the father's final word on the matter.

> 9. In Proverbs 7:26-27 (ESV) below, box people (26a). Wavy-underline the adulteress's actions (26a). Wavy-circle penalties (26ab, 27ab).
>
> 7:26   …for many a victim has she laid low,
>             and all her slain are a mighty throng.
> 27      Her house is the way to Sheol,
>             going down to the chambers of death.

*Death* may come at the hands of a jealous husband or after the final judgment.

Because Odysseus and his men remembered the consequences of allowing themselves to listen to the Sirens' songs, they made no provision for their flesh. The men allowed Odysseus to block their hearing with wax. Odysseus instructed them to tie him to the mast and not free him till they were past the danger. They helped each other.

> 10. ♥ What are some measures you can take to help you make no provision for the flesh?

In this lesson we read the seductress's call. It offered pleasure but not life. We discovered five ways to defeat temptation. Next we'll hear a different call.

## Day 3

# Lady Wisdom Calls

Odysseus listened to the Sirens' song and struggled to get free so he could go to them. He scowled at his men and demanded they free him. But they tied him tighter, as he'd told them to do when he could still think sanely. When they were finally out of earshot, he came to his senses. No longer struggling, he nodded to his men, and they released him. They all survived.

"He's not a Christian, so I'm not letting my heart love him."

Clay Jones writes about this in his book *Immortal*:

> Many Christians live their entire lives like Odysseus. They hear the music of this world and struggle against their Christian commitment. So many Christians lust after this world but manage, sort of, to not go headlong into sin. But too many escape their bonds and their lives are destroyed...We've all heard the Sirens' song. I've certainly heard the Sirens' song countless times and have felt like I'm tied to a mast by my commitments (and accountability!). But we don't have to live like that![10]

Jones then relates another, more hopeful story, this one about the musician Orpheus. When Orpheus "sang to his lyre the trees would listen and the beasts would follow him."[11] On a voyage passing the Sirens, he saw the men begin to succumb to the lulling, seductive songs. Orpheus took up his lyre and sang, reminding the men of who they were: "the strength of Greece...born for great labors and to face dangers that other men might not." He celebrated their accomplishments, "winners of the Golden Fleece" whose "story would be told forever." He pointed to what awaited, "the welcoming hands of the men and women of their own land." His was a better song, and the men listened and rowed to safety.[12]

A better song: who they were, what they'd accomplished, and the glorious welcome that awaited them.

We, too, need to listen to a better song when facing temptation. We need to remember who we are in Christ, what Jesus has already accomplished in us, and the glorious eternity that awaits us. As Jones writes, "The world plays a piercing song and if you follow its song throughout your life then it will draw you to your death and destruction. But there is a better music!"[13]

In the next poem, Lady Wisdom sings a magnificent melody to all who will hear.

**Wisdom Describes Her Call**

While the adulteress lurks in darkness, Lady Wisdom walks in public. The adulteress seduces with temporary pleasure, but Lady Wisdom reasons with eternal joys. The adulteress takes her victims down the path of death, but Lady Wisdom leads her followers up the path of life everlasting.

*Wisdom's Call Is for All*

> **11.** Read Proverbs 8:1-3 (ESV) below. Underline what wisdom does (1ab, 3b).
>
> 8:1  Does not wisdom call?
>        Does not understanding raise her voice?
>   2   On the heights beside the way,
>        at the crossroads she takes her stand;
>   3   beside the gates in front of the town,
>        at the entrance of the portals she cries aloud...

The adulteress seduces with temporary pleasure, but Lady Wisdom reasons with eternal joys.

*Wisdom* calls out—we just need to respond. And she calls out in public. *At the crossroads* is where one must decide between wisdom and folly. The city *gates* were where people gathered to talk and carry out business—a place Wisdom was needed.

## Wisdom's Call Is Personal

Wisdom's call may be public, but it's also personal.

> **12.** Read Proverbs 8:4-5 (ESV) below. Box the people to whom Wisdom calls (4ab, 5ab). Underline what she says they should do (5ab).
>
> 8:4    "To you, O men, I call,
>           and my cry is to the children of man.
> 5      O simple ones, learn prudence;
>           O fools, learn sense."

Wisdom calls to *the children of man* (that is, humankind) but particularly to the *simple ones* and *fools*. By heeding her call and listening to her voice, they can *learn prudence* and *sense*.

## Wisdom's Call Is Reliable

So much of what we hear and read is unreliable. An ad copywriter described his job to me as lying to convince people they need a product. Politicians are frequently caught misleading. Press secretaries spin bad news as good. The news media sometimes conflate opinion with facts. Conflicting reports can't all be true.

But Lady Wisdom assures us she offers something different.

> **13.** Read Proverbs 8:6-9 (ESV) below. Underline what Lady Wisdom calls us to do (6a). Double-underline what her words are and double-wavy-underline what they are not (6-9). Box who recognizes her words' worth (9ab).
>
> 8:6    "Hear, for I will speak noble things,
>           and from my lips will come what is right,
> 7      for my mouth will utter truth;
>           wickedness is an abomination to my lips.
> 8      All the words of my mouth are righteous;
>           there is nothing twisted or crooked in them.
> 9      They are all straight to him who understands,
>           and right to those who find knowledge."

Wisdom claims her *mouth will utter truth,* just as Jesus said of his own teachings, "Truly, truly, I say to you" (John 3:3 ESV). She assures us her words have no *wickedness* and are not *twisted or crooked. Crooked* "signifies to pervert, twist, or distort the ethical norm."[14] The simple and foolish may not recognize that *all* her words *are righteous*, but those who have walked in discernment will attest to their goodness. *They are all straight…and right* means her words follow God's commands.

## Wisdom Describes Her Benefits

After declaring her reliability, Wisdom explains what we gain from her words.

### Wisdom Describes Her Worth

Wisdom begins by comparing her worth to items most people value.

## The Little Details

### Mary Kassian on Three Categories of Fear:

The way I see it, the biblical concept of fear can be divided into three basic categories: apprehensive fear, respectful fear, and reverent fear.

FEAR says, *This is bigger and more powerful than me and beyond my control...*

1. Apprehensive fear adds... *and it will likely harm me.*

2. Respectful fear adds... *and it is worthy of my regard.*

3. Reverent fear adds... *and it is worthy of my veneration.*[15]

- - - - - - - - - - - - - - - - - - - -

In time I saw that God used my childlessness to mold my character and open ministries not available to homes with children.

- - - - - - - - - - - - - - - - - - - -

**14.** Read Proverbs 8:10-12 (ESV) below. Underline the verb in 10a. Circle what Wisdom says to choose instead of silver, gold, and jewels (10ab, 11a). Circle with whom she dwells and what she finds for us (12ab).

> 8:10 "Take my instruction instead of silver,
>     and knowledge rather than choice gold,
> 11 for wisdom is better than jewels,
>     and all that you may desire cannot compare with her.
> 12 "I, wisdom, dwell with prudence,
>     and I find knowledge and discretion."

Listening is not enough. One must *take* wisdom's *instruction* and *knowledge* over wealth. Jesus put it this way: "No one can serve two masters. Either you will hate the one and love the other, or you will be devoted to the one and despise the other. You cannot serve both God and money" (Matthew 6:24). *Wisdom* and *prudence* are inseparable. With wisdom comes *knowledge and discretion.*

After my second miscarriage, I was confused as to why God wasn't giving me a desire of my heart. But my greatest desire was knowing him and being conformed into Christ's image. In time I saw that God used my childlessness to mold my character and open ministries not available to homes with children. (Find a link to "The Journey of Childlessness" on DiscoveringTheBibleSeries.com.)

### Wisdom Describes Her Piety

The Creator designed the world and its inhabitants. He instructed us in how to live in that world in ways that bless us. Wisdom embraces those ways.

**15.** Read Proverb 8:13 (ESV) below. Underline the first five words. Double-wavy-underline what those who have that quality hate and the four things Wisdom hates.

> 8:13 "The fear of the LORD is hatred of evil.
>     Pride and arrogance and the way of evil
>         and perverted speech I hate."

Remember that Proverbs 1:7 reads, "The fear of the LORD is the beginning of knowledge, but fools despise wisdom and instruction." Now we see further what *the fear of the Lord* entails: *hatred of evil.* Wisdom hates *pride and arrogance,* for this pair exalts itself against God and claims to know better than God how the universe should run. Romans 12:16 (ESV) commands, "Live in harmony with one another. Do not be haughty, but associate with the lowly. Never be wise in your own sight."

Lady Wisdom also hates *the way of evil and perverted speech*: actions and words contrary to God's ways. If she hates those things, then the wise will as well.

### Wisdom Describes Her Competence

While the unchaste wife offered pleasure for a night, Wisdom offers enduring rewards.

16. Read Proverbs 8:14-16 (ESV) below. Circle what Wisdom has (14ab). Underline what those gifts enable leaders to do (15ab, 16ab).

> 8:14 "I have counsel and sound wisdom;
>         I have insight; I have strength.
> 15    By me kings reign,
>         and rulers decree what is just;
> 16    by me princes rule,
>         and nobles, all who govern justly."

Since Wisdom has *counsel, insight,* and *strength,* she can grant them to those who love her. Good leaders embrace godly wisdom to ensure they *decree what is just.*

17. ♥ What's one way you use wisdom in an area of leadership, whether in business, family, church, or friendship?

## Wisdom Describes Her Rewards

Wisdom rewards those who love her.

18. Read Proverbs 8:17-21 (ESV) below. Box the people Wisdom rewards (17ab, 21a). Circle her rewards (17a, 18ab, 19ab, 21ab).

> 8:17 "I love those who love me,
>         and those who seek me diligently find me.
> 18    Riches and honor are with me,
>         enduring wealth and righteousness.
> 19    My fruit is better than gold, even fine gold,
>         and my yield than choice silver.
> 20    I walk in the way of righteousness,
>         in the paths of justice,
> 21    granting an inheritance to those who love me,
>         and filling their treasuries."

Wisdom rewards those who love wisdom. Solomon learned this when he asked God for wisdom and the Lord granted him both wisdom and wealth (1 Kings 3:10-13). Wisdom knows the right way to *riches and honor.* Her *fruit is better* than purified *gold* and *silver.* She shows how to *walk in the way of righteousness* and *justice.* Those who seek wisdom find an *inheritance,* while those who seek wealth forgo wisdom.

19. ♥ Which of wisdom's rewards do you most desire today? Why?

In this lesson we've seen Wisdom's worth, piety, competence, and rewards. In the next we'll discover her credentials.

### The Little Details
*Allen P. Ross on Wisdom as Jesus Christ:*

Many interpreters have equated Wisdom in this chapter with Jesus Christ. The connection works only insofar as Jesus reveals the nature of God the Father, including his wisdom, just as Proverbs presents the personification of this attribute. Jesus' claims included having wisdom (Mt 12:42) and a unique knowledge of God (11:25-27). He even personified wisdom in a way that was similar to Proverbs (11:19; Lk 11:49). Paul saw the fulfillment of wisdom in Christ (Col 1:15-20; 2:3) and affirmed that Christ became our wisdom in the crucifixion (1 Co 1:24, 30). So the bold personification of wisdom in Proverbs certainly provides a solid foundation for the revelation of divine wisdom in Christ. But because Wisdom in Proverbs 8:22-31 appears to be a creation of God, it is unlikely that Wisdom can be identified as the preincarnate Jesus Christ.[16]

# Lady Wisdom's Credentials

**The Little Details**

*Bruce K. Waltke on Proverbs 8:22:*

The metaphor "brought me forth" signifies that Solomon's inspired wisdom comes from God's essential being; it is a revelation that has an organic connection with God's very nature and being, unlike the rest of creation that came into existence outside of him and independent from his being. Moreover, since this wisdom existed before creation and its origins are distinct from it, wisdom is neither accessible to humanity nor can it be subdued by human beings, but it must be revealed to people and accepted by them.[17]

Mere months before I married, the small business where I worked as a secretary unexpectedly closed, so I was scouring want ads for a full-time job. But every place I called wanted someone with more experience than I had. Desperate, I signed up with an employment agency. At my first interview with them, the middle-aged recruiter scowled and shook her head. She said because I lacked experience, I'd have to settle for less money than I wanted.

She sent me to an interview at a small company, where two men stared at my legs and then slowly looked me up and down. Later, the woman called and said the place was offering me the job, but I turned it down, citing the low pay. She berated me for wasting her time and said I'd better not turn down another offer or she'd drop me as a client. But I knew it wouldn't be wise to accept such a job, not only working with men like those but with such a low salary.

The next place she sent me was much better. The owner of the photography studio was professional and offered to match the salary I requested if I agreed to work as the receptionist there 45 hours per week. He even proposed giving me time off for my wedding and honeymoon if I agreed to make it up by working another three hours per week. When the agency called to say the studio made an offer, I accepted. The work was hard with long hours, but I gained both the pay and experience I needed.

Experience. We all want those who help us to have plenty of it. We want to see experience that shows not just accomplishments and knowledge but also wisdom.

## Wisdom Describes Her Experience

So what experience does Wisdom have? She explains in the next poem we'll read.

### *Wisdom Describes Her Length of Experience*

Job applications ask for length of employment. That's where Wisdom begins.

> **20.** Read Proverbs 8:22-29. Check which existed first:
>
> ☐ Earth ☐ Wisdom

The ESV translates *brought me forth* as "possessed me," the NRSVUE as "created me," and the HCSB as "made me" (see sidebar). God *formed* wisdom before creating the *world*. Wisdom, therefore, does not come from creation.

### *Wisdom Describes Her Tasks, Performance, and Attitude*

Potential employers want to know key accomplishments, read recommendations, and discern attitude toward work and people. Wisdom turns to those next.

**21.** Read Proverbs 8:30-31 (esv) below. Underline where Wisdom was during creation and box what she was like (30a). Circle God's opinion of her performance (30b). Double underline descriptions of her attitude (30c, 31ab). Box those she delighted in (31b).

> 8:30 "Then I was beside him, like a master workman,
> and I was daily his delight,
> rejoicing before him always,
> 31 rejoicing in his inhabited world
> and delighting in the children of man."

Wisdom was *beside* God and is not God. She was a *master workman* whose performance gave God *delight*. Wisdom was *rejoicing* in creation and *delighting* in humans. She got along with God and people. Creation was good! Yes, sin entered the world, but God set in motion his plan to redeem people from sin before creation (1 Peter 1:20).

## Wisdom Calls Again

Job applications ask for contact information. If we want to engage wisdom's services, that's what we'll need.

**22.** Read Proverbs 8:32-34. What should we do to find wisdom?

*Now then, my children, listen to me* are the words the father spoke in Proverbs 7:24, leading some scholars to view Lady Wisdom as a personification of the father.[19] Others see her as calling pupils *children*. Being *blessed* is more than being happy; it's "the joyful spiritual condition of those who are right with God and the pleasure and satisfaction that is derived from that."[20] *Watching daily* and *waiting* describe constant seeking.

### Wisdom Summarizes Her Offer

Years after that early job search, I worked as a computer consultant, crafting project proposals for potential clients. I routinely wrote executive summaries so upper management could quickly see the bottom line. That's what the poem offers next.

**23.** Use Proverbs 8:35-36 to fill in the blanks below.

Those who find Wisdom…
 1) find_____ .
 2) receive _____ from the Lord.
Those who don't find Wisdom…
 1) _____ themselves.
 2) love _____ .

Verse 35 contains terrific news. But notice that the poem's final word links back to the ending of the poem about the unchaste wife, which read, "Her house is the way to Sheol, going down to the chambers of death" (Proverbs 7:27 esv).

**The Little Details**
*Bruce K. Waltke on Proverbs 8:29's Sea:*
Many texts affirm that the Lord harnessed the sea by setting its limits (cf. Pss. 93; 104:6-9). *And the waters... cannot go beyond...his command...*reprises Job 38:11: "when I said: 'This far you may come and no farther.'" The reprise puts beyond reasonable doubt that Wisdom has in mind that the Creator established unalterable laws or ordinances that set the boundaries for the earth that the hostile sea cannot transgress (see Job 38:8-11). The chaotic energy of the sea operates within strict limits. Nevertheless, it retains an element of freedom within divine restraint and in that sense retains meaning in the cosmos, the scheme of things, the created "order." Whereas Proverbs emphasizes the restraining structures, the book of Job highlights the freedom associated with chaos, which makes human life within order relatively unpredictable and inexplicable.[18]

**The Little Details**

*Allen P. Ross on the Goddess Sophia:*

A number of feminist commentators take this passage [Proverbs 9:1] as referring to a goddess named Wisdom [or Sophia] who builds a palace, gives a feast, and inaugurates worship…There is no support for such a view, especially within the strict monotheism of Israel.[22]

24. ♥ What stood out to you most in Proverbs 8? Why?

In this lesson, we read Lady Wisdom's call to all who might seek her. She describes what she bestows on those who love her as well as her credentials. The poem ends with the hope of blessing for those who watch and wait at her door. In our next lesson we'll read about the banquet that awaits those who respond to her.

## Day 5

# Rival Invitations Calling

One year we received three invitations for parties on Christmas Eve, so we had to choose which one to joyfully accept and which two to sadly decline. Today we'll read invitations to two simultaneous parties. We can choose either, but they differ in guests and offerings. Indeed, most people will want to gladly decline one and joyfully accept the other. Old Testament professor Bruce K. Waltke describes the invites:

> Wisdom, out of true love, competes for the hearts of the uncommitted; Folly, out of erotic lust, competes for their bodies. Wisdom invites them to leave behind their old identification and become wise at her sumptuous feast; Folly lures those who have been going straight to turn aside, mindless of the consequences, at her profligate and self-indulgent meal. Those who accept Wisdom's invitation will live; the apostates will die.[21]

Proverbs 9 is the epilogue to the lengthy prologue we've now traversed. It employs an arrangement that's common in Hebrew poetry called *chiasm* (KEY-asm). In a chiasm, the theme is in the center, and elements equal distance from the center are linked by something that repeats. Below, I've identified linked elements by using the same letter. The first repeat of an element has a prime mark ('). In longer chiasms, the second repeat would have two prime marks ("), the third three ('''), and so on.

  A       Wisdom's invitation

      B       Consequences to wisdom teachers

          C       The beginning of wisdom

      B'      Consequences to responders to teachers

  A'      Folly's Invitation

**Lady Wisdom's Invitation**

Lady Wisdom is throwing a party and sending invitations.

25. Read Proverbs 9:1-6 (ESV) below. Box people (1a, 3a, 4ab). Underline Wisdom's actions (1-3) and admonishments (4-6). Circle what she offers (2ab, 5ab, 6a).

> 9:1 Wisdom has built her house;
>      she has hewn her seven pillars.
> 2 She has slaughtered her beasts; she has mixed her wine;
>      she has also set her table.
> 3 She has sent out her young women to call
>      from the highest places in the town,
> 4 "Whoever is simple, let him turn in here!"
>      To him who lacks sense she says,
> 5 "Come, eat of my bread
>      and drink of the wine I have mixed.
> 6 Leave your simple ways, and live,
>      and walk in the way of insight."

Lady Wisdom is incredibly industrious, strong, and hardworking. *House* may symbolize Solomon's book or the cosmos. Most houses had only three supporting pillars, so *seven pillars* "points to an exceptionally large, grand, and stately structure where numerous guests are expected. 'Seven' in this literary fiction symbolizes perfection."[23] *Mixed her wine* normally means one has added either honey and spices[24] or water,[25] but here *beasts* and *wine* symbolize her teaching and proverbs. *Set her table* is figurative for the arrangement of proverbs. A woman's servants would be female, so *her young women* ("servants" in the NIV) refers to all who call others to hear wisdom. *Eat...and drink* means listen to her teaching; the New Testament likewise symbolizes sound teaching as food (1 Corinthians 3:2). *Live,* she says, for she offers spiritual life.

## Everyone Faces Consequences

Our poem next tells Wisdom's messengers the types of responses they can expect when they invite others to her banquet.

26. Read Proverbs 9:7-9 (ESV) below. Box the people. Underline actions. Wavy-circle bad results and circle good results.

> 9:7 Whoever corrects a scoffer gets himself abuse,
>      and he who reproves a wicked man incurs injury.
> 8 Do not reprove a scoffer, or he will hate you;
>      reprove a wise man, and he will love you.
> 9 Give instruction to a wise man, and he will be still wiser;
>      teach a righteous man, and he will increase in learning.

*Scoffers* ("mockers" in the NIV) reject godly wisdom and *abuse* those who offer it because they are arrogant and hate correction. The wise embrace humility and appreciate a word that instructs them rightly. These verses give us a way to judge ourselves.

27. ♥ Think over how you respond to correction and which response from Proverbs 9:7-9 is most like you. How can you respond more like the wise?

### The Little Details
### *Allen P. Ross on Scoffers:*

We have met the scoffer before in the book (1:22; 3:34); he is the immoral or frivolous person who will not live by wise and moral teachings (13:1; 15:22; 21:24; 22:10). Moreover, he is not content to let others do so without his cynical mocking. The warning is that anyone who tries to correct a mocker is asking for trouble. "Strife" or "insult" ["abuse" ESV] (*qālôn*) *and "abuse"* ["injury" ESV] (*mûm*) are second nature to this cynical heckler (v.7). The only response such rebuke will receive is hatred... The idea of hatred is a spontaneous rejection as well as a dislike for the one trying to correct the mocker. One may perceive the potential to learn in such a person, but if met with such scorn the effort should be abandoned.[26]

**The Little Details**

*Mary Kassian on Reverent Fear:*

Reverent fear says: "God is bigger and more powerful than me, beyond my control, and worthy of my veneration."…This beautiful jewel is made up of five main facets: awe, obedience, devotion, worship, and trust.[27]

Now we come to the key verse in this chapter's poem.

> **28.** Read Proverbs 9:10 (ESV) below. Box the two names of God. Underline the two things we must start with. Circle what they bring.
>
> 9:10    The fear of the LORD is the beginning of wisdom,
>           and the knowledge of the Holy One is insight.

The Creator designed us to thrive in certain circumstances. Following his instructions is wise. Humbly submitting to the Lord's authority is the first step toward becoming wise. Not only that, but knowing *the Holy One*—God—makes sense of the world.

Next the poem describes the consequences of two extremes.

> **29.** Read Proverbs 9:11-12 (ESV) below. Circle Wisdom's benefits (11ab, 12a). Underline the good action and wavy-underline the bad one (12ab). Wavy-circle the penalty (12b).
>
> 9:11    For by me your days will be multiplied,
>           and years will be added to your life.
> 12    If you are wise, you are wise for yourself;
>           if you scoff, you alone will bear it."

Since "the fear of the LORD is the beginning of wisdom," wisdom takes us straight to God. In him we find eternal *life*. But those who *scoff* do not find life. Ultimately, they *alone will bear* responsibility for their choices and sin. Wisdom, on the other hand, rewards the *wise* in many ways (as we shall see), including *life*.

## Woman Folly's Invitation

Now we turn to the second invitation, this one from Woman Folly.

> **30.** Read Proverbs 9:13-18 (ESV) below. Box the people (13a, 15a, 16ab, 18ab). Double-underline Folly's flaws (13b). Wavy-circle her fare and guest room (17ab, 18b).
>
> 9:13    The woman Folly is loud;
>           she is seductive and knows nothing.
> 14    She sits at the door of her house;
>           she takes a seat on the highest places of the town,
> 15    calling to those who pass by,
>           who are going straight on their way,
> 16    "Whoever is simple, let him turn in here!"
>           And to him who lacks sense she says,
> 17    "Stolen water is sweet,
>           and bread eaten in secret is pleasant."
> 18    But he does not know that the dead are there,
>           that her guests are in the depths of Sheol.

While Lady Wisdom toils for her guests, Folly takes it easy and sits. *Seductive* could be translated "simple" (NIV, NKJV), "naive" (NASB), or "gullible" (HCSB). Old Testament professor Allen P. Ross writes, "The text of v. 13 is uncertain…The point of the passage seems to be a description of this woman as seductive and without knowledge of moral integrity."[28] Unlike Wisdom, Folly has not built her house, prepared a banquet, set her table, or sent out messengers. Instead, *she sits at the door of her house…calling to* gullible passersby. Notice that Folly's words in verse 16 are identical to Wisdom's in verse 4.

While Lady Wisdom offers mixed wine, Folly offers *stolen water*, claiming its illegitimacy sweetens it. Waltke notes, "An Arabic proverb says, 'Everything forbidden is sweet.'"[29] Wisdom prepares meat and bread, but Folly offers *bread eaten in secret.* We've already seen water and eating as metaphors for sex (Proverbs 5:15-16; 30:20). So *stolen water* and *bread eaten in secret* refer to adultery; what is stolen is that which legitimately belongs to her husband.

One more contrast: While Wisdom offers life, Folly brings death. *Sheol* can mean the grave, death, extreme danger, or hell/hades (the realm of the departed who "are cut off from fellowship with God"[30]). Ross writes, "Many 'eat' on earth what they 'digest' in hell."[31]

Jesus says something similar: "Enter through the narrow gate. For wide is the gate and broad is the road that leads to destruction, and many enter through it. But small is the gate and narrow the road that leads to life, and only a few find it" (Matthew 7:13-14).

In this lesson, we compared Lady Wisdom's invitation to Woman Folly's and discovered striking differences. We also saw the consequences of accepting each invitation.

## Wisdom's Worth

**31.** ♥ In what way did you apply wisdom from Proverbs to your life this week?

In this chapter we looked at how to defeat temptation and saw how qualified Wisdom is to aid us. In our next chapter, Proverbs shows us how the simple can become wise.

### Wisdom Worship

Find a quiet place and prepare your heart for grateful worship.

 Turn to Psalm 119:41-64 in your Bible and pray the passage aloud.

While Lady Wisdom toils for her guests, Folly takes it easy and sits.

## Karla's Creative Connection

*The fear of the LORD is the beginning of wisdom, and knowledge of the Holy One is understanding.*

Proverbs 9:10

Jean ended this week's study encouraging us to find a quiet place to be alone with God. A place to give him praise for being the source and supplier of the wisdom we need so desperately. A place where we can seek his wisdom for our everyday lives without distractions.

Our key verse for this week tells us if we want God's wisdom and understanding to lead us and guide our decisions, we need to know God and reverence him for who he truly is. Giving yourself a quiet time each day to worship him in prayer has the power and potential to bring greater peace and purpose to your life.

The Bible tells us Jesus often withdrew to a lonely, secluded, or out-of-the-way place to pray, and he is our perfect example. For some of us, finding a quiet place isn't difficult, but with such busy lives, going there can still be a struggle. For others, especially moms with little ones, even finding a quiet space can seem impossible. And then there's the challenge of finding not the space itself but the quiet place in our heart and thoughts.

Whatever the challenge, the ultimate goal is to create a way to be alone with God—to create a sacred space to pray. Now, don't let the word *sacred* scare you, because it's such a beautiful word and simply means "dedicated or set apart for the service or worship of a deity."[32] For Christians, that deity is the one true God. And that's what we're looking for—a time and place set apart and dedicated to creatively connect with him.

So this week try creating your own unique sacred space as simple or as elaborate as your heart desires. The goal is not so much how it looks but how it helps draw you to its purpose and provides you with the quiet you need. Prayer warrior Susanna Wesley, mom of 11 and mother of John and Charles Wesley (brothers whom God used mightily to impact the world) created her own sacred space by pulling her long white apron up over her head. That signaled to her little ones that she was not to be disturbed while she prayed.

Your sacred space may be your favorite chair by a window. Or maybe an outdoor swing where you can see God in nature. Wherever I am, I personally like to light a candle to help me focus on Jesus being the Light of the world and the Light of my life.

However and wherever you create your sacred space, may it draw you to a time devoted to being still and in awe of God as the Author of the wisdom and understanding you seek.

*Karla*

THE FEAR OF THE LORD IS THE BEGINNING OF WISDOM AND KNOWLEDGE OF THE HOLY ONE IS UNDERSTANDING. PROVERBS 9:10

## Chapter 4

## Proverbs 10:1–12:28
## The Wise, the Simple, and the Fool

How can the simple become wise?

**Day 1**

## Ouch!

As a child too short to reach my bedroom light switch even standing on tippy-toes, I would push my little red wooden chair against the wall, scramble up, stand on its seat, and flip the switch.

One night, the scrambling didn't go as planned. I tumbled backward to the floor with a yelp and a thud. The chair fell on top of me and whapped my face. I squirmed, struggling to untangle my legs from its legs.

Soon my mother was cradling me in her lap in the living room, gently pressing an ice cube wrapped in a washcloth to my face. My father came over to see the damage. Mom lifted the ice and murmured, "Looks like she's going to have a black eye."

"Mm-hmm," he replied.

Alarmed, I asked, "What's a black eye?!" I'd never seen anyone with an all-black eye. My mom placed the ice back on my face.

The next morning Mom lifted me above the bathroom vanity so I could see myself in the mirror. I was relieved to see my eye's white and brown parts were still white and brown. The large red and purple bruise surrounding my eye was interesting, though. I was curious as to why adults called these colors "black" and said "black *eye*" when the hues were clearly around the eye, not in it.

Not only did my black eye teach me that language can be odd but that gravity is strong. I went from knowing I could bounce a ball on the ground to knowing *I* could bounce on the ground too. I started out simple in gravity's ways and grew wiser about balancing while climbing. To this day I still test anything I step onto that's not a stair.

1. ♥ What childhood wisdom did you learn that has kept you safe and healthy?

Children start out simple and eventually become wise or foolish. If I'd ignored the fall and neglected to change how I scampered up my chair, I'd have scooched into the foolish category. But repeatedly testing my chair to see what would make it tip made me wiser.

This chapter will look at those three types of people: the wise, the simple, and the fool. So let's begin with our reading, after which we'll change things up a bit.

## God's Word to Us in Proverbs

Chapters 1–9 introduced us to the book of Proverbs and explained why we need wisdom. But chapters 10–30 contain collections of individual proverbs covering diverse topics. We can study these in two ways: in the order they're listed or topically.

One advantage to covering these chapters in the order they're listed is that we're likely to find a verse or passage that helps with a current situation. So today we'll read chapters 10–12 in one sitting. Watch for insights into what's happening in your own life.

Proverbs 10:1 has a heading: "The proverbs of Solomon." It starts ***Collection II: Proverbs of Solomon***, which spans 10:1–22:16. Most of the proverbs in the first half of Collection II are *antithetical*; that is, the second line contrasts with the first line.

> 🗯 Take a moment to pray for insight as you read God's Word.

> 2. ♥ Read chapters 10–12 in Proverbs. (a) What stood out to you in your reading? Why? (b) How can you apply that insight to your life this week?

Reading Proverbs' collections topically also has an advantage: We get a more well-rounded understanding of subjects and grasp nuances better. So for the Day 2 to Day 5 lessons, we'll select one broad subject addressed in the chapters we read and cover it in detail, reading verses from throughout Proverbs. We'll also find a few proverbs that are repeated in different collections. When that happens, the question will ask you to look up either verse.

## The Benefits the Wise Enjoy

This chapter's topic is "The Wise, the Simple, and the Fool." Let's begin by looking at some benefits the wise enjoy.

> 3. What results from getting wisdom and cherishing understanding (Proverbs 19:8)?

*Wisdom* brings confidence that can make *life* enjoyable and prosperous.

> 4. Use Proverbs 21:20-22 to fill in the blanks.
>
> Fools don't store
> 1) _____
> 2) _____
> Pursuers of righteousness and love find
> 1) _____
> 2) _____
> 3) _____
> The wise pull down
> _____

In Solomon's day, people harvested grain in the spring and pressed *olive oil* in the fall. They used oil in cooking, to moisturize skin and hair, and to light lamps. The wise made sure supplies lasted throughout the year. In more general terms, the wise practiced constraints that allowed them to accumulate wealth, while the foolish spent all they had without thought for tomorrow's needs.

The wise person's pursuit of *righteousness and love* brings fullness of *life, prosperity,* and *honor.* The wise dwell securely and can *pull down the stronghold in which* the wicked *trust.*

> **5.** In Proverbs 24:13-14 below, circle wisdom's benefits.
>
> 24:13    Eat honey, my son, for it is good;
>          honey from the comb is sweet to your taste.
> 14    Know also that wisdom is like honey for you:
>          If you find it, there is a future hope for you,
>          and your hope will not be cut off.

The father begins by telling his son to *eat honey* (something he probably wants to do anyway) and then uses honey as a metaphor for *wisdom.* Honey is *good* for its medicinal value as well as being *sweet to your taste.* Just as honey imparts goodness and sweetness to people, so *wisdom* gives a good and sweet *future hope.*

In this lesson we discovered more about Proverbs' arrangement and began to look at the advantages the wise have, a topic we'll return to in the Day 5 lesson. Next we'll find the differences between the wise, the simple, and the fool.

**The Little Details**
*For Budding Poets*

The poem at the end of this lesson is a **quatrain**, which means the rhyming pattern is *abab cdcd,* and so on. Its lines are ***iambic tetrameter***. *Iamb* means the meter has a light stress followed by a heavy stress. *Tetrameter* means there are four metrical feet. Here is the poem's first line with heavy stresses in bold and bars between metrical feet:

The **sim**|ple **an**|y**thing** | be**lieve**

## Pam's Simply Beautiful Wisdom

*Does not wisdom call out?...For those who find me find life and receive favor from the LORD.*

Proverbs 8:1, 35

I keep mementos of my desire to walk in integrity. In the Old Testament, God called his people to build altars to remind them of everything he'd done for them. On my desk, I have a figurine with a beach umbrella to remind me to stay under God's umbrella of blessing. In the margin in my art Bible is written "Every word of God is flawless; he is a shield to those who take refuge in him" (Proverb 30:5). Next to that verse, I doodled out a cartoon of Bill and me under a colorful umbrella as a reminder that I want the blessings that come with living out the Word.

I also have a collection of heart-shaped rocks and paperweights to capture a desire to seek God with a whole and pure heart. A compass points to God as my true North when I need direction. Photographs of my family, friends, and mentees prompt me to recall that every choice affects those I love. When I'm tempted to step out from God's will, I picture myself having to own up to some sin or failure to all those faces. I much prefer spending my time pouring positives into those lives instead of unravelling negative consequences I created by my own selfishness or rebellion.

I keep a clay turtle as a symbol of integrity. I also give one to each woman I mentor and say, "If you see a turtle on a fence post, what should you ask? 'How did it get there?' Turtles can't climb atop a post; someone had to put the turtle there. In the same way, God placed each of us on our platform of influence, and if we turn our back on him and his principles, he can remove us from ministry (even for a season). First Peter 5:6 (NASB) says, "Humble yourselves under the mighty hand of God, so that He may exalt you at the proper time."

The last memento on my desk is a frame filled with Bible verses. Just under the glass, I can see the commands and the promises of blessings if I obey what the verses say. What I and others can't see are the articles I've placed behind those verses about leaders who have spiraled out of control and crashed their lives, ministries, marriages, and children's lives. When I look at that frame, I say to myself, *Seek to be the blessings on the front, not the headlines on the back.*[1]

One day while researching for this study on wisdom, I inscribed all the verses in Proverbs about integrity in a special art notebook with black paper, writing cursive in white ink. I gathered pages and pages of instruction accompanied with the motivating blessings and benefits. (My friend Lisa Saruga used a black notebook and wrote in white pen for her quiet times after she was brutally attacked. Writing Scripture in white moved her healing forward out of darkness into God's light and life. Now she raises funds for her ministry to victims of violence by selling these sets. You can find that contact information and a worksheet in the extras on DiscoveringTheBibleSeries.com so you can do your own study of these verses on integrity, uprightness, righteousness, and wisdom.)

I taught my children that *integrity is who you are when no one is looking—except God.*

If the book of Proverbs has one major theme, it's that wisdom is achieved by a step-by-step pursuit of integrity, and each step brings you closer to God and the blessings of walking with him.

"Whoever walks in integrity walks securely" (Proverbs 10:9).

## PLANT and WATER God's Word

If we have a heartbeat of walking in wisdom, we must hunger after God's Word, then walk it out in obedience. My mother is a master gardener, and she's always out in her garden planting, weeding, trimming, pruning, fertilizing, and watering with tender loving care. Picture your own life as a garden. If you want it to blossom in beauty, here are a few simple steps you can take to cultivate growth in God's Word:

First, PLANT God's Word into your life consistently.

- *P*robe. Find a process of studying God's Word so it makes sense to you.
- *L*isten. Hearing other people teach the Bible and relate how it's affecting their lives will encourage growth in you.
- *A*cquaint yourself. There's no substitute for consistently reading God's Word for yourself.
- *N*ail it down. Memorizing specific verses makes them readily accessible when you need them.
- *T*hink it over. Asking yourself questions like *How do I live this out?* and *How does this apply to me?* energizes God's Word in your life.

Second, WATER your relationship with God through interactive prayer.

- *W*ait for God. Listen in prayer by saying, "God, you go first."
- *A*cknowledge your sin to God. Confess your sins and receive his forgiveness.
- *T*hank God. Praise him for the blessings he's given you.
- *E*xalt God. Worship him.
- *R*equest of God. Tell him your needs.

As you PLANT and WATER God's Word in your life daily, may you enjoy the fragrance and loveliness of your garden of a blessed life.[2]

*Pam*

### Experiencing Scripture Creatively (Optional)

If you have extra time, consider these suggestions for creatively engaging with verses from this week's reading. Check the appendix for more creative ideas.

- Identify a verse in today's reading that convicted you. Follow Karla's instructions at the end of this chapter for creatively imagining yourself on God's potter's wheel as he uses the verse's truth to mold you.
- Color Karla's full-page illustration at the end of the chapter while repeating the words of the verse aloud.
- Color the sidebar toppers using distinct color schemes. Choose your favorite to use on the bookmark on this chapter's opening page.
- Write a poem based on one or two proverbs that stood out to you. Here's an example based on question 6:

*A poem of Jean concerning Proverbs 14:15; 22:3.*
The simple anything believe;
The prudent stop their steps for thought.
The simple's soul does often grieve;
The other far from danger got.

## The Little Details
### Antithetical Parallelism

Proverbs 14 verses 15 and 18 employ *antithetical parallelism*. That's when the two halves of a proverb contrast. When reading such a proverb, look closely at parallel parts to see how they relate. For example, in Proverbs 10:13, the person who has understanding has wisdom on his lips, but the one who lacks sense has a rod on his back. The two types of people bear two different things on their bodies. This is the most common type of proverb in Proverbs.

---

*Just as fool's gold appears golden in sunlight, so do many false ways appear golden in this world's light.*

---

## Day 2

# Fool's Gold

When I was a child, my family often camped. At one campsite, I found rocks with golden sparkles. I picked one up and ran to my father, shouting, "Daddy! Daddy! Look! I found gold!" I was sure we'd be rich. But he smiled as he took the rock in one hand and shaded it with his other. The gold specks turned dark gray. He said, "See how it's no longer gold when the sun isn't shining on it? This is fool's gold."

Just as fool's gold appears golden in sunlight, so do many false ways appear golden in this world's light. But like fool's gold, they don't lead to that for which we hope. Then again, there is a way that leads to the heavenly city with streets of gold.[3]

### Spot the Simple

At the campsite, I was what Proverbs calls simple. I needed my father's wisdom. Indeed, all children start out simple in everything.

6. Contrast the simple and the prudent (Proverbs 14:15, 18; 22:3 or 27:12—they're identical).

| Simple | Prudent |
|---|---|
|  |  |

When Clay and I were in Yellowstone National Park recently, we paid attention to warning signs and were careful not to approach geysers or wild animals too closely. But the book *Death in Yellowstone* details the tragic consequences for people who *see danger* signs but *keep going and pay the penalty.*

### Know the Difference

We can distinguish gold from fool's gold, also known as pyrite, in several ways. A knife will scratch gold but flake pyrite. Gold weighs twice as much as pyrite. Beating gold forms it into sheets, while beating pyrite crumbles it.

Likewise, we have ways to distinguish the wise from fools. Knowing the distinctions can help us discern to whom we should turn for advice.

7. Contrast the wise with the fool (Proverbs 10:13-14, 23; 12:8; 15:21; 17:24).

| The Wise | The Fool |
|---|---|
|  |  |

Here are a few more ways to differentiate between the wise and foolish.

8. Contrast the wise with the fool (Proverbs 14:3, 8, 9, 16, 24, 33).

| The Wise | The Fool |
|----------|----------|
|          |          |

## Don't Mock True Gold

Now that we know how to distinguish the wise from the foolish, we'll look at one type of fool: mockers. These are the people whose foolishness has grown to the point that they mock God's commands and the people who follow them.

9. In Proverbs 14:6 below, box people. Wavy-circle what the mocker finds. Circle what the discerning finds.

   14:6    The mocker seeks wisdom and finds none,
           but knowledge comes easily to the discerning.

*The mocker* is cynical, arrogant, and so committed to folly that finding wisdom is impossible lest repentance paves the way. Indeed, any claims of seeking wisdom are deceptive since mockers think themselves wiser than all others. But mockers are useful to the simple. Let's see how.

10. What can the simple learn from others' responses to mockers (Proverbs 19:25, 29; 21:11)?

The *simple learn prudence* and *gain wisdom* when they see the mocker face consequences. In the nineteenth and twentieth centuries, many countries, including the United States and England, replaced corporal punishments such as flogging with fines, community service, jail time, and job loss for vandalism, theft, and other types of foolish misbehaviors.

11. ♥ Which difference between the wise and the fool most stands out to you? Explain.

In this lesson we learned how to recognize the simple, the wise, and the foolish. We also saw the importance of mockers facing consequences so that the simple become wise. Next we'll discover how to avoid being a fool.

**The Little Details**

*Formal Parallelism in Proverbs 15:16; 21:16; and 23:9*

When a proverb's second line completes its first line, it's using *formal parallelism*. This is the case in Proverbs 21:16: "Whoever strays from the path of prudence / comes to rest in the company of the dead." Here the subject is in the first line, and the predicate is in the second. Another example is Proverbs 23:9: "Do not speak to fools, / for they will scorn your prudent words." In this proverb, the first line gives advice, and the second explains the reason behind it. An additional form of formal parallelism is found in proverbs that explain that one thing is better than another: "Better a little with the fear of the LORD / than great wealth with turmoil" (Proverbs 15:16).

**The Little Details**
*"Dead" in Proverbs 21:16*

Ross notes that the Hebrew word for *dead* in Proverbs 21:16 is translated *spirits* in Isaiah 26:14 when speaking of the wicked: "They are now dead, they live no more; their *spirits* do not rise" (emphasis mine). The Hebrew word is used in Isaiah 26:19 to speak of saints who have died and have a different end: "Your dead will live, LORD; their bodies will rise—let those who dwell in the dust wake up and shout for joy—your dew is like the dew of the morning; the earth will give birth to her *dead*" (emphasis mine).[5]

*Day 3*

## Don't Be a Fool

Teens are still simple, and most if not all start down foolish paths at least a few times—I certainly did. Thankfully, God delights in those who leave foolish paths and start down wise ones. The consequences can be severe, however, which is why the father in Proverbs is so concerned that his son avoid doing risky things.

Parents today are still concerned, and for good reason. UCLA Health reports:

> The rate of overdose deaths among U.S. teenagers nearly doubled in 2020, the first year of the COVID pandemic, and rose another 20% in the first half of 2021 compared with the 10 years before the pandemic, even as drug use remained generally stable during the same period, according to new UCLA research.[4]

### The Dangers of Being a Fool

Proverbs aims to discourage the simple from becoming fools.

> **12.** What happens to those who abandon prudence (Proverbs 21:16)?

Every year many young people perish from foolish choices.

### The Difficulties of Being Around a Fool

The foolish who stray from prudence don't just affect themselves.

> **13.** What exhausts more than carrying stones and sand (Proverbs 27:3)?

*Deal with Fools Wisely*

Proverbs 26 contains a long series on fools. Much of it tells us how to deal with them.

> **14.** Compare how we should and shouldn't deal with fools (1, 3, 6, 8).
>
> Do | Don't

We ought not honor a fool, for it's as unfitting and catastrophic as *snow in summer* or *rain in harvest* and as useless as a *stone* tied in a *sling*. Indeed, giving a fool the honor of an elevated position brings harm and may mislead the simple. Just as riders can't reason with a *horse* or *donkey* but must use a *whip* to prompt and a *bridle* to guide, so leaders can't reason with rebellious fools but must use something to prompt and guide them into right behavior.

15. In Proverbs 26:10 (ESV) below, box the two people an employer might hire in 10b. Wavy-underline what such an employer is like in 10a.

> 26:10 Like an archer who wounds everyone
> is one who hires a passing fool or drunkard.

Hiring a *fool* puts people in danger, especially in fields involving construction, transportation, and government.

16. Proverbs 26:4-5 delivers a conundrum. (a) Why shouldn't you answer a fool according to his folly? (b) On the other hand, why should you?

While we shouldn't answer a fool in the same foolish way as a fool, nonetheless, we should make clear what the folly is so the fool won't be arrogant.

17. Why shouldn't fools speak when there's serious business to discuss (Proverbs 24:7)?

### Don't Bother Teaching Fools

Proverbs teaches wisdom to the simple and wise. It advises against trying to teach wisdom to fools, however.

18. In the Proverbs verses below, wavy-underline reasons it's useless to try to teach a foolish person who doesn't want to learn. Box people.

> 17:16 Why should fools have money in hand to buy wisdom,
> when they are not able to understand it?
> 23:9 Do not speak to fools,
> for they will scorn your prudent words.
> 26:7 Like the useless legs of one who is lame
> is a proverb in the mouth of a fool.
> 26:9 Like a thornbush in a drunkard's hand
> is a proverb in the mouth of a fool.
> 26:11 As a dog returns to its vomit,
> so fools repeat their folly.
> 27:22 Though you grind a fool in a mortar,
> grinding them like grain with a pestle,
> you will not remove their folly from them.

While Proverbs 4:7 admonished the son to get wisdom even if "it cost all you have," in Proverbs 17:16 the teacher notes with exasperation that it does fools no good to try to buy wisdom, for they have no ability to understand it. Further, Proverbs 27:22 warns that while a *mortar* and *pestle* can crush *grain* into useful flour, no discipline can *remove folly* and so make a fool useful.

## The Little Details
### Slings

Proverbs 26:8 reads, "Like tying a stone in a sling / is the giving of honor to a fool." Bruce K. Waltke explains that "a sling was made of a leather or textile strip that had been broadened in the middle and into which the stone was placed, but never bound. A person held the ends of the strip together and swung it until he loosed one of its ends so that the stone could fly."[6] To bind a stone in a sling defeats the purpose of the sling! Likewise, giving a fool honor defeats the purpose of honor: rewarding behavior that one wants others to imitate.

The most well-known story of a warrior using a sling is David's defeat of Goliath in 1 Samuel 17:49: "Reaching into his bag and taking out a stone, he slung it and struck the Philistine on the forehead. The stone sank into his forehead, and he fell facedown on the ground."

**19.** ♥ (a) Describe a time you witnessed someone facing the consequences of foolishness. (b) How did that affect you? (c) How did the person react?

### Know What's Worse Than a Fool

Many of the proverbs we read in this lesson come from Proverbs 26. Its section on fools concludes with what's worse than a fool.

**20.** Who has less hope than a fool (26:12)?

That verse always shocks me.

**21.** ♥ (a) Describe a time someone you know faced the consequences of being wise in their own eyes (or a time you did). (b) What did that teach you?

In this lesson we looked at the dangers of being a fool, the difficulties of being around a fool, and what's worse than a fool. Our next lesson builds on the last proverb we read by examining the importance of hearing advice.

*Day 4*

# Listen Up!

When Clay and I were first married, I wanted to cook a wonderful meal every night. But I kept forgetting to start the vegetables before I finished the main dish. While I was preparing dinner one evening, Clay asked, "Did you start the vegetables?" I fought back tears as I responded, "You think I'm a terrible wife and wish you'd never married me!"

Okay, that reveals some major insecurities. But it also showed I took correction as rejection. Thankfully, Clay responded wisely by calmly asking me to distinguish between what I thought he meant and what he actually said.

As we'll read in this lesson, I needed to learn to embrace correction.

### Take Advice

Today we're looking at something essential for becoming wise: taking advice.

Today we're looking at something essential for becoming wise: taking advice.

22. In the Proverbs verses below (NRSVUE), wavy-underline foolish actions and underline wise actions. Box people.

> 12:15 Fools think their own way is right,
>     but the wise listen to advice.
> 13:10 By insolence the empty-headed person makes strife,
>     but wisdom is with those who take advice.
> 15:14 The mind of one who has understanding seeks knowledge,
>     but the mouths of fools feed on folly.
> 18:15 An intelligent mind acquires knowledge,
>     and the ear of the wise seeks knowledge.
> 28:26 Those who trust in their own wits are fools,
>     but those who walk in wisdom come through safely.

*Fools* confidently assert that their ways are *right*, even when they reject God's commands. They arrogantly *trust in their own wits* and, if questioned, explode, causing *strife*. (We all know someone like that, don't we?) In contrast, the *wise listen to advice* and weigh it. If the advice doesn't seem right, they can seek advice from others.

23. In the ESV Proverbs verses below, underline what's needed to successfully plan.

> 15:22 Without counsel plans fail,
>     but with many advisers they succeed.
> 20:18 Plans are established by counsel;
>     by wise guidance wage war.
> 24:5 A wise man is full of strength,
>     and a man of knowledge enhances his might,
> 6 for by wise guidance you can wage your war,
>     and in abundance of counselors there is victory.

Solomon knew a wise woman had prevented his father's commander from destroying her city (2 Samuel 20:15-22). He also had to prepare his son for *war*. Though we may not engage in physical battles, we do face spiritual battles against spiritual enemies, sinful desires, and arguments against knowing God (see sidebar).

## Follow Instructions

We've all faced the consequences of not reading directions or of reading them but then either ignoring or not understanding them. My professor husband has returned many students' papers because they weren't completed according to the syllabus's directions. I've ripped out countless stitches because I skipped the instructions about basting before sewing. When I tried to renew my driver's license and registered first online, I missed the last step: print everything out. The DMV insisted I stand in yet another long line and register again, this time using one of their computers.

24. ♥ Describe a time when something went awry because you didn't follow instructions.

### The Little Details
### *The New Testament on Our Battles:*

***Ephesians 6:12:*** Our struggle is not against flesh and blood, but against the rulers, against the authorities, against the powers of this dark world and against the spiritual forces of evil in the heavenly realms.

***1 Peter 2:11:*** Dear friends, I urge you, as foreigners and exiles, to abstain from sinful desires, which wage war against your soul.

***James 4:1:*** What causes fights and quarrels among you? Don't they come from your desires that battle within you?

***2 Corinthians 10:3-5:*** For though we live in the world, we do not wage war as the world does. The weapons we fight with are not the weapons of the world. On the contrary, they have divine power to demolish strongholds. We demolish arguments and every pretension that sets itself up against the knowledge of God, and we take captive every thought to make it obedient to Christ.

## The Little Details

### David A. Hubbard on Proverbs 10:8 (NKJV):

"*Heart*" is the seat of choice, the part of the person that says, "I will" or "I won't." If wise (10:8), it is open to the commands of the knowledgeable and experienced; if foolish, it encourages "*pratting*" back talk which resists authority and causes a person to "*fall*," or, even worse, come to total ruin (see Hos. 4:14).[7]

The "*pratting fool*" (lit., "a fool in lips") talks much and listens little. Left to his own devices he and all he plans come to ruin ("*will fall*"; see the same Hebrew verb in Hos. 4:14). Success is impossible because his thinking—in contrast to the wise in heart, the one who makes wise decisions that lead to success—is limited to his own resources and not enriched by the "*commands*" of the prudent people around him. Success depends on listening.[8]

Many mistakes from not following instructions are funny—but not all.

**25.** Compare the wise with the fool and mocker (Proverbs 10:8; 13:1).

| The Wise | The Fool and Mocker |
|---|---|
|  |  |

While those who are wise in their own eyes are *chattering* about God's *commands* being misguided or not right for today, the *wise in heart accept commands*. The *wise son* not only *heeds* his parents' *instructions* but responds properly to *rebukes*, unlike the rebellious *mocker*.

**26.** To what should we apply our heart and ears (Proverbs 23:12)?

In other words, the *ears* must listen to *words of knowledge*, and the *heart* must love and store *instruction*. Hubbard writes:

> "*Knowledge*" serves as a summation of God's will and way (see 1:2; 22:19-21). "*Apply*" implies deliberate discipline. Literally it says, Take your heart in hand and bring it into the presence of "*instruction*." The latter word pictures the cost of learning: correction, even punishment and pain.[9]

**27.** What happens if you stop listening to instruction (Proverbs 19:27)?

All our lives we must not *stop listening to instruction*. Otherwise, we shall surely *stray*. Sadly, near the end of his life, Solomon stopped listening to his own advice. He married foreign wives and amassed wealth and horses despite God's commands forbidding these things. He built temples for his wives to worship their gods in and eventually worshiped those gods with them. In other words, because he stopped *listening to instruction*, he strayed.

### Heed Correction

We don't just need advice and instruction. The wise also heed correction. This holds true in relationships, business, and spiritual matters.

**28.** To the left of each reaction below, write the letter of the results that go with it (Proverbs 10:17; 13:18). Each reaction has two unique results.

| | Reaction to Discipline and Correction | Result |
|---|---|---|
|  | Heed them | A. Are honored |
|  | Ignore them | B. Find poverty and shame |
|  |  | C. Lead others astray |
|  |  | D. Show the way to life |

We don't live in a vacuum, and one benefit of taking *correction* is that our actions can then help others. Another benefit is that it leads to being *honored*.

Think about how you usually react to correction before reading the next question.

> **29.** In the verses from Proverbs below, box people. Underline wise actions. Wavy-underline foolish actions. Double-underline character qualities. Double-wavy-underline flaws.
>
> 12:1 Whoever loves discipline loves knowledge,
> but whoever hates correction is stupid.
>
> 15:5 A fool spurns a parent's discipline,
> but whoever heeds correction shows prudence.
>
> 17:10 A rebuke impresses a discerning person
> more than a hundred lashes a fool.

A third benefit of taking correction is that our response to it *shows* our character. We're either *a stupid fool* who *hates correction* or we possess *prudence*, are *discerning*, and love *discipline* and *knowledge*. (My husband sometimes jokes from the pulpit, "If you want to see if your friends are fools, give them sincere advice and see how they respond.")

The most important source of life-giving correction is the Bible: "All Scripture is God-breathed and is useful for teaching, rebuking, correcting and training in righteousness, so that the servant of God may be thoroughly equipped for every good work" (2 Timothy 3:16-17).

> **30.** Contrast the mocker's and the wise person's reactions to correction (Proverbs 15:12, 31).
>
> | The Mocker | The Wise |
> |---|---|
> | | |

*Mockers* keep away from *the wise* because they *resent correction*, but those who take *correction* are comfortable around them.

> **31.** In the NASB Proverbs verses below, wavy-underline foolish actions. Underline wise actions. Circle what those who take the wise actions gain.
>
> 15:32 He who neglects discipline despises himself,
> But he who listens to reproof acquires understanding.
>
> 19:20 Listen to counsel and accept discipline,
> That you may be wise the rest of your days.

Allen P. Ross explains "despises himself":

> The person who despises discipline slights or "despises himself" ([the Hebrew] means that he rejects himself as though he were of little value and so fails to grow). One must acquire understanding, especially about oneself, to grow spiritually, intellectually, and emotionally.[11]

**The Little Details**
*David A. Hubbard on Proverbs 13:18 (NKJV):*
To guard and cling to ("*regards*") "*a rebuke*" was not grounds for shame but for respect and even material reward. The Hebrew root for "honor" can mean both glory and wealth. To welcome reproof and let it change our ways is a mark of maturity that people will admire and that may make our work more effective and perhaps more profitable. To disdain correction, in contrast, abandons us to our own resources, severs us from the wisdom and regard of our associates, and may well lead to "*poverty and shame.*" Poverty here implies losing wealth that one had earlier acquired and losing it by making bad decisions based on ignoring ("*disdains*") sound correction. In such circumstances—though certainly not in all circumstances—the poverty would inevitably lead to shame.[10]

**The Little Details**
*Proverbs 13:12-19 Outline*

The verses in Proverbs 13:12-19 are arranged such that those equal distance from the middle are linked:

A    A longing fulfilled is a tree of life (12)

  B   Whoever respects a command is rewarded (13)

    C  The teaching of the wise is a fountain of life (14)

      D Good judgment wins favor (15)

      D' All who are prudent act with knowledge (16)

    C' A trustworthy envoy brings healing (17)

  B' Whoever heeds correction is honored (18)

A'   A longing fulfilled is sweet (19)

The good news is that the one who takes correction *acquires understanding* that leads to being *wise* for *the rest of* their *days*.

> **32.** In the ESV Proverbs verses below, wavy-circle penalties for foolish actions. Wavy-underline foolish actions. Underline three things that "lie open before the Lord."
>
> 15:10   There is severe discipline for him who forsakes the way;
>          whoever hates reproof will die.
>
> 11   Sheol and Abaddon lie open before the Lord;
>          how much more the hearts of the children of man!
>
> 29:1   He who is often reproved, yet stiffens his neck,
>          will suddenly be broken beyond healing.

*Sheol and Abaddon* are the current realm of the dead. Since *hearts* lie *open before the Lord*, the judgment that follows death will expose every rejection of *discipline* and *reproof*. While the Lord disciplines his children now to correct them, there will come a time when all who have continued to reject him *will suddenly be broken beyond healing* in the final realm of the dead: hell.[12] Thankfully, God offers an alternative to death: "God so loved the world that he gave his one and only Son, that whoever believes in him shall not perish but have eternal life" (John 3:16).

Before I read Proverbs, I hated correction. But reading so many proverbs about the necessity of it drove me to change. I began seeking advice, even when it was hard. I admit it took time, but I grew wiser, bit by bit. I also grew in patience.

> **33.** ♥ (a) What is something about which you could seek advice, instruction, or correction? (b) How have you sought help on this so far? (c) Who might advise you?

In this lesson we discovered why taking advice is essential to becoming wise. Our next lesson discovers how to fulfill our deepest longings.

## Day 5

# Fulfill Your Longings

When I misidentified pyrite as gold, I thought my parents' money woes would be over. Then they would stop fighting, and our family could be happy. It wasn't so much gold that I wanted as the happiness I thought gold might bring. I didn't yet know that something much deeper than a lack of money caused their unhappiness.

Proverbs 15:17 (ESV) puts it like this: "Better is a dinner of herbs where love is than a fattened ox and hatred with it." Frankly, hatred poisoned our house. No amount of money would have changed that. Though I couldn't put it into words, what I longed for deeply was love, peace, grace, and joy.

## A Longing Fulfilled

In the next passage, Proverbs speaks to our deepest longings. These verses have many connections that invite comparing and contrasting to uncover deeper meanings, so we'll label repeated elements. (See the sidebar for more links).

34. Read Proverbs 13:12-19 below. Draw a heart (♥) or write "LONGING" next to mentions of "longing fulfilled" (12b, 19a). Draw an up arrow (▲) or write "LIFE" next to mentions of "life" and "healing" (12b, 14a, 17b). Draw an ear (👂) or write "HEAR" by 13b and 18b. Draw a sad face (☹) or write "PENALTIES" by 13a, 14b, 15b, 16b, 17a, 18a. Draw a star (★) or write "BLESSINGS" next to 13b, 15a, 18b.

> 13:12 Hope deferred makes the heart sick,
>      but a longing fulfilled is a tree of life.
> 13 Whoever scorns instruction will pay for it,
>      but whoever respects a command is rewarded.
> 14 The teaching of the wise is a fountain of life,
>      turning a person from the snares of death.
> 15 Good judgment wins favor,
>      but the way of the unfaithful leads to their destruction.
> 16 All who are prudent act with knowledge,
>      but fools expose their folly.
> 17 A wicked messenger falls into trouble,
>      but a trustworthy envoy brings healing.
> 18 Whoever disregards discipline comes to poverty and shame,
>      but whoever heeds correction is honored.
> 19 A longing fulfilled is sweet to the soul,
>      but fools detest turning from evil.

As we read in chapter 1, a *tree of life* can refer to eternal life. Verse 19b seems odd by itself but makes sense in the context of the previous verses. Everyone wants their deepest *longing fulfilled*, but because fools *scorn instruction* and *detest turning from evil*, they will experience a *heart sick* from *hope deferred*.

35. Complete the sentences below by comparing verses in Proverbs 13:12-19 above that have the same labels.

    ♥ LONGING fulfilled is

    ▲ LIFE comes from

    👂 HEAR, respect, and heed

    ☹ PENALTIES for not hearing are

    ★ BLESSINGS for hearing are

### The Little Details
#### Eternal Life in Proverbs?

While Solomon may have been speaking in Proverbs 13:12-14 mostly of the shortened lives the foolish and reckless sometimes encounter, he may also have had in mind what his father, King David, wrote: "You will not abandon me to the realm of the dead, nor will you let your faithful one see decay. You make known to me the path of life" (Psalm 16:10-11) and "From the depths of the earth you will again bring me up" (Psalm 71:20). David as a prophet had some of the earliest glimpses of eternal life.

All long for eternal life, so let's look more deeply at the tree of life and its significance.

### The Tree of Life

The tree of life was in the garden of Eden. When Adam and Eve sinned, God cast them out of the garden and set cherubim in place to block the way to the tree of life.[13] The tabernacle (and later, the temple) had a curtain embroidered with cherubim that blocked the way to the Most Holy Place, showing the way to God and eternal life was blocked.[14] But when Jesus died, the curtain ripped in two.[15]

But that's not all. After the judgment, God will create a new heaven and earth.[16] All whose names are written in the Lamb's book of life will dwell there with God and Jesus forever.[17] The new Jerusalem will have a foundation of jewels, gates of pearl, and streets of pure gold.[18] Revelation 22:1-2 describes Eden's restoration:

> Then the angel showed me the river of the water of life, as clear as crystal, flowing from the throne of God and of the Lamb down the middle of the great street of the city. On each side of the river stood the tree of life, bearing twelve crops of fruit, yielding its fruit every month. And the leaves of the tree are for the healing of the nations.

Access to the tree of life is restored. Hallelujah!

## Wisdom's Value

Some proverbs discuss the value of wisdom for the life we now live on earth.

> **36.** In Proverbs 15:24 below, circle where the path of life leads the prudent. Wavy-circle what it keeps them from.
>
> 15:24 The path of life leads upward for the prudent
>           to keep them from going down to the realm of the dead.

Prudence keeps people on *the path of life*, while foolishness can shorten life. For example, some engage in risky behaviors to gain social media followers—and perish.

> **37.** In Proverbs 24:3-4 below, circle what wisdom, understanding, and knowledge enable for a house.
>
> 24:3 By wisdom a house is built,
>           and through understanding it is established;
> 4       through knowledge its rooms are filled
>           with rare and beautiful treasures.

While builders need the skills in these verses to construct a sound *house*, we all need them to build homes of love.

> **38.** Complete the phrases below from Proverbs 16:16.
>
> Better than getting gold is getting _____ .
> Better than getting silver is getting _____ .

While we can have both wisdom and wealth, if we must lack one, it's better to lack wealth. Wisdom imparts spiritual and relationship blessings necessary for joy in life.

**39.** ♥ Review the benefits of wisdom in this lesson and the Day 1 lesson. Which do you long for most? Why?

In this lesson, we saw how wisdom leads to fulfilled longings and life.

## Wisdom's Worth

**40.** ♥ In what way did you apply wisdom from Proverbs to your life this week?

In this chapter, we explored the benefits of wisdom and the attributes of the wise, the simple, and the fool. We saw why it's okay to be simple but not okay to remain so. We noticed the danger of both being a fool and being around a fool, and we learned what's worse than a fool. We uncovered why taking advice is essential to becoming wise. And we saw why wisdom leads to fulfillment. Next we'll look at who the righteous are in Proverbs.

### *Wisdom Worship*
Find a quiet place and prepare your heart for grateful worship.

 Turn to Psalm 119:65-80 in your Bible and pray the passage aloud.

## Karla's Creative Connection

*Whoever loves discipline loves knowledge, but whoever hates correction is stupid.*

Proverbs 12:1

Ouch! This week's key verse has a little sting to it, doesn't it? The word *stupid* seems jarring. In fact, as I was illustrating this verse, I shared it with a few people, and their response was the same: No one wanted to believe God would use a word as harsh as *stupid*. So I looked up the verse in a different translation. And then another. They all used the same word—*stupid*—except for the King James Version, which translates it *brutish*, and that means the same thing.

I think God chose this word because he wanted to jar us, to shake us into listening to the wisdom of this verse. Growing in any area of our lives requires discipline and a willingness to submit to the correction of someone who has more knowledge or wisdom than we do. If we rebel against discipline and refuse correction, we become stuck in believing our way is the right way, causing us to sadly suffer the consequences of our own poor choices.

A story in the Bible illustrates this truth so wonderfully. God reveals himself to the prophet Jeremiah as the Potter and we, his people, as the clay in his hands. When we say yes to Jesus and invite him into our lives, God lifts us up out of the miry clay of sin and death, sets us upon his glorious potter's wheel of life everlasting, and begins molding and shaping us into the image of his Son.

God's Word and wisdom become tools of discipline, instructing us in choosing what is right and good. He places people along our path who love us and speak truth into our hearts or are godly examples for us to follow. And he provides us with ample trials and life experiences, including the consequences of our actions, to bring valuable correction and learning opportunities.

As the wheel turns and we're willing to yield to his discipline and correction and allow him to have his way in us and through us, his hands are loving yet firm. He shapes our lives into uniquely beautiful vessels to be used for his glory and the blessing of others. If we refuse his discipline or correction and put our feet down, wanting our own way rather than his, we can too easily become set in our ways and hardened. Then we miss out on the beauty and blessings he's prepared for us.

As you spend time in your sacred quiet space throughout this next week, creatively connect with God by imagining yourself climbing up on his potter's wheel. Confess any area where you've been resisting his correction. Pick up your feet, rejoice in his love, and enjoy the ride!

*Karla*

## Chapter 5

# Proverbs 13:1–15:33
## Walk This Way!

What does godly character look like?

## Who Are the Righteous in Proverbs?

Proverbs mentions the righteous and wicked often. For example, here's Proverbs 13:5: "The righteous hate what is false, but the wicked make themselves a stench and bring shame on themselves." This confused me when I first read it. After all, didn't Paul write that no one is righteous (Romans 3:10)? Doesn't that make everyone wicked?

Eventually, I discovered that when Proverbs talks about the righteous, it's not talking about someone who's never sinned (which is the sense that Paul meant in Romans 3:10). Rather, it means someone who strives to live the way God commands and confesses wrongdoing to him when that effort fails.

In both the Old and New Testaments, the standard for righteousness is God's righteousness, but no one can obtain that righteousness on their own because "all have sinned and fall short of the glory of God" (Romans 3:23). As Solomon put it in Ecclesiastes 7:20, "Indeed, there is no one on earth who is righteous, no one who does what is right and never sins."

Scripture, however, calls some people *the righteous*: those whose faith in and love for God cause them to order their lives according to his laws (Psalm 1:2; 1 John 3:7). God bestows righteousness on them because he counts faith as righteousness (Genesis 15:6; Philippians 3:9).

In the New Testament, God makes righteous those who put their faith in Jesus. In both Testaments, the righteous aren't sinless, but when they sin, they seek God's forgiveness, and God cleanses them of unrighteousness (Psalm 51:9-10; 1 John 1:9).

In contrast, the wicked are those who live as they see fit. The word translated *wicked* in Proverbs can refer to those who simply don't love God, those who reject God's laws,[1] or those who are committed to violence and oppression.

### Righteous Living Versus Righteous Standing

When I first became a Christian, I thought God saved and cleansed me so I could be a good Christian and never sin again. Never sinning turned out to be impossible, so praise God, what I thought was false.

You see, I thought righteous standing before God depended on my living righteously. But

WHOEVER IS PATIENT HAS GREAT UNDERSTANDING, BUT ONE WHO IS QUICK-TEMPERED DISPLAYS FOLLY.

PROVERBS 14:29

The basic meaning of "righteous" has to do with conforming to the standard; in religious passages that standard is divine revelation. The righteous are people who have entered into covenant with God by faith and seek to live according to his word. The covenant that they have makes them the people of God—God knows them, and because God knows them, they shall never perish. They may do unrighteous things at times, but they know to find forgiveness because they want to do what is right.[2]

*righteous standing* is the righteousness God gives people who live by faith. The theological term is *justification*. It doesn't depend on how good we are; it's a gift.

On the other hand, *righteous living* is ordering one's life by God's commands. It's something God wants us to do, so he sends the Holy Spirit to help us. The theological term for this is *sanctification*.

Justification—righteous standing—happens the moment we're saved. Sanctification—righteous living—is an ongoing process.

Here's an important key: Righteous living without faith (simply keeping a certain moral code) *never* leads to righteous standing, whereas righteous standing based on faith *always* leads to righteous living. Just keeping a moral code can't lead to righteous standing, because no person is sinless and God gives righteous standing only to those with faith in him.[3]

Additionally, those without faith in God always break the greatest command, which Jesus quotes in Matthew 22:37-38: "Love the Lord your God with all your heart and with all your soul and with all your mind. This is the first and greatest commandment."

On the other hand, righteous standing always leads to righteous living, because those with faith in God love and trust him enough to obey him (albeit imperfectly) and because God works in them to change them.[4] It may take time to overcome weaknesses and old habits, but the Holy Spirit will produce growth as people live what they believe.[5]

1. Summarize the difference between righteous living and righteous standing.

### God's Word to Us in Proverbs
As you read Proverbs today, keep in mind what it means by *righteous* and *wicked*.

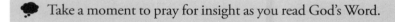 Take a moment to pray for insight as you read God's Word.

2. ♥ Read chapters 13–15 in Proverbs. (a) What stood out to you in your reading? Why? (b) How can you apply that insight to your life this week?

### The Way That Appears Right
A problem faces the young and the simple: The world often presents going against God's commands as beneficial and right. Yet how wise can it be to reject what the Creator who designed the world says is the way to live a blessed life?

3. What's the problem with people deciding right and wrong for themselves (Proverbs 14:12 or 16:25—they're identical)?

Proverbs explains the ways that can and cannot bring life, whether abundant and long life on earth or life after the grave.

4.  In the Proverbs verses below, underline what brings life. Wavy-underline what cannot. Box people.

    10:2   Ill-gotten treasures have no lasting value,
           but righteousness delivers from death.
    10:16  The wages of the righteous is life,
           but the earnings of the wicked are sin and death.
    11:4   Wealth is worthless in the day of wrath,
           but righteousness delivers from death.
    11:19  Truly the righteous attain life,
           but whoever pursues evil finds death.
    14:32  When calamity comes, the wicked are brought down,
           but even in death the righteous seek refuge in God.
    16:17  The highway of the upright avoids evil;
           those who guard their ways preserve their lives.
    19:16  Whoever keeps commandments keeps their life,
           but whoever shows contempt for their ways will die.

In 11:4, *the day of wrath* may be divine judgment in this life (as when the earth opened and swallowed the rebellious Korah) or the final judgment.[6] In 11:19, *life* and *death* may refer to this life or to the eternal life and death that follow the final judgment. Although all face physical *death*, those who *seek refuge in God* have comfort even then, because they desire and expect eternal life.

Thus, from Proverbs we learn that the righteous—those who follow God's commands as best they can and confess wrongdoing when they fail—are on the path to life.

In this lesson we looked at who the righteous and wicked are in Proverbs. In our next lesson we'll see how the wicked act and the unwelcome consequences they face.

**The Little Details**
*David A. Hubbard on*
**Righteous *and* Wicked:**
Righteous (Hebrew *ṣaddîq*) speaks of loyal, reliable conduct based on a commitment to God and the covenant which God made with Israel. It is a term of relationship which describes a desire to live a life pleasing to God and fitting to the members of God's family. It means behaving toward God and His people with the same care, compassion, and integrity that the righteous God has shown them...

Wicked (Heb. *rāshā*) is best defined as the opposite of all that "righteous" entails: disloyalty to the Lord, rebellion against the covenant standards, disregard for the welfare of the people.[7]

# Pam's Simply Beautiful Wisdom

*By wisdom a house is built, and through understanding it is established;*
*through knowledge its rooms are filled with rare and beautiful treasures.*

Proverbs 24:3-4

When we pursue wisdom, understanding, and committed concern, our homes are filled with what is precious, splendid, pleasant, lovely, and delightful. Wow! This promise is better than any interior design magazine. A relationship full of beautiful treasures has three vital components: words, body language, and tone of voice.

## Words

Proverbs 25:11 says, "A word fitly spoken is like apples of gold in a setting of silver" (ESV). Using an earlier NIV translation of that verse, author Anthony Selvaggio writes in his book *A Proverbs Driven Life*, "'A word aptly spoken is like apples of gold in settings of silver'...'Apt'...means 'exactly suitable; appropriate'...speech that is biblically wise—can be seen as involving three essential components: thoughtfulness, timeliness, and truth."[8]

In our book *The Marriage Code,* Bill and I share words that *RAISE a Safety Net for Love* and create a gentle approach to your spouse:

*R*espect: Use statements of honor and respect. You can say, "I am proud of you" or "You are remarkable at _____ (fill in the blank)" at any time, regardless of how you feel at the moment. The best traits of your spouse don't change with the current emotional climate of your relationship, so speak out statements of honor.

*A*ffirmation. Simple statements such as "You're safe with me," "I will guard whatever you share with me," and "We don't need to be perfect—let's just work on being a little better by this time next year," give your spouse the confidence to share with you. A promise to protect the confidentiality of your spouse is a valuable gift.

*"I"* statements. Most conversations go better when you speak about your needs and how life is affecting you, but the tendency is to point out what you don't like in your spouse. That breeds defensiveness. "For some reason, it's very upsetting to me when we arrive late" is much different from "You make me so mad because you're always late." The first statement allows your spouse to safely enter the conversation. The second statement forces your spouse to put up defenses.

*S*incerity. In the Bible we're told to "speak the truth in love" (Ephesians 4:15 NLT). This means you get to say some really nice things to your spouse, and it means you'll have to share some tough things with your spouse. You can usually navigate the tougher conversations well if you seek your spouse's best interests. We all have a tendency to play games to gain attention or just to smooth things over. Either of these approaches eventually gives the impression that you have an agenda. Instead, choose to love your mate from a sincere heart.

*E*ncouragement. Look for ways to build up your spouse. "Encourage one another and build each other up" is a command from God (1 Thessalonians 5:11). This is a picture of building a solid home by laying a strong foundation, constructing solid walls with 2 x 4s of kindnesses, compliments, praise, and reassurances, then sheltering it with a reliable roof.

An example in our relationship happened when the COVID-19 pandemic shut down not only our speaking careers but also the marina where we enjoyed living on a boat close enough to Bill's then 90-year-old parents for us to care for them. When COVID hit, we knew we were the safest people to continue their care, but we had to move into a 300-square-foot RV on their property to help them 24/7. We enjoy living "tiny," but this was *teeny-tiny!* To multiply the stress, Bill's dad experienced strokes that continued to cripple his body and then his mind. Dad was not a "happy camper." Each night, as I hugged Bill before our bedtime prayers, I would whisper, "Our today is not our forever." Holding out words of hope is also a gift of encouragement.[9]

## Body Language

A bit of advice I give women in *Red-Hot Romance Tips for Women*, a book Bill and I wrote together, is to try a SOFTER approach with their husbands:

- *S*top what you're doing and turn toward your mate
- *O*pen up your body language
- *F*ind key words and phrases to repeat as you listen
- *T*ry not to take comments so personally
- *E*xpress affirming emotions
- *R*espond with loving actions[10]

## Tone of Voice

One day a few years into our marriage, Bill reached over and took my hand. Then he calmly said, "Honey, I know you love me, and that you never intend to hurt me, but, sweetie, you have a tone of voice that hurts my feelings and shuts me down."

"What tone of voice?" I replied—sharply.

"Well, that tone of voice."

"I don't have a tone!" I said. "Record me! I'll prove to you that I do *not* have a tone!"

Bill did record me, and after listening to the playback, I immediately replied, "I *do* have a tone! I am so sorry, honey. I'll ask God to help me break this hurtful habit." Each day for decades I've asked God to help me mindfully live out Proverbs 15:1: "A gentle answer turns away wrath."

*Pam*

### Experiencing Scripture Creatively (Optional)

If you have extra time, consider these suggestions for creatively engaging with verses from this week's reading. The appendix has even more ideas.

- Cut out the bookmark at the back of the book that displays this chapter's key verse. Color it and place it where you can see it each morning.

- Use your answers to a comparison question to write a wisdom psalm using the structure of Psalm 1. Here's an example based on question 25:

*A psalm of Jean concerning Proverbs 10:12; 14:17, 29; 15:18; 16:32; 29:22.*
Blessed is the one
     who possesses not a quick temper
     nor fuels anger to spread conflict
     nor stokes a hot temper into sins,
but her delight is covering wrongs with love
     and calming quarrels with patience.
She is like an ocean breeze
     that cools the sun's hot rays
        and caresses the bright flowers of friendship.
     In all her relationships, she's cherished.

**The Little Details**
*For Budding Poets*

Psalm 1 is a *wisdom poem* that contrasts the righteous and the wicked. Proverbs that contrast two people (such as the quick tempered and the patient) can be turned into a psalm that follows Psalm 1's structure.

You can download my worksheet with step-by-step instructions and find more sample poems at DiscoveringTheBibleSeries.com.

Not so the quick-tempered.
> They are like blistering Santa Ana winds
>> that suck moisture and life from all in their path
> and drive destructive red fires before them.
Therefore the hot-tempered scorch friendships
> and leave tears and anguish behind.

For the Lord blesses the patient,
> but the relations of the quick-tempered turn to ashes.

## *Day 2*

## The Paths of the Wicked

Identifying some people as wicked can feel icky. I struggled with it for years, partly due to being told as a child that if I thought bad thoughts about people, that's what I'd become. Eventually, I realized that wasn't true.

But does it matter whether we recognize those whom Scripture calls wicked as being such? Yes. And for many reasons. Recognizing that someone's traits put them into Scripture's category of wicked...

1. is part of being like Jesus (Luke 11:29) and lets us know that this is someone who needs the gospel's message of hope;
2. keeps us from naively trusting the untrustworthy and getting hurt;
3. helps us more clearly recognize our sin, understand why Jesus had to die, and appreciate Jesus's sacrifice to purify us;[11]
4. helps us forgive malicious, intentional sin for what it is instead of excusing all sin as unintentional;
5. keeps us from chasing earthly utopias through politics; and
6. helps us understand the doctrine of original sin (see sidebar on the next page).

> **5.** ♥ Which of the reasons for recognizing the wicked is most difficult for you? Why? Or with which reason have you seen others struggle?

### How the Wicked Act

In California, con artists targeted the churchgoing elderly because they were particularly trusting. They convinced my father-in-law and many others to invest in their phony firm. By the time the U.S. Securities and Exchange Commission intervened, the thieves had spent most of the "investments" on themselves. One reason we need to recognize the wicked is so that we don't fall into their traps, as the next passage warns.

6. In Proverbs 16:27-30 below, wavy-underline the actions of the wicked. Box people.

> 16:27 A scoundrel plots evil,
>         and on their lips it is like a scorching fire.
> 28 A perverse person stirs up conflict,
>         and a gossip separates close friends.
> 29 A violent person entices their neighbor
>         and leads them down a path that is not good.
> 30 Whoever winks with their eye is plotting perversity;
>         whoever purses their lips is bent on evil.

Ross defines *scoundrel*:

> The "scoundrel" is literally a "man of belial"…The meaning of "worthless" has been frequently given…but that is too weak. The term describes deep depravity and wickedness…This is a wicked person, for "he digs up evil."[13]

The *scoundrel* is like a *fire*-breathing dragon. A *perverse person* is literally "a man of falsehoods, a liar."[14] This one invents bad press, spreads it through *gossip*, and in so doing *separates close friends*. The *perverse person* also *entices* a gullible *neighbor* like my father-in-law into following *down a path that is not good* for the neighbor. Beware of those who signal to each other behind someone's back; they may be *bent on evil*.

Proverbs 21:10 reads, "The wicked crave evil; their neighbors get no mercy from them." Proverbs 29:10 warns, "The bloodthirsty hate a person of integrity and seek to kill the upright." Whereas Jesus commands his followers to love even enemies and to give mercy, the wicked do neither.[15]

7. Below, box the description of the person and his name in Proverbs 29:24a. Wavy-underline the person's behavior in 24b.

> 21:24 The proud and arrogant person—"Mocker" is his name—
>         behaves with insolent fury.

The *arrogant* disdain God's person and commands. They mock the Bible. Even believers can become *proud*, responding *with insolent fury* to any who disagree with them. God doesn't allow his children to remain proud, though.

8. In these Proverbs verses, wavy-underline wrong actions. Box people.

> 17:23 The wicked accept bribes in secret
>         to pervert the course of justice.
> 28:21 To show partiality is not good—
>         yet a person will do wrong for a piece of bread.

*Bribes in secret* makes clear the wrongdoer knows he wrongs the innocent. *A piece of bread* shows how little it takes to incentivize people to wrong others.

## The Penalties of Wickedness

Proverbs exposes the consequences of wickedness, both to deter the simple from taking that path and to assure all that justice will come.

**The Little Details**
*Clay Jones on Original Sin:*

Historically for Protestants original sin has two commonly held components: humankind is guilty for the sin of their first parents and humankind inherited a corrupted nature, since they are sexual reproductions of their first parents.

Although the words "original sin" aren't found together in Scripture, the doctrine is taught in many passages: "Therefore, just as sin came into the world through one man, and death through sin, and so death spread to all men because all sinned" (Rom. 5:12); "one trespass led to condemnation for all men" (Rom. 5:18); and "in Adam all die" (1 Cor. 15:22). So it is no wonder that David wrote in Psalm 51:5, "Behold, I was brought forth in iniquity, and in sin did my mother *conceive* me" (emphasis added).

That humans are born corrupted makes sense of Jesus' proclamation in John 6:63 (NIV) that "the Spirit gives life; the flesh *counts for nothing*" (emphasis added) and his later telling the Jews in John 8:44 (NIV) that "you are of your father, the devil."[12]

## The Little Details
### Passages on Partiality

**Leviticus 19:15:** Do not pervert justice; do not show partiality to the poor or favoritism to the great, but judge your neighbor fairly.

**Deuteronomy 1:17:** Do not show partiality in judging; hear both small and great alike. Do not be afraid of anyone, for judgment belongs to God.

**Deuteronomy 10:17:** The LORD your God is God of gods and Lord of lords, the great God, mighty and awesome, who shows no partiality and accepts no bribes.

**Deuteronomy 16:19:** Do not pervert justice or show partiality. Do not accept a bribe, for a bribe blinds the eyes of the wise and twists the words of the innocent.

**2 Chronicles 19:7:** Now let the fear of the LORD be on you. Judge carefully, for with the LORD our God there is no injustice or partiality or bribery.

**1 Timothy 5:21:** I charge you, in the sight of God and Christ Jesus and the elect angels, to keep these instructions without partiality, and to do nothing out of favoritism.

### The Social Penalties

People often turn to family and friends when they need refreshment.

> **9.** In the Proverbs verse below, wavy-underline what a formerly righteous person can become like and their wrong action. Box people.
>
> 25:26 Like a muddied spring or a polluted well
>     are the righteous who give way to the wicked.

Instead of refreshing others like a glass of clean water, the one who turns from righteousness becomes as foul as filth flowing from faucets.

> **10.** Compare others' reactions to the righteous and wicked (Proverbs 10:6-7; 18:3; 22:5; 24:8-9; 29:27).
>
> | Righteous | Wicked |
> | --- | --- |
> | | |

People pour *blessings* on the *righteous* but recognize that *violence* is in the *mouth* (speech) of the wicked. People's *name* becomes associated with their fame or infamy; thus, we name children after Matthew, Mark, Luke, and John but criticize with statements like "He's a Judas" or "She's a Jezebel." The righteous *stay far from* the *paths* that *the wicked* trod, because they each *detest* the way each other lives.

> **11.** Compare others' reactions to the fortunes of the righteous and wicked (Proverbs 11:10; 28:12, 28).
>
> When the righteous prosper: _____ .
> When the wicked perish: _____ .
> When the wicked rise to power: _____ .

Queen Athaliah murdered the royal family and usurped the throne for seven years. But Jehosheba took her nephew, the youngest prince, *into hiding* at the temple. When the priest hiding the child revealed him publicly and ordered Athaliah killed, "All the people of the land rejoiced, and the city was calm, because Athaliah had been slain with the sword at the palace" (2 Kings 11:20).

Today Christians often *go into hiding* in nations where Christianity is illegal.

### The Natural Penalties

Some consequences are natural to life, as when gang members turn on each other.

> **12.** In the Proverbs verses below, wavy-underline the consequences that face the wicked.
>
> 17:13 Evil will never leave the house
>     of one who pays back evil for good.

| 17:20 | One whose heart is corrupt does not prosper; |
| | one whose tongue is perverse falls into trouble. |
| 21:7 | The violence of the wicked will drag them away, |
| | for they refuse to do what is right. |
| 22:8 | Whoever sows injustice reaps calamity, |
| | and the rod they wield in fury will be broken. |

*The rod* is their ability to harm others.

## The Divine Penalties

People take the path of wickedness to fulfill their desires.

**13.** Compare what happens to the desires of the righteous and wicked (Proverbs 10:3, 24, 28; 11:18, 23; 13:25; 15:6, 29).

| Righteous | Wicked |
| --- | --- |
| | |
| | |

*Hungry* refers to any kind of *craving*. The choices before us are clear: *dread* versus *desire, joy* versus *nothing, good* versus *wrath*. Over time, the righteous desire what God desires, and God fully blesses them. The *income of the wicked* is "a thing troubled,"[16] being "either too uncertain or too tainted to provide confidence."[17] *The wicked* keep *far from the LORD* who delights to answer *the prayers of the righteous*.

Still, some think the consequences don't matter if you get rich. But Proverbs 16:8 observes, "Better a little with righteousness than much gain with injustice." Yes, your conscience can bother you and relationships can suffer. The main reason righteousness with little is better, however, is that the wicked face divine consequences.

**14.** In these Proverbs verses below, wavy-circle what faces the wicked. Box names and people.

| 14:34 | Righteousness exalts a nation, |
| | but sin condemns any people. |
| 17:11 | Evildoers foster rebellion against God; |
| | the messenger of death will be sent against them. |
| 21:12 | The Righteous One takes note of the house of the wicked |
| | and brings the wicked to ruin. |
| 21:27 | The sacrifice of the wicked is detestable— |
| | how much more so when brought with evil intent! |

Sacrifices meant for the repentant to seek cleansing from sin obtain no mercy when the unrepentant offer them. Sometimes people get away with wickedness in this life, but the Bible promises that all will be made right at the final judgment.[18]

### The Little Details
### *Examples of Paying Evil for Good*

Before David became king, he guarded the wealthy Nabal's sheep and shepherds. But when David asked Nabal to share food with his men during festivities, Nabal refused and insulted David (1 Samuel 25:2-17). Fortunately, Nabal's wife Abigail found out and loaded donkeys with provisions she then took to David with an apology.

Later, when David was king, Uriah was one of his faithful, elite soldiers. But David slept with Uriah's wife Bathsheba, and when she became pregnant, he had Uriah killed in battle so he could marry Bathsheba and conceal the adultery (2 Samuel 11). God knew, though, and disciplined David.

## The Little Details

**Thaddeus J. Williams on Pursuing Justice in Spirit-Led Ways:**

Here are some clues that we may have been taken in by an anti-Spirit ideology: Instead of being love-filled, we're easily offended, ever suspicious, and preoccupied with our own feelings. Instead of being filled with joy, we're filled with rage and resentment, unable to forgive. Instead of striving for peace, we're quarrelsome—dividing people into oppressed or oppressor groups instead of appreciating the image-bearer before us. Instead of having patience, we're quickly triggered and slow to honestly weigh our opponents' perspectives. Instead of being kind, we're quick to trash others, assuming the worst of their motives. Instead of showing gentleness, we use condemning rhetoric and redefined words to intimidate others into our perspective. Instead of showing self-control, we blame our issues exclusively on others and their systems, not warring daily against the evil in our own hearts.[19]

---

15. Box the descriptions of people in Proverbs 11:7 (NRSVUE) below. Wavy-circle what ultimately happens to their hope and expectation.

> 11:7 When the wicked die, their hope perishes,
> and the expectation of the godless comes to nothing.

We learned how the wicked act and what penalties they face. Next we'll look at the traits of the righteous.

## Day 3

# The Traits of the Righteous

Before I made Jesus Lord of my life, I was heading down the paths of the wicked. I didn't know it, though. Some things I thought wrong were right, and some things I thought right were wrong. But there came a time when I trespassed my moral system enough that shame and regret overwhelmed me. How thankful I was when in the Gospel of John I read that Jesus died to cleanse us from our sins so we could have both righteousness and eternal life.

So far, we've looked at the paths of the wicked and the penalties they face. You've probably ventured into those paths, too, perhaps testing them tentatively or maybe barreling boldly down them. Either way, God's offer of cleansing and eternal life is there for the taking. When we turn from sin and ask God's forgiveness, he not only forgives and purifies us but also begins to change us to make us more like him. That process is called *sanctification*.

When Proverbs lists traits of the righteous, it shows us what the Holy Spirit intends to work in us as he sanctifies us.

### The Righteous Are Secure

In Proverbs, we see that the righteous are secure and avoid the pitfalls that entrap the wicked.

---

16. In the following Proverbs verses, wavy-underline what traps evildoers. Underline what happens to the righteous. Box people.

> 11:6 The righteousness of the upright delivers them,
> but the unfaithful are trapped by evil desires.
> 12:13 Evildoers are trapped by their sinful talk,
> and so the innocent escape trouble.
> 28:10 Whoever leads the upright along an evil path will fall into their own trap,
> but the blameless will receive a good inheritance.
> 29:6 Evildoers are snared by their own sin,
> but the righteous shout for joy and are glad.

When investigations into accusations reveal innocence, then *righteousness...delivers*. Nonetheless, the *upright* must take care not to let evildoers lead them onto *an evil path*. After the final judgment, true worshipers of God *will receive a good inheritance* in the new heavens and earth.

17. Compare the troubles of the righteous and wicked (Proverbs 11:8; 12:21; 13:6; 28:18).

| Righteous | Wicked |
|-----------|--------|
|           |        |

Innocence protects the *righteous* from judgments too.

18. Compare the security of the righteous with the fear of the wicked (Proverbs 10:9; 11:5, 21).

| Righteous | Wicked |
|-----------|--------|
|           |        |

Some bemoaned that convicted sex offender Jeffrey Epstein escaped justice by dying before his trial for sex trafficking could occur. But Proverbs 11:21 assures those who have suffered at the hands of the wicked that ultimate judgment comes.

## The Righteous Persevere
One benefit of pursuing righteousness is the ability to persevere.

19. In the Proverbs verses below, underline ways the righteous persevere.

10:25   When the storm has swept by, the wicked are gone,
              but the righteous stand firm forever.

10:30   The righteous will never be uprooted,
              but the wicked will not remain in the land.

12:3    No one can be established through wickedness,
              but the righteous cannot be uprooted.

12:7    The wicked are overthrown and are no more,
              but the house of the righteous stands firm.

13:9    The light of the righteous shines brightly,
              but the lamp of the wicked is snuffed out.

14:11   The house of the wicked will be destroyed,
              but the tent of the upright will flourish.

24:15   Do not lurk like a thief near the house of the righteous,
              do not plunder their dwelling place;

16      for though the righteous fall seven times, they rise again,
              but the wicked stumble when calamity strikes.

29:16   When the wicked thrive, so does sin,
              but the righteous will see their downfall.

Proverbs 10:30 reflects God's covenant with Israel. If the people keep his covenant, they *will never be uprooted*, but if they abandon God, they *will not remain in the land*. Indeed,

**The Little Details**
*David A. Hubbard on Proverbs 28:18:*
To walk *"blamelessly"* includes following the pattern of confession and abandonment of sin described in 28:13. "Blamelessly" means "maturely," depending on God and seeking His help and strength to be what He wants us to be. It includes trust and faithfulness and, hence, carries with it the blessings of salvation. God's arm is there to rescue us from the narrow places and to snatch us from falling off life's tight ledges (see 20:22). The who *"is perverse in his ways"* has the opposite experience. He *"will suddenly fall"* and keep falling at every turn. He neither acknowledges his sin, seeks God's mercy, nor obeys God's will. Therefore he has cut himself off from God's resources and is open to all that life throws at him. The divine order has become his enemy because he does not acknowledge any accountability to the Lord of creation and covenant.[20]

## The Little Details
### Scriptures on Perseverance

***Matthew 7:24-27:*** Everyone who hears these words of mine and puts them into practice is like a wise man who built his house on the rock. The rain came down, the streams rose, and the winds blew and beat against that house; yet it did not fall, because it had its foundation on the rock. But everyone who hears these words of mine and does not put them into practice is like a foolish man who built his house on sand. The rain came down, the streams rose, and the winds blew and beat against that house, and it fell with a great crash.

***2 Peter 1:5-7:*** Make every effort to add to your faith goodness; and to goodness, knowledge; and to knowledge, self-control; and to self-control, perseverance; and to perseverance, godliness; and to godliness, mutual affection; and to mutual affection, love.

after many warnings, God exiled the people from the land.[21] *Light* represents "life, joy, and prosperity" in 13:9; *snuffed out* "signifies adversity and death."[22]

## The Righteous Are Humble

A high school teacher told me I needed to develop more self-confidence. So I searched my Bible concordance for "confidence" and discovered the Bible doesn't promote self-confidence. Instead, it extols confidence in the Lord. In fact, Paul wrote that he boasted "in Christ Jesus" and "put no confidence in the flesh" (Philippians 3:3).

The verse that stunned me most, however, was Philippians 2:3 (GNT): "Don't do anything from selfish ambition or from a cheap desire to boast, but be humble toward one another, always considering others better than yourselves." That didn't mean I should consider someone who didn't like math to be better than me (I had a natural knack for it), but it did mean I should value others more than I value myself.

David A. Hubbard summarizes the Bible's teaching on pride:

> Pride is pagan behavior. It should have no place in the lives of God's people. Israel's teachers, psalmists, chroniclers, and prophets were unanimous on that point. Pride was, for them, a rejection of creatureliness, a declaration of independence from God if not an announcement of war against Him. Pride drew God's scorn, sparked His ire, and guaranteed His judgment. Moreover, it did not make friends for the haughty nor raise their esteem in their communities. Hard it is to love our neighbor as ourselves when we have an exaggerated sense of our own importance. We can easily sop up our total supply of love for our own needs, given our exalted ideas of how lovable we are.[23]

As I started valuing others over myself by reaching out to them no matter how insecure I felt, I made friends and gained more confidence in relationships. That grew my confidence in the Lord.

---

**20.** Double-wavy-underline what Proverbs 21:4 below labels sin.

21:4    Haughty eyes and a proud heart—
           the unplowed field of the wicked—produce sin.

---

*Haughty eyes* describe disdain. *A proud heart* describes those who think too highly of themselves. *Unplowed field* might also be translated *lamp*—the Hebrew is challenging, and so Bible translations vary. Either the *wicked* are like fields that can't be plowed to produce good fruit or the haughtiness that guides them and "'lights' their way" is a sin.[24] Either way, the verse's main thought is that this type of pride is *sin*.

---

**21.** Check the box next to what, according to Proverbs 16:19, is better to be.

☐ Humble and oppressed      ☐ Rich and proud

---

The next verses explain why.

---

I should value others more than I value myself.

---

22. In the ESV Proverbs verses below, circle humility's benefits and wavy-circle pride's penalties.

   11:2 When pride comes, then comes disgrace,
       but with the humble is wisdom.
   16:18 Pride goes before destruction,
       and a haughty spirit before a fall.
   18:12 Before destruction a man's heart is haughty,
       but humility comes before honor.
   29:23 One's pride will bring him low,
       but he who is lowly in spirit will obtain honor.

*Bring him low* means *pride* brings humiliation (see sidebar).

We've looked at three traits of the righteous: security, perseverance, and humility.

23. ♥ Which of the traits of the righteous would you most like to see more of in your life? Why?

In the next lesson, we'll see how the righteous act and what they do.

## Day 4

# The Paths of the Righteous

Clay and I love walking paths. The hills around us abound with flowering shrubs, singing birds, and rustling squirrels. The coastal sage scrub and ocean breezes smell earthy and clean. Many trails lead to soaring vistas of ocean waves and rocky bluffs. Others meander among California chapparal and woodlands that offer shade and food to mule deer, Black Phoebe flycatchers, and crimson-throated Anna's hummingbirds. Red-tailed hawks, turkey vultures, crows, and mockingbirds enliven the sky.

One week we followed the creek at the foot of our hill to where it joins another creek and then empties into a lake. We also followed it in the other direction to its start. The paths are physically invigorating and emotionally refreshing. Like them, the paths of the righteous are spiritually invigorating and refreshing.

## How the Righteous Act

As we dive into how the righteous act, remember that righteous living is a process. The Holy Spirit helps us by convicting, encouraging, and strengthening us. Our part begins with confessing sin, turning from it, and asking for help.

### The Righteous Act Kindly

The righteous and wicked treat others differently.

**The Little Details**
*Jesus on Pride and Humility in Luke 14:7-11:*
When he noticed how the guests picked the places of honor at the table, he told them this parable: "When someone invites you to a wedding feast, do not take the place of honor, for a person more distinguished than you may have been invited. If so, the host who invited both of you will come and say to you, 'Give this person your seat.' Then, humiliated, you will have to take the least important place. But when you are invited, take the lowest place, so that when your host comes, he will say to you, 'Friend, move up to a better place.' Then you will be honored in the presence of all the other guests. For all those who exalt themselves will be humbled, and those who humble themselves will be exalted."

## The Little Details
### *Thaddeus J. Williams on Finding Real Community:*

Real community—something we all long for and were created for—does not come easy. Think of how easily our hearts harbor grudges and assume the worst of others to feel better about ourselves and our clans. That is what our hearts do in their fallen default mode. That is one reason Paul talks so much about *schismata*—the sin of divisiveness—and why he talks about "the fruit of the Spirit." For quick-to-quarrel, easy-to-offend, clique-forming people to have any hope of experiencing real community, of gathering, of doing *church* together, then we need love, joy, peace, patience, kindness, faithfulness, goodness, gentleness, and self-control to deal with other far-from-perfect people. These "fruits" must be Spirit-produced. Without the Spirit's fruit, we fall into tribal default mode. That is why any approach to social justice that encourages suspicion and rage instead of the fruit of the Spirit has no place in Jesus's church.[25]

24. In the ESV Proverbs verses below, double-underline qualities, double-wavy-underline flaws, circle good consequences, and wavy-circle bad consequences (11:17). Underline what the righteous do, and wavy-underline what the wicked do (12:10; 29:7).

    11:17 A man who is kind benefits himself,
        but a cruel man hurts himself.

    12:10 Whoever is righteous has regard for the life of his beast,
        but the mercy of the wicked is cruel.

    29:7 A righteous man knows the rights of the poor;
        a wicked man does not understand such knowledge.

*Kind* could also be translated *merciful* (NASB).

### The Righteous Act Patiently

Here's an area I struggled with for years: patience.

25. Compare how patient and quick-tempered people handle conflict (Proverbs 10:12; 14:17, 29; 15:18; 16:32; 29:22).

| Patient People | Quick-Tempered People |
| --- | --- |
|  |  |

First Peter 4:8 quotes Proverbs 10:12: "Above all, love each other deeply, because love covers over a multitude of sins." *Love* forgives *wrongs*. In fact, Jesus said, "If you forgive other people when they sin against you, your heavenly Father will also forgive you. But if you do not forgive others their sins, your Father will not forgive your sins" (Matthew 6:14-15).

### The Righteous Act Honestly

Here's another area where the righteous and wicked differ.

26. Compare the actions of the righteous and wicked (Proverbs 11:3; 13:5; 28:5).

| Righteous | Wicked |
| --- | --- |
|  |  |

Honesty about ourselves enables us to grow spiritually. Honesty with others builds trust and shows love. Only *those who seek the Lord* can *understand what is right* because the Creator reveals it, while *evildoers* are self-serving.

### The Righteous Act Boldly

The righteous and wicked even differ in boldness.

> **27.** Compare the attitudes of the wicked and righteous (Proverbs 21:8; 28:1).
>
> | Wicked | Righteous |
> |---|---|
> | | |

*The guilty* are *devious*, always covering up their ways. The *wicked* live in constant fear that their sins will be found out. Indeed, if they're not uncovered now, the judgment will display them before all. The righteous can be *bold as a lion* because they have nothing to hide. They don't have to keep track of lies.

> **28.** ♥ Which of the actions of the righteous inspires you most? How can you plan to incorporate that action into your life—and soon?

## What the Righteous Do

The righteous act kindly, patiently, honestly, and boldly. But what do they do?

### The Righteous Plan to Do Good

Fairness, justice, and honesty mark the righteous.

> **29.** Compare the plans of the righteous and wicked (Proverbs 11:27; 12:5; 14:22; 21:29).
>
> | Righteous | Wicked |
> |---|---|
> | | |

In 11:27, either the one who *seeks good* for others *finds favor* with them or the one who *seeks good finds favor* with the Lord. Nonetheless, the *one who searches* for *evil* toward others meets with *evil*. In 21:29, *a bold front* masks dishonesty and contempt.

### The Righteous Rejoice in Justice

The righteous and wicked differ in their reactions to justice.

> **30.** In the Proverbs verse below, underline how the righteous react to justice. Wavy-underline how evildoers react.
>
> 21:15    When justice is done, it brings joy to the righteous
>        but terror to evildoers.

---

**The Little Details**

***Mary Kassian on Proverbs 21:29:***

Presumption is excessive self-confidence. Overconfidence, one might say, though ironically, it can manifest in a low view of self. For example, if God says he loves and accepts me, and I claim that he doesn't, then I am being presumptuous. I am setting my opinion up as higher than his. Scripture tells us that a wicked man "puts on a bold face" or puts up a bold front (Prov. 21:29). He is overly sure of himself. He figures that he is thinking and doing the right thing. But his boldness is presumptuous. Disrespectful. Insolent. What's more, it is extremely sinful.[26]

*The Righteous Confess Sins*

Here's an action crucial to sanctification.

> **31.** In the ESV Proverbs verse below, wavy-underline the action that doesn't prosper. Underline the actions that find mercy.
>
> 28:13  Whoever conceals his transgressions will not prosper,
>     but he who confesses and forsakes them will obtain mercy.

We grow spiritually when we recognize, confess, and renounce our sins. When we ignore or justify sin, sin stunts us.

In summary, the righteous are kind, patient, honest, and bold. They plan good things, rejoice in justice, and confess and renounce their sins. Next we'll look at the many blessings that come to the righteous.

## Day 5

# The Blessings of Righteousness

One of our former foster children as an adult asked why God allowed her to be born to a bad mom. I explained that's not how births work. God gave good commands designed to protect women and children. For instance, they forbid adultery and command dads to care for their wives and children. But her birth parents ignored those commands. Her mom had an affair with a married military superior. Then she lost her job when she became pregnant, and without financial support from the child's father, she couldn't find adequate work while expecting. She didn't have the support, guidance, or resources to raise a child alone. I told her I was extremely happy that her mom did what God wanted by not getting an abortion, however, because God and we all loved her dearly.

That God gives good commands designed to protect people is one of this chapter's key messages. When we ignore those commands, we and others suffer.

On Day 2, we looked at negative consequences when people ignore God's commands. Some of the passages also showed the blessings of following those directives. Now let's examine those blessings more thoroughly. We'll divide them into the same categories we used for penalties: social, natural, and divine.

**The Social Blessings**

In Day 2's lesson we saw how wickedness adversely affects relationships, earning the wicked shame and the contempt of others. But we also read that righteousness blesses relationships. For example, others crown the righteous with blessings (Proverbs 10:6) and use their name in blessings (verse 7). Additionally, cities rejoice when the righteous prosper and the wicked perish (Proverbs 11:10). Let's see what else righteousness brings socially.

> **32.** In the following Proverbs verse, circle what good judgment wins a person.
>
> 13:15  Good judgment wins favor,
>     but the way of the unfaithful leads to their destruction.

People love a person with good judgment.

God gave good commands designed to protect women and children.

**33.** In this verse, circle how children are affected by having righteous parents.

> 20:7   The righteous lead blameless lives;
> blessed are their children after them.

The Bible commands husbands to love their wives and children and to not abandon them. It commands wives to respect and love their husbands. Additionally, it instructs parents to teach God's ways to their children. And it forbids sex outside of marriage, which often results in children growing up in poverty. All these commands help bless children with a stable, nurturing home life.

## The Natural Blessings

Just as going against God's commands brings natural penalties, so following them brings natural blessings.

**34.** In Proverbs 12:12 (esv) below, wavy-underline what the wicked do and circle what the righteous bear.

> 12:12   Whoever is wicked covets the spoil of evildoers,
> but the root of the righteous bears fruit.

Ross writes that verse 12:12 is difficult to translate and "seems to be saying that there are good rewards for the righteous, but the wicked are dangerous and perhaps get caught in their own devices."[27] The righteous, however, bear good fruit. Galatians 5:22-23 lists such fruit: "The fruit of the Spirit is love, joy, peace, forbearance, kindness, goodness, faithfulness, gentleness and self-control."

## The Divine Blessings

In Day 2's lesson we read that the wicked face calamities and evil, but the righteous have full stomachs (Proverbs 13:25), treasure-filled houses (15:6), and joy (10:28). Additionally, the desires of the righteous will be granted and will end in good (10:24; 11:23).

**35.** In the Proverbs verse below, circle what else comes to the righteous.

> 11:31   If the righteous receive their due on earth,
> how much more the ungodly and the sinner!

This may seem counterintuitive. But the verse means that if God disciplines *the righteous* when they sin *on earth*, *how much more* can we expect to see *the ungodly* meet justice. God's discipline blesses us because it "produces a harvest of righteousness and peace" (Hebrews 12:11). Divine discipline is a blessing to his children.

**36.** What rewards can the righteous expect (Proverbs 13:21; 14:14, 19; 21:18)?

Proverbs 14:19 is similar to Philippians 2:10: "At the name of Jesus every knee should bow, in heaven and on earth and under the earth." The *wicked become a ransom* when what they

## The Little Details
### Clay Jones on What Happens When You Die:

So what happens to your soul when you die? The answer is that your soul will be immediately transferred into the spiritual realm: "to the city of the living God, the heavenly Jerusalem, and to innumerable angels in festal gathering, and to the assembly of the firstborn who are enrolled in heaven, and to God, the judge of all, and to the spirits of the righteous made perfect, and to Jesus, the mediator of a new covenant" (Hebrews 12:22-24). As Jesus said to the thief being crucified next to Him, "Truly, I say to you, *today* you will be with me in paradise" (Luke 23:43) and "paradise" is one of the Biblical names for heaven. There will be no delay. In fact, your transition into the unseen realm will be so smooth, so seamless, so natural, that it may take you a while to realize that you've died. It won't be like the reboot of a computer. You will never lose consciousness. If you happen to turn and see your body lying on the floor, or in a mangled car, or on an operating table then you can take that as evidence of your passing.[28]

planned for the righteous comes upon them, as when Haman desired to hang Mordecai but was himself hanged (Esther 7:10).

In Day 1's lesson, we saw that the righteous are on the path of life while the wicked are on a path that may appear to be a path of life but in actuality is a path to death. When the Bible talks about death, it doesn't always mean the death of our bodies. Sometimes it's speaking of not inheriting eternal life. In Solomon's day, God hadn't fully revealed the gift of eternal life. But Proverbs speaks of it nonetheless.

> **37.** Circle references to life and immortality in the proverbs below.
>
> 11:30 The fruit of the righteous is a tree of life,
> and the one who is wise saves lives.
>
> 12:28 In the way of righteousness there is life;
> along that path is immortality.

The tree of life will be restored in the new heavens and earth, where all those whose names are written in the Lamb's book of life will live with God eternally.[29]

In this lesson, we saw the social, natural, and divine blessings of the righteous.

> **38.** ♥ Which of this lesson's blessings do you desire most? Why?

## Wisdom's Worth

> **39.** ♥ In what way did you apply wisdom from Proverbs to your life this week?

In this chapter, we examined what Proverbs means when it calls people righteous. We looked at the paths of the righteous and wicked, and we saw the consequences of both. We saw a model of how the righteous act.

But even though many blessings adorn the righteous, that doesn't mean they don't face adversities. In our next chapter we'll discover the key to strength in adversity.

### Wisdom Worship

Find a quiet place and prepare your heart for grateful worship.

> 🧠 Turn to Psalm 119:81-96 in your Bible and pray the passage aloud.

## Karla's Creative Connection

*Whoever is patient has great understanding, but one who is quick-tempered displays folly.*

Proverbs 14:29

As much as I hate to admit it, I was an angry, quick-tempered young woman, so this week's key verse really struck a chord.

Although I didn't understand it at the time, my mother was a classic narcissist. And I was her favorite object of abuse that escalated to her legally disowning me when I was 17 and my becoming a ward of the state of Illinois. Her verbal and emotional abuse, rejection, and final act of abandonment triggered an uncontrollable anger in me, and I saw myself and my world through the eyes of a victim. I felt trapped in a prison of my own emotions with no way out.

And then, seven years later at a neighborhood Bible study, I met Jesus. For the first time in my life, I felt completely and unconditionally loved. My sins, including my quick-tempered outbursts of anger, were forgiven, and I was set free! I no longer saw myself as a victim as I began to see myself—and my mother—through God's eyes, not just my own.

I still remember the evening I sat sobbing as I heard Jesus say, "Forgive others as I have forgiven you." I was so overwhelmed with his forgiveness for my own sins that I was able to forgive my mother for her treatment of me and ask her to forgive me for my anger toward her. It was the first step in my journey of allowing the Lord to heal my heart and make me more like Jesus.

We've all been hurt, haven't we? You might be thinking of someone who has hurt you right now. Offended you in some way. Made you angry. The offense may have been totally unwarranted, but the hurt is real. I know. And I'm sorry. I also know if you hold on to that hurt, allowing that anger to settle in your heart, it will, over time, affect your spiritual, mental, and physical health. And it will eventually come out. Somewhere. And at someone.

One way I've found to creatively connect with God when I've been hurt or offended is to ask him to allow me to use my imagination to see myself, the situation, or the offense through his eyes and not my own. When you can look at the offense and your own emotional response through the lens of God's Word and wisdom, you might be surprised to see how you might have overreacted. Or you might be reminded of how much God has forgiven you, giving you the grace you need to forgive your offender. And still other times he might gently prompt you to love the person anyway, be patient, and trust him with the resolve.

I hope you'll take time this week to explore this creative way to connect with God and trust him to bring renewed hope and healing to your beautiful, wounded heart.

*Karla*

WHOEVER IS PATIENT HAS GREAT UNDERSTANDING, BUT ONE WHO IS QUICK-TEMPERED DISPLAYS FOLLY.

PROVERBS 14:29

## Chapter 6

# Proverbs 16:1–18:24
## The Keys to Strength in Adversity

What are the keys to strength in adversity?

## Day 1

## Encountering Adversity

As I sat squeezed between my two siblings in the back seat of the white Mazda, I gripped the edge of the seat so hard that my joints hurt. My mom was careening around hairpin turns in the Santa Ana Mountains—drunk. She had threatened suicide many times, but now my heart pounded as I realized she meant to kill us with her. I prayed over and over that God would save my siblings and me and do whatever was best for my mother.

God acted on my prayers. Mom suddenly braked, turned the car around, and drove slowly home.

Proverbs 18:10 says, "The name of the Lord is a fortified tower; the righteous run to it and are safe." God kept three children safe.

1. ♥ Describe a time God protected you or a loved one.

### God's Word to Us in Proverbs

As you read Proverbs today, notice how active God is in the lives of those who love him. Also notice how the second half of Collection II holds a variety of proverb types.

🗯 Take a moment to pray for insight as you read God's Word.

2. ♥ Read chapters 16–18 in Proverbs. (a) What stood out to you in your reading? Why? (b) How can you apply that insight to your life this week?

### Discover What the Fear of the Lord Looks Like

Adversity. Sometimes it's a flat tire on the way to an important meeting. Other times it's from a person who opposes or even hates us.

## The Little Details
### For Budding Poets

The last page of this lesson has another example of forming proverbs that compare people into a **wisdom psalm** based on Psalm 1. This one compares those who forgive offenses with those who don't.

As mentioned previously, you can download my worksheet with step-by-step instructions and find more sample poems at DiscoveringTheBibleSeries.com.

When it comes to strength in adversity, the first place to start is with the fear of the Lord, as these next verses explain.

> **3.** In Proverbs 14:26-27 (ESV) below, circle the three things the fear of the Lord offers. Underline what it enables us to do.
>
> 14:26  In the fear of the LORD one has strong confidence,
>           and his children will have a refuge.
> 27      The fear of the LORD is a fountain of life,
>           that one may turn away from the snares of death.

Those who fear the Lord not only have a *strong confidence* that God will protect them but also supply a *refuge* for their children. This refuge is like a military fortress.[1] And speaking of military fortresses, let's look at our key verse again—Proverbs 18:10.

> **4.** Circle what the name of the Lord is. Box people. Circle what they become.
>
> 18:10  The name of the LORD is a fortified tower;
>           the righteous run to it and are safe.

No matter how adverse our circumstances, those who belong to the Lord can rely on his protection and *safe* care. Does that mean nothing bad can happen to one faithful to God? No, bad things can and will happen. Indeed, Christians in some countries are killed for their faith. But nothing will happen that the Father can't work for good and use for his ultimate purposes. He decreed it necessary for people to crucify Jesus to pay for our sins. But Jesus rose from the dead and showed that he has the final victory.

The Lord can and will protect us from much, and one day he will raise us from the dead to be with him forever.

> **5.** Compare the actions of those who fear the Lord with the actions of those who despise him (Proverbs 14:2).
>
> | Those Who Fear the Lord | Those Who Despise the Lord |
> | --- | --- |
> | | |

The person who *fears the LORD* respects his power and authority and therefore obeys him. That person *walks uprightly*; that is, consistently lives according to God's ways.

In this lesson we saw from our key verse that the righteous—those who make every effort to live the way God commands and who confess wrongdoing when they fail—can find safety in the name of the Lord. We discovered that those who fear the Lord have a secure fortress in him in the middle of adversity. In our next lesson we'll read many more benefits that God gives to those who fear him, benefits that help us when we face adversity.

# Pam's Simply Beautiful Wisdom

*The horse is made ready for the day of battle, but victory rests with the L*ORD*.*

Proverbs 21:31

We long for the thrill of victory, the adrenalin rush of a win, the feeling of reaching the summit. But for most of us, victory comes in the form of:

- Landing that big client, reaching a sales goal, or signing an important contract
- Purchasing that new home, boat, or RV
- Hearing you got the new job, the promotion, the raise, the scholarship, or the deal
- Learning you, your kids, or grandchildren got that straight *A* report card

Sometimes victories are raw and real:

- Reading a positive blue line signaling the expectation of a long-awaited baby
- Overcoming a nagging negative habit that's held you back from life's best
- Healing an emotional hurt that's been haunting you
- Shedding the weight that's put your health and wellness at risk
- Repairing a relationship so it's healthy and whole
- Seeing a prodigal return to Christ and the family
- Helping a child overcome an obstacle to move forward in life
- Returning home from deployment *alive*
- Crawling, wheeling, shuffling forward with assistance until you can solo
- Breathing on your own after a near-death illness

During a difficult season, one of my friends encouraged me with, "Sometimes it's victory to just stand!" Ephesians 6:13 (ESV) concurs: "Having done all, to stand firm."

No matter what victories you long to achieve, know that if that desire matches God's heart and Word, he's in it with you! God plants the seed for the goal, empowers your path, and celebrates the victory with you.

In the book of Proverbs, we gain a glimpse into God's battle plan to victory (God's part is italicized):

- *He holds success* in store for the upright, *he is a shield* to those whose walk is blameless (Proverbs 2:7).
- Be sure of this: The wicked *will not go unpunished*, but those who are righteous will *go free*" (Proverbs 11:21).
- The wicked *are overthrown* and *are no more*, but the house of the righteous *stands firm* (Proverbs 12:7).
- The name of the LORD is a *fortified tower*; the righteous run to it and *are safe* (Proverbs 18:10).

Do you notice a common thread in what is *our part*? Living *righteously and uprightly.*

*Righteousness* capsulized means blameless, innocent, and just. Living *uprightly* is to live on the straight path. Victory comes when we seek to live in congruence with God's principles.

# Circle Up for Victory

To live in agreement with God's *way*, we should dwell in God's *Word*. Since reading *The Circle Maker* by Pastor Mark Batterson, I write a goal or prayer in my journal, draw a circle around it, and then write a verse to pray over that heart's desire. For example, I might pen "Get a contract to publish a children's book" and then around that prayer request jot "My God will supply every need of yours according to his riches in glory in Christ Jesus" (Philippians 4:19 ESV). After I write the prayer request and verse, I ask myself, *What will it take to get there? Who do I need to become so I can manage well the "Yes" should God decide to grant it?* Then I circle up the answers into new prayer requests:

- *Lord, as I research bestselling children's books, give me insights on how to write an excellent one.*

- *Lord, show me what I need to learn and from whom I need to learn to succeed at writing a life-impacting work for children.*

- *Lord, fine-tune my children's book ideas and help me prioritize other things to gain more time to write.*

- *Lord, give me more time with my grandchildren as they inspire and fine-tune me.*

I repeat the process of selecting verses to pray over these stepping stones toward the realization of my hopes, goals, and prayers. In a margin of this study, draw circles in which to record the dreams, desires, and prayers for which you hope to gain God's victories in your future. Below is a Scripture prayer, with some of the verses paraphrased, to kick-start you out of the blocks on your run to victory:

> God says, "I am able to do immeasurably more than all you ask or imagine, according to my power that is at work within you. Mine is the greatness and the power and the glory and the majesty and the splendor, for everything in heaven and earth is mine. Mine is the kingdom; I am exalted as head overall. Wealth and honor come from me; I am the ruler of all things. I am beyond your reach and exalted in power; in my justice and great righteousness, I do not oppress. I, the Sovereign LORD, come with power, and my arm rules for me. See, my reward is with me, and my recompense accompanies me. I give strength to the weary and increase the power of the weak. I, the Sovereign LORD, have made the heavens and the earth by my great power and out-stretched arm. Nothing is too hard for me. I rescue and save." [2]

First Corinthians 15:57 says, "Thanks be to God, who gives us the victory through our Lord Jesus Christ" (ESV). May God empower you to many victories!

## Experiencing Scripture Creatively (Optional)

If you have extra time, consider these suggestions for creatively engaging with verses from this week's reading.

- If you're struggling to forgive someone, sketch a weighing scale representing justice on a card and write Proverbs 29:26b next to them. Place it where you can see it regularly.

- Follow Karla's instructions at the end of this chapter for imagining yourself safe in God's presence.

- Use your answers to a comparison question to write a wisdom psalm based on Psalm 1's structure. Begin the title with "A psalm of" followed by your name and the verses it concerns. This poem is based on question 37:

  > *A psalm of Jean concerning Proverbs 19:11; 20:22; 25:21-22.*
  > Blessed is the one
  >      who threatens not revenge
  >      nor slanders an offender
  >      nor refuses a wrongdoer help.

But her glory is in overlooking an offense
      and her hurts she patiently takes to the Lord.
She is like bubbling springs
      that quench thirst
          and wash wounds.
In all that she does, she cares.

The bitter are not so,
      but are like polluted, putrid ponds buzzed by flies.
Therefore revenge seekers will not forgive,
      nor will they humbly admit wrongdoing.

For the Lord avenges and rewards forgivers,
      but the way of revenge seekers he judges.

# Our Strong Confidence

A girlfriend showed up to Bible study one morning with portions of her eyebrows, bangs, and arm hair missing. Trying to use her outdoor grill for the first time the night before, she'd had trouble lighting it. She leaned close to see what was wrong, and when it suddenly lit, the flames singed her hairs.

She hadn't properly feared the consequences of mistreating the grill.

Likewise, many people don't properly fear the consequences of mistreating the Lord. To counter this, Proverbs motivates us to fear the Lord. We read one such motivation in the last lesson: "In the fear of the Lord one has strong confidence" (Proverbs 14:26 ESV). Let's look at more.

## The Many Motivations for Fearing the Lord

The incentive in Proverbs 15:33 below is simple.

> 6. Underline what wisdom teaches. Double-underline the character quality that comes before line 2's blessing. Circle the blessing.
>
> 15:33   Wisdom's instruction is to fear the Lord,
>          and humility comes before honor.

Those with *humility* embrace *wisdom's instruction* to *fear the Lord* and receive *honor*. The first clause can also be translated "The fear of the Lord teaches a man wisdom," in which case the humble fear of the Lord brings wisdom and honor.[4] Either way, this proverb partners wisdom, the fear of the Lord, humility, and honor.

Why is fearing the Lord wise? Proverbs offers many reasons.

### It's Wise Because God Sees All

One reason people don't fear the Lord is that they believe they're good, contrary to Romans 3:23: "All have sinned and fall short of the glory of God." Without God people create their own moral systems that make them feel good about themselves and support their belief that they *are* good (see sidebar).

## The Little Details

### David A. Hubbard on Proverbs 29:13:

I sat enthralled as I listened to Benjamin Mays. The distinguished preacher-educator and former president of Morehouse College in Atlanta described his pilgrimage from the fields of South Carolina to the halls of Academe. What helped the young black child, born in the last century, gain perspective on himself in a time and place when second-class status was the best that a kid like him could hope for? His Sunday school teacher had told him that he was made in God's image, and he sensed at that tender age that he was as good as anybody else no matter what the practices and practitioners of segregation said about him. The lamp of the Lord burned bright with him, and in that light he lived his long, full life, as he taught thousands of African-Americans to live the same way.[5]

7.  (a) Over whom does the Lord keep watch (Proverbs 15:3)? (b) What can he see (20:27)?

We can hide wrongdoing from people and ourselves but not from *the eyes of the LORD*. Indeed, as we read in chapter 4, "Sheol and Abaddon lie open before the LORD; how much more the hearts of the children of man!" (Proverbs 15:11). The Lord knows and judges our thoughts and motives. He ferrets out hypocrisies. The Lord gives each person a *spirit* that serves as a conscience. When we walk with him, he *sheds light* on our *inmost* thoughts, convicting and encouraging us so that we grow in godliness and trust.

### It's Wise Because the Lord Is Creator of All

God's status as the Creator means we're accountable to him.

8.  Below, to the left of the people, write the letter of what they have in common (Proverbs 22:2; 29:13).

| People | Have This in Common |
| --- | --- |
| Poor and oppressors | A. The LORD gives them sight |
| Rich and poor | B. The LORD is their Maker |

Thus, the *rich* shouldn't despise the *poor*. *Sight* (or "light," ESV) is either the conscience or a metaphor for life. The *Maker* will judge those he made for how they treat each other, not by their own standards but by his. It is best, therefore, to fear the Lord.

### It's Wise Because the Fear of the Lord Brings Blessings

The Lord gives us a strong confidence and refuge. But there's more.

9.  In Proverbs 15:16 below, underline what's better, and wavy-underline what's worse.

> 15:16 Better a little with the fear of the LORD
> than great wealth with turmoil.

While the earth's riches offer benefits, they pale in comparison with spiritual riches.

10. In the Proverbs (ESV) verse below, double-underline the qualities God rewards. Circle rewards.

> 22:4 The reward for humility and fear of the LORD
> is riches and honor and life.

Hubbard writes that *riches* "here and elsewhere in Proverbs...means something like having enough material goods to care for one's own family and to give generously to those around you who may be in want."[6] *Honor* is the esteem others give one.

11. What comes to those who fear the Lord according to Proverbs 10:27, 16:6, and 28:14?

☐ Avoidance of evil     ☐ Favor     ☐ Love

☐ Blessings     ☐ Longer life     ☐ Riches

Modern medicine has alleviated much of what used to *cut short* rebellious lives, but violence, substance abuse, and recklessness still kill. *Love and faithfulness* to others had to go with sin sacrifices for them to make *sin atoned for*, and an unrepentant heart was never cleansed. *Evil is avoided* altogether *through the fear of the Lord.*

But what if an unbeliever seems more blessed than we are? Proverbs addresses that.

12. In Proverbs 23:17-18 below, underline what should replace envy (17b). Circle what you should set your heart on instead (18ab).

> 23:17 Do not let your heart envy sinners,
>           but always be zealous for the fear of the Lord.
> 18 There is surely a future hope for you,
>           and your hope will not be cut off.

### It's Wise Because the Lord Is Trustworthy

Proverbs 22:19 explains the above passage's purpose: "So that your trust may be in the Lord." His trustworthiness is the reason for our strong confidence amid adversity.

13. In the Proverbs verses below, underline wise actions. Wavy-underline foolish actions. Circle blessings. Wavy-circle negative consequences. Box people.

> 16:20 Whoever gives heed to instruction prospers,
>           and blessed is the one who trusts in the Lord.
> 28:25 The greedy stir up conflict,
>           but those who trust in the Lord will prosper.
> 29:25 Fear of man will prove to be a snare,
>           but whoever trusts in the Lord is kept safe.

The *greedy* trust in wealth, and their selfishness will *stir up conflict*. Compromise comes when we *fear* offending someone more than we trust God. Those with fickle favor aren't worth pursuing. Plus, *fear of man* makes us easy to manipulate.

14. ♥ What most motivates you to fear the Lord?

### Discover in What the Lord Delights and Detests

Those who want the strong confidence that comes from the fear of the Lord will want to know in what he delights and what he detests.

15. To the far left of what's found in each Proverbs verse cited below, write the letter of the result that goes with it. Note that some Bibles translate "the Lord detests" as "is an abomination to the Lord." Each item found in a verse matches to one result.

| Verse | What's Found in Verse | Result |
|---|---|---|
| 11:1 | Accurate weights | A. Do not please the Lord |
|  | Dishonest scales | B. Please the Lord |
| 11:20 | People with blameless ways | C. The Lord delights in |
|  | People with perverse hearts | D. The Lord detests |

Chart continues on the next page.

**The Little Details**
*James 3:13-18 (NRSVUE) on Envy:*

Who is wise and knowledgeable among you? Show by your good life that your works are done with gentleness born of wisdom. But if you have bitter envy and selfish ambition in your hearts, do not be arrogant and lie about the truth. This is not wisdom that comes down from above but is earthly, unspiritual, devilish. For where there is envy and selfish ambition, there will also be disorder and wickedness of every kind. But the wisdom from above is first pure, then peaceable, gentle, willing to yield, full of mercy and good fruits, without a trace of partiality or hypocrisy. And a fruit of righteousness is sown in peace by those who make peace.

---

Those who want the strong confidence that comes from the fear of the Lord will want to know in what he delights and what he detests.

---

**The Little Details**
*Mary Kassian on Arrogance and Insecurity:*

All of us have a sinful tendency to value our own opinions above God's. But when it comes to confidence, this can land us in one of two opposite and equally dangerous ditches—the ditch of arrogance or the ditch of insecurity. We become arrogant when we think higher of ourselves than we ought to think. We become insecure when we think lower of ourselves than we ought to think. To build strong confidence, we must humbly check our over-confidence at the door and let Christ renew our minds so that we can think about everything, including ourselves, the way God says we should (Rom. 12:2–3).[8]

| | | | |
|---|---|---|---|
| 12:22 | Lying lips | | E. The LORD favors |
| | Trustworthy people | | F. The LORD loves |
| 15:8 | Prayers of the upright | | G. The LORD sees as pure |
| | Sacrifices of the wicked | | |
| 15:9 | People pursuing righteousness | | |
| | The way of the wicked | | |
| 15:26 | Gracious words | | |
| | The thoughts of the wicked | | |
| 16:5 | All the proud of heart | | |
| 17:15 | Acquitting the guilty | | |
| | Condemning the innocent | | |
| 20:10 | Differing measures | | |
| | Differing weights | | |
| 20:23 | Differing scales | | |
| | Dishonest weights | | |

*Dishonest scales* cheat by using two sets of weights or mismarked scales. *Perverse hearts* are "a twisted mind, i.e., the whole spiritual being is influenced toward evil."[7] The *sacrifice of the wicked* is detestable because it seeks forgiveness with neither repentance nor a sincere desire to draw close to God, making the sacrifices rituals of fake piety. The *proud of heart* are those who arrogantly oppose God. *Condemning the innocent* happens when witnesses lie before juries and when laws forbid what God commands.

In this lesson we read proverbs that motivate us to fear the Lord with a healthy reverence and respect for his power and authority. We also looked at what the Lord delights in and detests. Next we'll discover the attitudes that strengthen us in adversity.

## Day 3

## Attitudes That Strengthen

When I first became a Christian, I had a mix of good and bad attitudes. A learning attitude served well to strengthen me. But pessimism, negativity, hopelessness, and distrust of people weakened me, especially in hardship. As I grew spiritually, though, the Holy Spirit replaced hindering attitudes with helpful ones. Let's look at what Proverbs says about adopting attitudes that strengthen.

### Embrace a Learning Attitude

Proverbs 22:17-21 is the introduction to a section of Proverbs known as Thirty Sayings of the Wise. The collection prepared young court officials to convey messages and get answers, but it has great advice for everyone.[9] It begins with a learning attitude.

> As I grew spiritually...the Holy Spirit replaced hindering attitudes with helpful ones.

**16.** Read Proverbs 22:17-21 (ESV) below. Underline the actions to take (17ab, 18ab). Circle the benefits you'll receive (18a, 19a, 21ab).

> 22:17  Incline your ear, and hear the words of the wise,
>            and apply your heart to my knowledge,

<sup>18</sup> for it will be pleasant if you keep them within you,
    if all of them are ready on your lips.
<sup>19</sup> That your trust may be in the LORD,
    I have made them known to you today, even to you.
<sup>20</sup> Have I not written for you thirty sayings
    of counsel and knowledge,
<sup>21</sup> to make you know what is right and true,
    that you may give a true answer to those who sent you?

If we approach Scripture with an attitude of eagerness to learn, bending our *ear* to *hear*, listening attentively, seeking to *apply* it with a responsive *heart*, and memorizing it, the results will be *pleasant*. We'll grow in our *trust in the LORD*, we'll know what is *right and true*, and we'll be able to *answer* others well.

### Break Bad Attitudes

When I started reading the Bible as a teen, I learned that many of my attitudes had to change. For instance, I envied girls in my high school who had nicer clothes, even though some of them qualified for a role in *Mean Girls*. But the Thirty Sayings of the Wise collection warns against that and other attitudes that weaken.

**17.** Why shouldn't we desire a wicked person's company (Proverbs 24:1-2)?

A woman who escaped an abusive situation told me much of her story. In high school, she got involved with a gang of thieves partly because she envied what they had but also because giving her friends gifts made her feel important and liked. After high school, she moved in with one of the boys, not realizing he would be untrustworthy, eventually aim the anger he aimed at others at her and their kids, and be in and out of jail.

*Envy* can tempt us to gloat when troubles strike those who've wronged us.

**18.** Read Proverbs 24:17-18. (a) What shouldn't we do when someone who doesn't like us falls? (b) Why not?

Jesus told us the attitude God wants us to have toward enemies: "Love your enemies and pray for those who persecute you" (Matthew 5:44).

**19.** Why shouldn't we fret over or envy evildoers (Proverbs 24:19-20)?

Both fretting over and envying the wicked signal a need to shift our focus to the eternity Jesus has secured for us. The final judgment will bring final justice.

### Replace Harmful Attitudes with Healing Attitudes

When I became a Christian, I read in 1 Thessalonians 5:16-18 that I was supposed to rejoice always and give thanks in all circumstances. So I embarked on a journey to give

### The Little Details
**Thaddeus J. Williams on Oppressors:**

Howard Zinn's *A People's History of the United States* rewrites history from the perspective of the oppressed, as Zinn imagines their perspective. A biblically informed reading of history would tell us to care for the oppressed and to take their stories seriously as God's downtrodden image-bearers, but it would also do something Zinn never dreamed of. It would inspire us to see history not purely through the perspective of the oppressed but also through the lenses of the oppressors. Why? Because the same human nature in the Aztec slayer, the Atlantic slave trader, and the Auschwitz executioner resides in us too. If we don't seriously reckon with that uncomfortable truth, then we can all too easily become the next round of self-righteous oppressors.[10]

## The Little Details
### David A. Hubbard on Cheerfulness:

The medicinal effects of cheerfulness were explored by Norman Cousins in his famous experiment with comedy films and the therapeutic impact of laughter during his painful recovery from an inflammation of the nervous system. So dramatic were his findings that he has served on the faculty of the UCLA School of Medicine sharing his experiences with the neophyte physicians. His personal research anticipated the discovery of endorphins and other hormonal secretions which are the body's own pain blockers, released by the act of laughter and other expressions of hopeful positive outlook.[11]

thanks more often and to look for how God worked good out of bad situations. I even thanked God for the good he would somehow bring through adversity. This dissolved much of my pessimism, negativity, and hopelessness. Healing attitudes replaced harmful ones.

20. To the far left of each attitude below, found in the Proverbs verses cited, write the letter of the result that goes with it. Then in the Strengthen or Weaken column, check "S" if the attitude strengthens or "W" if the attitude weakens. Each attitude matches to one unique result.

| Verse | Attitude Found in Verse | Strengthen or Weaken | | Result |
|---|---|---|---|---|
| 14:30 | Envy | ☐ S | ☐ W | A. Are good medicine |
| | Peaceful hearts | ☐ S | ☐ W | B. Continually feast |
| 15:13 | Happy hearts | ☐ S | ☐ W | C. Crush spirits |
| | Heartaches | ☐ S | ☐ W | D. Dry up bones |
| 15:15 | Cheerful hearts | ☐ S | ☐ W | E. Endure sickness |
| 17:22 | Cheerful hearts | ☐ S | ☐ W | F. Give life |
| | Crushed spirits | ☐ S | ☐ W | G. Make cheerful faces |
| 18:14 | Crushed spirits | ☐ S | ☐ W | H. Rot bones |
| | Human spirits | ☐ S | ☐ W | I. Who can bear? |

Ongoing *envy* can make one sick. *A crushed spirit* "suggests a broken will, loss of vitality, despair, and emotional pain" and includes depression.[12] *Oppressed* in 15:15 is opposite *cheerful heart* and thus means inward oppression.[13]

A crushed spirit describes my teenage years well. But as I gave thanks and looked for the good God was working, a cheerful heart replaced my crushed spirit. When I memorized verses about God's love and faithfulness, negativity turned to hope. As I sought to value others over myself instead of hiding, I gained friends. God's Word proved true!

## Maintain a Submissive Attitude

If we want God's strength in our adversity, then keeping a submissive attitude is vital. That's because God hinders some plans and blesses others.

21. In these NRSVUE Proverbs verses, wavy-circle ways God might hinder the wicked.

22:14 The mouth of a loose woman is a deep pit;
     he with whom the LORD is angry falls into it.
22:22 Do not rob the poor because they are poor
     or crush the afflicted at the gate,
23   for the LORD pleads their cause
     and despoils of life those who despoil them.

*Mouth* is the *loose* woman's seductive speech. The godly avoid her, but those who seek her fall into the trap of a *deep pit* and will face God's anger. Oppressors who exploit the *poor* may think their plans secure but will likewise face God's wrath.

**22.** Box the two descriptions of people in the Proverbs verse below. Circle the blessing (12:2a). Wavy-circle the penalty (12:2b).

> 12:2 Good people obtain favor from the LORD,
> but he condemns those who devise wicked schemes.

People plan what they want to do in life, the type of person they want to marry, and where they want to live. Life often surprises us, though.

**23.** To the left of each attribute of the Lord below, write the letter of the matching result for people's plans (Proverbs 10:22; 18:22; 19:14, 17). Each attribute matches one unique result.

| Attribute of the LORD | Result for People's Plans |
|---|---|
| The LORD's blessing | A. Brings wealth |
| The LORD's favor | B. Is a prudent wife |
| The LORD's gift | C. Is on one who finds a wife |
| The LORD's reward | D. Is on those kind to the poor |

The Lord gives wisdom, skill, protection, and opportunities that bring *wealth*. A good marriage is the Lord's blessing. Being *kind to the poor* should be in our plans if we want the Lord to *reward* us.

**24.** ♥ What's one attitude you'd like to swap for a better one? What can you do to work on that attitude this week?

This lesson compared attitudes that weaken us when we face adversity with attitudes that strengthen us. Next we'll discover more about how to meet adversity in ways that please the Lord and strengthen us.

## Day 4

## Victory Rests with the Lord

When hardships hit, how do we decide what to do? Proverbs offers lots of advice on plan making. In chapter 5, we read that the righteous plan to do good. In this chapter we'll look at how to plan to meet adversity in ways that please God.

### Take Proper Refuge

Proverbs 10:29 tells us our refuge.

**25.** Underline the first five words in the verse below. In 29a, circle what the five words are (one word) and box whom they're for. In 29b, wavy-circle what the first five words are (one word) and box the person described.

> 10:29 The way of the LORD is a refuge for the blameless,
> but it is the ruin of those who do evil.

The *way of the* LORD keeps us from the natural consequences of wrongdoing. But it also protects us from those who reject his way.

For example, a new boss once told me to lie to a competitor to get information. I said I wasn't comfortable lying but would try to get the information another way. I prayed for God's help and was able to get what my boss wanted. Yet that night he told his wife he planned to fire me for not doing what he'd asked.

That's when God intervened. His wife asked him why he would fire someone he now knew for certain was honest. He realized she was right and relented. I had kept to the *way of the Lord*, and the Lord was my *refuge*.

When this boss told me the story a year later, seeing how God had protected me strengthened my faith, helping me greet future adversity with strong confidence.

### Weigh Your Motives

When making plans, we must examine what drives us. The Proverbs verses below tell us why.

> **26.** If you think your plans are right, underline what you should remember the Lord does.
>
> 17:3 The crucible for silver and the furnace for gold,
> but the LORD tests the heart.
> 21:2 A person may think their own ways are right,
> but the LORD weighs the heart.

The LORD *tests the heart* to refine us. Since he knows what my motives are better than I do, I ask the Holy Spirit to reveal to me any sin of which I'm unaware. For instance, am I trying to get revenge or acting out of envy? If I discover a sinful motive, I can repent and reexamine my plans.

When talking about going forth with a good idea, computer pioneer Admiral Grace Hopper said, "It's easier to ask forgiveness than it is to get permission."[15] But some take this idea to mean we can do *whatever* we want and ask for forgiveness later. After all, first seeking permission may not get us what we want. Indeed, some who identify as Christians have a similar attitude toward sin: Just sin and ask for forgiveness later. But God dislikes that cavalier attitude.

> **27.** In the proverb below, underline what's more acceptable to the Lord than sacrifice (that is, than seeking forgiveness after doing wrong).
>
> 21:3 To do what is right and just
> is more acceptable to the LORD than sacrifice.

A *sacrifice* was how the Israelites sought God's purifying, forgiveness, favor, and fellowship. But sacrifices untethered to a heart wanting *to do what is right* were worthless. Indeed, in 1 Samuel 15:22-23, the prophet Samuel said something similar to Israel's first king, Saul, after Saul disobeyed God's commands twice, claiming he did so to offer sacrifices:

> Does the LORD delight in burnt offerings and sacrifices
> as much as in obeying the LORD?
> To obey is better than sacrifice,
> and to heed is better than the fat of rams.

For rebellion is like the sin of divination,
    and arrogance like the evil of idolatry.
Because you have rejected the word of the Lord,
    he has rejected you as king.

## Seek God's Guidance

God guides us in many ways. Numerous times I've talked to someone who needed encouragement and discovered that just that morning I'd read the Bible passage they needed. That's God's anticipatory guidance, planting in us what we'll need later.

More often, God guides us after we ask him for aid. For example, often I've asked God to help me understand something or help me through some problem, and the next time I opened the Bible, there was the answer. Or a pastor's sermon was just what I needed to hear. These incidents strengthen my faith that God is acting.

In all these examples, God puts before our eyes and ears what we need to know.

> 28. Why do we need God's guidance for our plans (Proverbs 20:12; 22:12)?

In Proverbs 20:12, *hear* includes heed, and *see* includes perceive and understand. In Proverbs 22:12, the Lord keeps *watch over knowledge*, bringing out truth and exposing falsehoods. Jesus offers this assurance to those facing persecution for their testimony: "Do not be afraid of them, for there is nothing concealed that will not be disclosed, or hidden that will not be made known" (Matthew 10:26).

## Commit Your Plans to the Lord

While Clay was working on his undergraduate degree, we discussed and prayed over whether we should marry. He wanted to know God's will. One morning he prayed, *God, please give me a sign as to whether I should marry Jean.* With eyes closed, he opened his Bible, pointed at a page, and read these words: "His mother Mary was pledged to be married to Joseph" (Matthew 1:18). That gave him confidence that we should marry, and we became engaged on my next birthday.

Sometimes God uses what might seem like chance to guide us and strengthen our faith.

(Although this really did happen, I'm not recommending this decision-making method as a substitute for reading your Bible, prayerfully seeking wisdom, or getting advice from wise friends when you need to make an important decision. Occasionally, though, God does help in this way.)

> 29. Read the Proverbs 16 and 19 verses cited below. Then to the far left of what people do, write the letter of what the Lord does that contrasts with it. Each human action contrasts with one action of the Lord.

| | Verse | What People Do in the Verse | What the Lord Does in Contrast |
|---|---|---|---|
| | 16:1 | Have plans of the heart | A. Establishes their plans |
| | 16:2 | View their ways as pure | B. Establishes their steps |
| | 16:3 | Commit actions to the Lord | C. Gives decisions to lots |
| | 16:4 | Become wicked | D. Gives proper answers |

Chart continues on the next page.

## The Little Details
### *Lots, Urim, and Thummim*

The Bible doesn't describe what the Urim and Thummim looked like. It does describe their purpose: "Also put the Urim and the Thummim in the breastpiece, so they may be over Aaron's heart whenever he enters the presence of the Lord. Thus Aaron will always bear the means of making decisions for the Israelites over his heart before the Lord" (Exodus 28:30). Thus, the high priest used them to learn the Lord's decisions, apparently like lots: "Then Saul prayed to the Lord, the God of Israel, 'Why have you not answered your servant today? If the fault is in me or my son Jonathan, respond with Urim, but if the men of Israel are at fault, respond with Thummim.' Jonathan and Saul were taken by lot, and the men were cleared" (1 Samuel 14:41).

Some scholars equate the Urim and Thummim with the breastplate's stones, while the Jewish historian Philo before the time of Christ "seems to have in mind two small symbols representing Light and Truth embroidered on" a cloth pouch perhaps hung from the high priest's neck.[16]

## The Little Details
### Omnipotence and Omniscience

Two of God's attributes are omnipotence and omniscience. Theologian Millard J. Erickson writes that *omnipotence* means "that God is able to do all things which are proper objects of his power." But "he cannot do the logically absurd or contradictory. He cannot make square circles." Neither can he create a rock so heavy he cannot pick it up. His "inability to do evil or to lie or to fail is a mark of positive strength rather than of failure."[18]

Erickson also writes that *omniscience* means that God's "understanding is immeasurable (Ps. 147:5)…He sees and knows us totally. And he knows all genuine possibilities, even when they seem limitless in number." Additionally, "God has access to all information. So his judgments are made wisely."[19]

Sometimes people wonder why an all-powerful, all-good God allows evil in this world. You can probably guess the short answer: He values free will and wants people to freely choose to love him. For an in-depth treatment of this subject, see the book *Why Does God Allow Evil?* by Clay Jones.

| | | |
|---|---|---|
| 16:9 | Plan their course | E. Makes his purpose prevail |
| 16:33 | Throw lots | F. Weighs motives |
| 19:21 | Make many plans | G. Works all to its proper end |

The Lord helps us give *the proper answer* he knows people need. Our *motives* show whether our *ways* are *pure*. "The verb 'commit' is literally 'roll'…as in rolling one's burdens onto the Lord."[17] *Everything* will receive its *proper end*, whether reward or *disaster*. High priests and others used a *lot* to find God's selections, though this practice seems to have stopped after the coming of the Holy Spirit. We can take comfort from knowing that whatever we plan, *the Lord's purpose prevails*.

### Embrace Humility

Even as a child, I loved making plans. But it took until well into adulthood for me to learn two important lessons: (1) plan for tasks to take much longer than expected, and (2) plan for interruptions. That last one was particularly hard. I've never been able to multitask, and interruptions confuse me. I had to learn that sometimes God sends interruptions, so I need to leave room for them.

In other words, I needed more humility about my plans.

> **30.** Why should we be humble about our plans (Proverbs 15:25; 20:24; 27:1)?

The wicked might try to move *boundary stones* to steal a defenseless widow's land, but the Lord intervenes to vindicate her even as he moves against *the proud*. For a modern equivalent, I twice had clients try to change terms *after* I finished the work, but the Lord saw that I was paid.

We are responsible for our plans and decisions, but God is ultimately in charge in ways we can't fully *understand*. For example, Clay and I planned to have children, but we couldn't, so we took in foster children instead. To *boast about tomorrow* is acting as if we're in charge instead of God. James 4:13-16 expands on this:

> Now listen, you who say, "Today or tomorrow we will go to this or that city, spend a year there, carry on business and make money." Why, you do not even know what will happen tomorrow. What is your life? You are a mist that appears for a little while and then vanishes. Instead, you ought to say, "If it is the Lord's will, we will live and do this or that." As it is, you boast in your arrogant schemes. All such boasting is evil.

The year 2020 proved this when a pandemic struck and everyone's plans changed. Pam, Karla, and I all had our many trips canceled. When we're humble about plans, God strengthens us when he shows us his better plans.

### Remember God's Sovereignty

Proverbs 16:7 assures us of God's power and knowledge.

> **31.** Underline what the Lord does when he's pleased with you.
>
> 16:7   When the Lord takes pleasure in anyone's way,
>       he causes their enemies to make peace with them.

God can smooth affairs for us even with our *enemies* when our *way* pleases him, as he did with my former boss who wanted me to lie. Still, we need to remember this is a general truism. Jesus perfectly pleased the Father, but his enemies crucified him. Those who repented, though, found *peace* through and with Jesus.

> **32.** In this next verse from Proverbs, underline the comfort you can find when you go before a leader.
>
> 21:1   In the LORD's hand the king's heart is a stream of water
>            that he channels toward all who please him.

When politics are crazy, we can have peace knowing that God has reasons for allowing rulers to go against his stated will, such as proving the folly of rejecting his ways.

> **33.** Read Proverbs 21:30-31 (ESV) below. Wavy-underline the three things that cannot succeed against the Lord (30a). Underline what a person does before a battle (31a). Circle "victory." Box the name of the One to whom victory belongs (31b).
>
> 21:30   No wisdom, no understanding, no counsel
>             can avail against the LORD.
> 31      The horse is made ready for the day of battle,
>             but the victory belongs to the LORD.

God is sovereign. His plans will prevail. He's told us what the end will look like, with evil defeated and banished. He is making all things new, and those whose names are written in the Lamb's book of life will live with him eternally.

> **34.** ♥ What security do you have knowing that the Lord is in charge?

In this lesson, we found how to meet adversity in ways that please God and strengthen faith. Next, we'll see the kind of self-reflection that strengthens us in adversity.

## *Day 5*

## Self-Reflection That Strengthens

Delusions are strange things in that they offer a way to feel better about ourselves even though we aren't aware of them. For instance, as the lead in a restaurant, I thought I was behaving fairly until another employee pointed out I wasn't. I'd acted in a way that helped me at her expense. She was kind and respectful, and I quickly resolved the issue. This wasn't the only time I thought I was completely in the right until someone's exhortation followed by prayerful reflection showed me I wasn't.

Sometimes self-deceptions last a long time. For years I held on to delusions about my abusive mother's motivations. I told myself she didn't know her words and actions were wrong. That not only lessened the hurt but helped me forgive her. I'd pray, *God, I forgive her because she doesn't know what she's doing is wrong.*

**The Little Details**
***Ojo Okoye on Respectful Disagreements:***
With this surge in social justice discourse there has been a steady increase in cynicism, aggression, and in some cases downright hatred toward people who are guilty of thinking about things in the "wrong way." Worse still is the unfortunate trend in people of my age group starting to see discussions and debates of social justice as an us-versus-them, zero-sum, winner-take-all battle. Instead of diverse perspectives being welcome at the table, daring to think outside the ideological confines runs you the risk of being "canceled," meaning declared null and void or having your career prospects erased. Disagreement is no longer taken as something that can be done respectfully and is seen instead as a rejection or attack on someone's personhood. The scary thing is that this is not happening just in the secular world but also within much of the church.[20]

## The Little Details

### *Proverbs 19:3 in Different Translations*

**ESV:** When a man's folly brings his way to ruin, his heart rages against the LORD.

**GNT:** Some people ruin themselves by their own stupid actions and then blame the LORD.

**KJV:** The foolishness of man perverteth his way: and his heart fretteth against the LORD.

**NASB:** The foolishness of man subverts his way, and his heart rages against the LORD.

**NIV:** A person's own folly leads to their ruin, yet their heart rages against the LORD.

**NKJV:** The foolishness of a man twists his way, and his heart frets against the LORD.

**NRSVUE:** One's own folly leads to ruin, yet the heart rages against the LORD.

It's easier to forgive offenses if we blame them on ignorance or weakness and thereby categorize them as unintentional. That's why bromides such as "Hurt people hurt people" are so popular. The Bible, however, plainly teaches that much sin is intentional, and we must forgive even that sin.

The problem with delusions is that truth keeps poking its way in. After years of telling myself my mother didn't know what she was doing was wrong, in my twenties I discovered she knew perfectly well. Sudden rage engulfed me. Now I had to do the much harder job of forgiving intentional sin.

Initially, I thought she'd fooled me into thinking her ignorant. But as I prayed and sought God's help to forgive, I remembered an incident weeks after my siblings and I made it safely home from my mother's first terrifying drunk drive with us. I was in the front seat next to her as she drove to the foothills to pick up one of my sister's friends. A security guard wrote down her car's license plate number, her name, and her driver's license number. Then he rebuked her for all the times he'd seen her speeding up the mountain with her kids in the back seat. He yelled, "How dare you put children in danger like that?" He warned her if she ever did it again, he would call the police and give them her details.

My mother hung her head in shame.

Deep inside, I did know she knew better. I deluded myself because it was easier than admitting my mother really hated me like she said she did. When I came to Christ and sought to forgive her, I clung to that lie because it helped me manage my emotions and believe I'd actually forgiven her. Not only that, but the delusion let me believe my siblings and I were better people than the mother I thought ignorant.

### Identify Delusions

My mother often told me I'd ruined her life, so she was paying me back by ruining mine. I believed her when I was five. But she was deluding herself and me.

35. Using the verses from Proverbs cited below, in the far left column write the letter of the delusion that goes with the people type. Each people type matches one or more delusions.

| | Verse | People | Delusion |
|---|---|---|---|
| | 19:3 | The Foolish | A. Blame God for what's their fault |
| | 28:11 | The Rich | B. Think they're better than others |
| | 30:11-14 | The Arrogant | C. Think they're pure |
| | | | D. Think they're wise |

Proverbs 19:3 so influenced me that I've put it in multiple translations in a sidebar. I thought about this verse when a man told me that when he was first learning his job and kept failing, he was sure God was causing the failures to mock him. Only later did he discover he wasn't processing the material correctly. I thought of it again when a single woman who'd slept with her boyfriend asked, "How could God let me get pregnant?" And I've thought about it every time I've humiliated myself and started to ask God, *How could you let this happen?* (It has always turned out to be for good reasons, such as my needing more humility.) Blaming God for our blunders may feel better initially, but it doesn't help us become better.

People who *are pure in their own eyes* attack in others the *filth* that is *not cleansed* in their own hearts. Thus, manipulators accuse people of trying to manipulate them, those who seek to control people accuse them of being controlling, and liars denounce others' dishonesty. In conflict, the egotistic hotly blame everyone but themselves.

*Those whose eyes are ever so haughty* and *whose teeth are swords* are all around us—sometimes they even are us. Those *wise in their own eyes* deem disagreement disrespectful and habitually put others in their place. Their feelings are easily hurt, but instead of looking inward to see if their wounded pride needs correcting, they accuse people of wrongs and slander to get even. Convinced they're owed more than they have, they *devour the poor...and the needy*—anyone holding less power than they.

> **36.** In the ESV proverb below, wavy-underline what the person who isolates himself seeks and breaks out against.
>
> 18:1    Whoever isolates himself seeks his own desire;
>           he breaks out against all sound judgment.

Those who think themselves pure distance themselves from any who disagree. The antisocial are quick-tempered and cut off relationships, believing the problem is always with others. But that's delusional, and they eventually run out of relatives and friends to reject.

## Seek Freedom from Delusions

The delusional are weak because truth relentlessly spotlights the lies they tell themselves. That's why they react so angrily when truth threatens their beliefs.

Freedom from delusions requires two actions. The first is honest, prayerful self-reflection. Psalm 139:23-24 offers a helpful prayer:

> Search me, God, and know my heart;
>     test me and know my anxious thoughts.
> See if there is any offensive way in me,
>     and lead me in the way everlasting.

Jesus explained the second requirement for escaping delusions: "If you hold to my teaching, you are really my disciples. Then you will know the truth, and the truth will set you free" (John 8:31-32). As we hold to his teaching, reflecting on how to apply it to our lives and then acting on it, truth replaces delusions and frees us from their chains. When we repent over our angry outbursts and apologize for them, humility replaces pride, and we grow stronger.

Nonetheless, we will face adversity from those clinging to deceptions. How do we respond, then, when we've been wronged?

## Responding When We're Wronged

When video of the George Floyd murder in 2020 went viral, people demanded justice. Our spirits naturally yearn for it.

> **37.** Compare what we should and shouldn't do when we've been wronged (Proverbs 19:11; 20:22; 25:21-22).
>
> | Should Do | Should Not Do |
> | --- | --- |
> |  |  |

### The Little Details
### *Thaddeus J. Williams on Self-Justifications:*

Biblically, there is such a thing as being damned by belonging to a people group—namely, the group called *people*. This damnation has nothing to do with our gender, our income, our national origin, or the melanin in our skin cells. It has to do, on the deepest level, with being a human being. According to Paul, every person on planet earth—rich or poor, male or female, black or white, religious or secular, right or left—stands united in this scandalous group identity. "All have sinned and fall short of the glory of God," say the Scriptures. We are, each and all of us, born under the curse of Genesis 3. Adam's sin has affected all of us from our days in diapers. None of us had to be taught how to be selfish, how to bend the truth in our favor, how to worship things that are not God, how to be ungrateful for what we have and jealous of what others have, how to push others down in an attempt to bump ourselves up, or how to make up absurd self-justifications when we know deep down we're wrong. All of that comes quite naturally to us, all of us in the dysfunctional human family.[21]

## The Little Details
### *Forgiving When Forgiving Is Hard*

You can find links to my five-part series on forgiving on DiscoveringTheBibleSeries.com:

1. "What Forgiving Isn't: 5 Stand-ins That Masquerade as Forgiving"

2. "Must I Forgive THIS Sin?"

3. "What Makes Confessing and Forgiving Inseparable"

4. "Four Sins That Require Faith to Forgive"

5. "The Ultimate Reason Behind Unforgiveness"

You'll also find links to these posts:

- "I Don't Feel Forgiven"
- "Six Offenses to Overlook"
- "Joseph: Triumph over Betrayal"

*To overlook an offense* means "to forgive."[22] When adversity comes in the form of a person wronging us, we crave justice. That desire for justice sometimes tempts us to take matters into our own hands and *pay* wrongdoers *back.* That always ends badly because only God can execute justice perfectly. If one who hates us is in need, we are to care for their necessities such as *food* and *water.* *Burning coals* "represents pangs of conscience, more readily affected by kindness than by violence."[23] Romans 12:20-21 quotes Proverbs 25:21-22 and concludes, "Do not be overcome by evil, but overcome evil with good" (Romans 12:21 ESV).

**38.** ♥ What positive thing could you do for someone who opposes you?

As a teen, I prayed for the Holy Spirit to draw my mom to know God. I shared the gospel with her. And I prayed for God to protect my siblings and me until we were old enough to move out of the house. Still, when I first faced the truth that my mother had intentionally wronged us, I struggled to forgive her. My heart cried out for justice.

**39.** In this next proverb, box the persons. Circle what we get from the Person in 26b.

> 29:26 Many seek an audience with a ruler,
> but it is from the LORD that one gets justice.

We may not receive deserved apologies. We may not get *justice* from courts and leaders. But we can be assured that justice will come. Psalm 37:7 says something similar: "Be still before the LORD and wait patiently for him; do not fret when people succeed in their ways, when they carry out their wicked schemes."

What finally calmed my heart was the realization that justice would be done. Either my mom would continue in rebellion and pay for her sins at the final judgment, or she would turn to Jesus in repentance, and he would pay for them on her behalf.

Take this assurance deep into your heart: Justice will be done.

In this lesson, we identified ways we delude ourselves and discovered how to strengthen ourselves through godly, prayerful self-reflection and holding to Jesus's teaching. We also discovered wise ways to respond when someone wrongs us.

### Wisdom's Worth

**40.** ♥ In what way did you apply wisdom from Proverbs to your life this week?

This chapter showed that the righteous find safety in the name of the Lord. Proverbs motivated us to fear the Lord with a healthy reverence and respect for his power and authority. We saw what the Lord delights in and detests. We compared weakening and strengthening attitudes. We saw how to meet adversity in ways that please God and strengthen faith. We learned how to strengthen ourselves through godly self-reflection and wise ways to respond to wrongs. Next we'll discover how to handle money wisely.

*Wisdom Worship*

Find a quiet place and prepare your heart for grateful worship.

 Turn to Psalm 119:97-112 in your Bible and pray the passage aloud.

## Karla's Creative Connection

*The name of the LORD is a fortified tower; the righteous run to it and are safe.*

Proverbs 18:10

This week's key verse takes me back in time and puts a song on my lips! I met Jesus during the era of Scripture-based praise choruses, and the song featuring Proverbs 18:10 was one of my favorites. Whatever trial I was facing or battle I was fighting, as I sang this simple song I could see myself running into a castle-like tower—the strong, fortified, impenetrable presence of the Almighty God—and knew I would be safe and okay there.

If you think about it, when you hear someone you know referred to by name, you immediately picture them because their name reflects all you know about them: what they look like and how they dress, whether they're kind and generous or mean-spirited and greedy, whether they're honest or untrustworthy. At the mention of their name, all they are to your knowledge of them comes to mind.

In the same way, the name of the Lord—or the name of Yahweh—refers to the entirety of who God is. Just the mention of his name brings to our hearts the assurance of his prevailing power and might, his love and faithfulness, and his worthiness and wisdom. Hearing his name stirs up our faith and reminds us of who God is and who he is to us.

Proverbs 18:10 describes God in a visual way, and I'm sure that if you're like me, you envision a tall tower with thick stone walls designed to protect the people of the kingdom from all harm. You may also see a few openings where the sentries could keep vigil and a watchful eye for any approaching enemies. This is the place of safety and security God is calling you to. This place in his presence is more safe and secure than any earthly tower could ever be.

The Bible clearly says you have an enemy who comes to steal your joy, destroy your faith, and kill your testimony of God's goodness and glory. He uses everything going on in the world and your own personal life to lure you into a life of darkness, despair, and depression. He seeks to fill your heart with fear and anxiety over what you cannot control. But in his great wisdom, in this verse God is calling to you to run—not walk, but run—into his presence and find the peace and sense of security your heart longs for.

So for this week, I encourage you to think about what battles you're fighting or what's causing you to be afraid and anxious. Then creatively connect with God by imagining yourself running into the fortified, impenetrable tower of his power and presence. No one can touch you there. You are safe and secure. Sense his peace wash over you as you worship his holy name: the name above all names.

Now breathe.

*Karla*

## Chapter 7

# Proverbs 19:1–22:16
## Money Matters

How can we be wise financially?

THE PLANS OF THE DILIGENT LEAD to PROFIT AS · SURELY · AS HASTE LEADS to POVERTY.

MY PLANS

PROVERBS 21:5

## Day 1 _____

### Starting Out

I didn't get an allowance in high school, so at 16 I got my first job. I served sodas and hot dogs in the snack bar at the giant swap meet that sprouted in a drive-in theater's parking lot most weekends. On breaks, I walked the aisles where sellers displayed macramé plant hangers, handmade jewelry, and music record collections.

I deposited my paychecks in my first checking account and carefully followed my bank's instructions on how to balance it each month. I was thrilled to be doing grown-up things. I told my mom not to worry about buying clothes for me, because now I could buy my own. (Finally, I could choose clothes for myself!)

I also saved enough for a down payment on a used, sky-blue Toyota Corona so my mom wouldn't have to drive me to work. My dad cosigned a loan for me, and I was on my way to building a credit score I didn't yet know would be valuable.

Today's chapter is all about money. Proverbs teaches us how to set financial priorities, make money, and manage our finances. In this lesson we'll look at foundational principles that young adults should know when they're just starting out on their own.

1.  ♥  What was your first job?

### God's Word to Us in Proverbs

Today's reading of three and a half chapters in Proverbs addresses many of the topics we'll cover in this book's chapter, including wealth and diligence. Some verses address shepherds, so look at the principle behind the verse that relates to your financial situation. Collection II ends at Proverbs 22:16, which is where we'll stop our reading today.

🗯 Take a moment to pray for insight as you read God's Word.

## The Little Details
### *For Budding Poets*

This lesson's sample poem is based on Hebrew poetry. Hebrew poetry uses poetic lines that usually have two line segments. A few have only one, and some have three or four. In many Bible translations, all but the first segments are indented.

Poetic lines in Hebrew poetry are either linear or parallel. In linear lines, the second segment completes the thought begun in the first segment.

***Linear*** (verse 2):

A B / C D

Many poetic lines place similar or contrasting thoughts parallel to each other within the segments. We can symbolize parallelism by using letters to represent units in a poetic line and a ***prime mark*** (') to show how many times a unit has been repeated.

***Normal parallelism*** (verse 1):

A B C / A' B' C'

***Incomplete parallelism*** (verse 4):

A B C / B' C'

***Chiastic parallelism*** (verse 5):

A B / B' A'

To learn more about Hebrew poetry, see our book *Discovering Hope in the Psalms*.

2. ♥ Read Proverbs 19:1–22:16 (note that we're reading only half of chapter 22). (a) What stood out to you in your reading? Why? (b) How can you apply that insight to your life this week?

## Preparing to Leave Home

After high school, I started college full-time. But my home situation again turned dangerous. So I postponed college and got a full-time job as a hostess at an all-you-can-eat buffet that served food like fried chicken, gelatin salads, and pies so I could save money to move out of the house.

Soon the manager promoted me to lead hostess. I set schedules, opened the restaurant each morning, balanced the cash register, and made sure everything was clean. He told me he promoted me because I never stood around talking, and I meticulously cleaned tables, booths, and condiment bottles. He asked me to teach the others to do the same.

### *Making Mistakes*

Unfortunately, I didn't yet have the experience to lead well. Since I didn't see the night workers except during shift changes, I left them notes when things weren't right. They were messy. But I didn't realize I was irritating them, so I didn't understand why they were leaving things even messier as the days went on. Thankfully, my supervisor—a kind, Christian woman who wore her silvery-white hair in a bun atop her head—sat me down and explained how it's more important to compliment good work than to criticize bad work.

That was news to me. My dad had told us he seldom complimented anyone because only perfection deserves compliments. I had unwittingly accepted this as true.

3. Is merely telling workers what needs to be done sufficient (Proverbs 29:19)?

☐ Yes  ☐ No

We can motivate workers in many ways, including through praise and rewards.

Knowing what Proverbs teaches about humility and admitting errors, I called a staff meeting and apologized to everyone. I asked their forgiveness and said I would change. I didn't ask them to change anything. But the next morning, I was shocked to see the restaurant was cleaner than it had ever been.

Learning to lead with encouragement wasn't the only lesson I learned.

4. In the NKJV proverb below, wavy-circle what's not fitting for fools and servants.

> 19:10 Luxury is not fitting for a fool,
> Much less for a servant to rule over princes.

Someone who lacks leadership training and experience shouldn't *rule* over experienced governmental officials. Hubbard writes that this is advice not to "strive for power beyond your reach, but work and wait until those who merited it are willing to share it."[1] In my case, both my supervisor and manager helped me grow into the position.

## Making Changes

On top of my salary at the restaurant, I was making good tips, so Clay and I got formally engaged. Then a friend of a relative called to say she had a job opening at a secretarial service she'd taken over from her prior boss. Two people at her church had suggested she hire me. I was ecstatic and took the job.

But just months before our scheduled wedding, the business abruptly and unexpectedly shut down. I scrambled to find another job that would pay enough to cover the basics so we wouldn't have to postpone the wedding. By doing that, we were following the advice of the next proverb we'll read.

> **5.** Underline the two things to do before setting up a home.
>
> 24:27  Put your outdoor work in order and get your fields ready;
>           after that, build your house.

The *outdoor work* and *fields* are the farmer's income streams. *House* can mean a dwelling or family. So the proverb means we should have a source of income in place before starting a family or making large purchases on things not needed to make money.

I carefully budgeted what I thought we'd need so I'd know what salary I had to make. I sought the services of that employment agency I mentioned in chapter 3. The receptionist position they found me at a photography studio paid the salary I needed if I worked 45 hours per week. The owner even offered to give me a paid week off for my wedding and honeymoon if I agreed to make up the extra time by working another three to five hours per week. I gladly accepted.

## Making Progress

Working that many hours was much harder than I expected. Plus, the receptionist job was mostly making cold-call sales. The owner listened through speakers to everything I said and criticized every mistake. (Thus, I learned what it was like working for someone who motivated mainly through criticism!) Initially, I hated the job, but I stuck with it because I needed the money.

It was right where the Lord wanted me. He was training me, but he also had spiritual work for me to do. I shared the gospel with my coworkers, and two of them came to know Jesus as their Savior.

In this lesson we discovered foundational principles that young adults (and older ones too) should know when they're just starting out on their own. In the next lesson we'll look at how to prioritize money.

**The Little Details**
*Jesus on Knowing Costs in Luke 14:28-30:*

Suppose one of you wants to build a tower. Won't you first sit down and estimate the cost to see if you have enough money to complete it? For if you lay the foundation and are not able to finish it, everyone who sees it will ridicule you, saying, "This person began to build and wasn't able to finish."

# Pam's Simply Beautiful Wisdom

*A generous person will prosper; whoever refreshes others will be refreshed.*

Proverbs 11:25

In Proverbs 11:25 is a principle of generosity leading to an anointed life: The key that unlocks your refreshment is to refresh or saturate others with encouragement, acceptance, and love. One avenue of application is to consider the following money motivation styles, especially when considering marriage. Deep-seated differences can arise when couples spend and save money according to their individual personalities and inner drives.

***Inner Drive #1: Authority.*** For those who are motivated by having authority, money is power. It represents options and opportunity. They spend money on whatever goals they consider worthwhile. They invent a plan and take calculated risks to see it become reality.

They are highly productive, visionary, focused, and fearless. These hard-working, hard-driving people have the capacity to handle large budgets and large challenges. With spiritual depth and maturity, they can accomplish much for a family, a marriage, a community, or a church. The danger for those motivated by authority is the temptation to become power hungry workaholics. The pursuit can become so important that people slip down their priority list.

One compromise might be to set aside a certain amount each month to save toward the big dreamer's long-term goal while a stable amount is used for regular family needs. In this way, the visionary makes headway on the dream, but the family's bread and butter is not at risk.

***Inner Drive #2: Attention.*** Money is all about people. This person spends money to make memories. The heartfelt question they ask over and over is *Will this person* [spouse, child, family member, or friend] *feel happy and loved if I spend money on them* [or give them money]*?*" They're very generous; they'll give you the shirt off their own back. But their shortcoming is that they like to appear as though they have a lot of money—whether or not they do! They love to pick up the tab, throw the lavish party, take others on shopping sprees, or provide a day of recreation.

Your family finances work out easier if this person is given the freedom to work very hard to earn extra money that is then set aside as discretionary funds to enhance relationships. If, however, you handcuff this person too much and take away the ability to "bless" the people they love most, they can become hard to live with. For the spouse married to the generous heart, create a line-item fund they can spend.

***Inner Drive #3: Acceptance.*** This person purchases peace. The goal is to create a simple process toward money and resources. When the money is there, they're cooperative. If finances are tight, they get stubborn, because they feel like a crisis that will disrupt the peace in their lives is being created. At this point, they'll either work harder, argue, or dig their heels in to find a path out of the crisis.

If the family is spending less than they're making, this person relaxes. If, however, more is being spent than they earn, they'll grow to resent the family's spending habits. They may feel more like a paycheck than a person. They are peacemakers and natural mediators, so they're good at solving financial issues to enrich relationships and pay the bills.

You'll find your marriage is better when you commit to a savings account, because it helps this motivational style relax.

***Inner Drive #4: Accuracy.*** This person is all about a system, and they're emotionally attached to the process. When a budget is set, they take it literally. So if the budget says $50 for groceries, he or she means $50—not $55 and not $60. The budget is a mandate they live by. Because they love managing money and resources, however, they often have money and resources to manage! They are savers, planners, and investors. They spend money according to a cautious, practical, and wise long-range plan. But because they can be inflexible and rigid about the plan, they can miss great financial opportunities.

This person will make sure you're never without funding for your life, but cooperating with the budgeting plan might be a challenge for your own personality. The key is to discuss any foreseen changes or adaptations that might need to occur ahead of time. This person values consistent encouragement and appreciation. The upside: It's highly unlikely you will ever be in a financial bind, because they are savvy financially.

***Motivations in Marriage.*** By discussing and then budgeting in a way that includes your motivation, there will be fewer arguments. For example, I (Pam) am motivation style #2, and for me, making memories with family and friends is what makes life worth living and working so hard for. We created a line item in our budget to give me freedom to make a few memories. Bill is motivation style #3, so I've agreed to ways of money management that make his life a little easier when it comes to monthly bill paying.

No money motivation style is right or wrong as long as you keep in mind biblical mandates of respect, honor, love, and desire to create a spirit of unity by valuing the way God wired your mate.[2]

*Pam*

## Experiencing Scripture Creatively (Optional)

If you have extra time, consider these suggestions for creatively engaging with verses from this week's reading. The appendix has even more ideas.

- Follow Karla's instructions at the end of this chapter for designing a spiritual life budget.

- Color Karla's full-page illustration at the end of the chapter while repeating the words of the verse there aloud.

- Color the sidebar toppers using distinct color schemes. Choose your favorite to use on the bookmark on this chapter's opening page.

- Create a poem from one or more proverbs. See examples in other chapters' Day 1 lesson.

- Form your answer to question 38 into proverbs based loosely on Proverbs 27:23-27. Here's an example:

*The words of Jean.*
1    To know the condition of your finances
           and to track the status of your investments,
2    invest in financial software
           that downloads bank transactions.
3    It will balance your accounts with ease
           and pay your bills when due.
4    You will know what fits your budget
           and what must wait for now.
5    You can plan ahead for vacations,
           and for emergencies you can prepare.

# Funds, Fun, and Faith

**The Little Details**

***Jesus in Luke 12:16-21 on Funds First:***

The ground of a certain rich man yielded an abundant harvest. He thought to himself, "What shall I do? I have no place to store my crops."

Then he said, "This is what I'll do. I will tear down my barns and build bigger ones, and there I will store my surplus grain. And I'll say to myself, 'You have plenty of grain laid up for many years. Take life easy; eat, drink and be merry.'"

But God said to him, "You fool! This very night your life will be demanded from you. Then who will get what you have prepared for yourself?"

This is how it will be with whoever stores up things for themselves but is not rich toward God.

When Clay and I were engaged, we worked out a budget. We prioritized the basics, of course. But we also hoped for fun nonessentials, like Fig Newton cookies, two-for-one hamburgers, and vacations in Yosemite National Park.

Thankfully, Proverbs explains how to wisely prioritize funds, fun, and faith. Still, it's surprising how subtly priorities can shift even when families begin wisely. So let's look at reasons and ways people put each of these three first.

## Funds First

Wealth offers advantages, so it's no wonder many seek it first.

> 6.   List reasons people value wealth (Proverbs 10:15; 14:20; 18:16).

Genesis 43:11 illustrates Proverbs 18:16: Jacob gave his sons *a gift* for Egypt's *great* governor so they could buy grain during a famine (Genesis 43:11).

### The Pitfalls

With wealth's advantages, it's easy to see why people chase it. But it comes with pitfalls.

> 7.   In the Proverbs ESV verses below, box the persons. Circle what the poor hear (13:8b) and what the faithful receive (28:20a). Wavy-circle what the rich imagine their wealth is (18:11ab) and what those who hurry to be rich receive (28:20b).
>
> 13:8   The ransom of a man's life is his wealth,
>              but a poor man hears no threat.
> 18:11   A rich man's wealth is his strong city,
>              and like a high wall in his imagination.
> 28:20   A faithful man will abound with blessings,
>              but whoever hastens to be rich will not go unpunished.

Those with great *wealth* encounter blackmailers, kidnappers, and lawsuits that *a poor man* never faces. Wealth tempts the *rich* to trust riches over God. But anyone who *hastens to be rich* through unfaithful practices will face punishment. We'll look at some of those unfaithful practices next.

> 8.   In the left column, write the letter of the result that goes with the people types (Proverbs 15:27; 17:8; 21:14). Each people type has one unique match.

|  | People Who | Result |
|---|---|---|
|  | Bribe others | A. Live |
|  | Hate bribes | B. Sooth anger |
|  | Secretly bribe | C. Think bribes are success-bringing charms |

*Bribes* influence people to do what they otherwise wouldn't, and *the greedy* are susceptible to them. *A bribe* is a way to pervert justice and stop others from exposing the briber's wrongdoing.

> **9.** In Proverbs 28:22a (NASB) below, box the description of the person and wavy-underline what he does. In 28:22b, wavy-circle what will come upon that person.
>
> 28:22    A man with an evil eye hastens after wealth,
>          And does not know that want will come upon him.

NIV and ESV translate *an evil eye* "stingy." It's the person who bears ill will toward others out of jealousy, greed, and stinginess. Get-rich-quick schemes and gambling tempt the one in a rush for riches but bring poverty to most.

If putting funds first has so many pitfalls, how does putting fun first fare?

## Fun First

In her book *Faithfully Different*, Natasha Crain summarizes the nature of most secular worldviews: "Feelings are the ultimate guide, happiness is the ultimate goal, judging is the ultimate sin, and God is the ultimate guess."[3] Media promote these views constantly, so it's no wonder that they creep into Christians' thoughts.

When happiness is the greatest good, we prioritize pleasure. Debt secures feasts, Rolexes, and Mercedes. A YOLO (You Only Live Once) attitude takes risks and maximizes today's happiness without giving much thought to tomorrow.

> **10.** What do the following people pretend (Proverbs 13:7)?
>
> Person who has nothing pretends to be: _____
> Person who has great wealth pretends to be: _____

Some pretend *to be poor* as a cover for stinginess. Others pretend *to be rich* to gain status, escape embarrassment, or gain wealth's trappings without waiting for wealth.

### The Pitfalls

Fun first has pitfalls too.

> **11.** What happens to those who prioritize pleasure (Proverbs 21:17; 22:7; 23:19-21)?
>
>
>
>
>

The one who *loves pleasure* becomes *poor* through living beyond means or neglecting work. In Israel, people could work off debt by becoming a servant to the *lender*; today, some people must work well into the traditionally retirement years to pay off debt. *Drunkards and gluttons* prioritize pleasure *too much* and end up *poor*.

## Faith First

Proverbs teaches that some things in life are more valuable than riches and temporary pleasures.

**The Little Details**
*Jesus on Money in Matthew 6:24-27:*

No one can serve two masters. Either you will hate the one and love the other, or you will be devoted to the one and despise the other. You cannot serve both God and money.

Therefore I tell you, do not worry about your life, what you will eat or drink; or about your body, what you will wear. Is not life more than food, and the body more than clothes? Look at the birds of the air; they do not sow or reap or store away in barns, and yet your heavenly Father feeds them. Are you not much more valuable than they? Can any one of you by worrying add a single hour to your life?

## The Little Details

### Jesus on Money in Matthew 6:28-33:

And why do you worry about clothes? See how the flowers of the field grow. They do not labor or spin. Yet I tell you that not even Solomon in all his splendor was dressed like one of these. If that is how God clothes the grass of the field, which is here today and tomorrow is thrown into the fire, will he not much more clothe you—you of little faith? So do not worry, saying, "What shall we eat?" or "What shall we drink?" or "What shall we wear?" For the pagans run after all these things, and your heavenly Father knows that you need them. But seek first his kingdom and his righteousness, and all these things will be given to you as well.

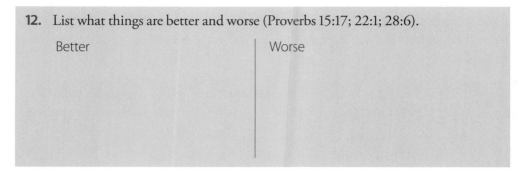

12. List what things are better and worse (Proverbs 15:17; 22:1; 28:6).

| Better | Worse |
|--------|-------|
|        |       |

What is *better* brings better results and more happiness in the end. These proverbs aren't saying there are no *blameless* people who are *rich* or no *poor* people who are *perverse*, but if we must choose, take the better choice.

13. Read Proverbs 11:28. (a) Why shouldn't we put our trust in riches? (b) What character quality should we pursue instead?

Prioritizing faith affects the entire family.

14. What's a penalty for pursuing wealth over righteousness (Proverbs 13:22)?

The blessings God bestows on *a good person* can be passed on to children and grandchildren. But the penalties *a sinner* receives can consume what might have been passed on, particularly if fraud or theft is involved. Children of those who don't know God may not learn how to properly treat finances.

15. Proverbs 30:7-9 contains a prayer penned by a sage named Agur. Wavy-circle what he wants God to keep from him (8ab). Circle what he wants God to give him (8c). Wavy-underline the reasons why (9).

> 30:7 Two things I ask of you, LORD;
>      do not refuse me before I die:
> 8 Keep falsehood and lies far from me;
>      give me neither poverty nor riches,
>      but give me only my daily bread.
> 9 Otherwise, I may have too much and disown you
>      and say, "Who is the LORD?"
> Or I may become poor and steal,
>      and so dishonor the name of my God.

Agur's prayer prioritizes faith in the Lord over prosperity and pleasure.

### The Pitfalls

No surprise: There are no pitfalls! Prioritizing God brings blessings in this life, spiritual growth, and heavenly rewards.

16. ♥ Which proverb about prioritizing funds, fun, and faith stood out to you the most? Explain.

In this lesson, we looked at the reasons and ways people prioritize funds, fun, and faith. In the next lesson, we'll discover how to make money wisely.

## Day 3

## Making Money

I'd always wanted to work from home so I'd have more time to write. Then I unexpectedly got that opportunity when a company I'd been with for only a year downsized, laid me off, and hired me back as an independent contractor three months later. I'd taken another job by then, but I was able to split my time between them.

When I launched out on my own, Clay and I kept the book of Proverbs firmly in mind as we made decisions. In this lesson I'll share some of the ways Proverbs guided us and some of the ways it would have guided us if we'd better understood a proverb's principle.

In this lesson I'll share some of the ways Proverbs guided us and some of the ways it would have guided us if we'd better understood a proverb's principle.

As you go through this lesson—and so you can share later—think about how the proverbs we read helped you or would have helped you if you'd better understood them.

### Invest in Good Tools

One of the first decisions we made was to invest in quality tools. I didn't know yet how much work I'd have as a contractor, but we based our decision on the principle behind Proverbs 14:4's farming advice.

17. Underline what a farmer needed to earn money (14:4b). Circle what that brought.

14:4    Where there are no oxen, the manger is empty,
            but from the strength of an ox come abundant harvests.

In Solomon's day, farmers invested in and cared for *oxen* so they could reap *abundant harvests*. The harvest filled the *manger*. With my new business, I didn't need an ox, but I did need the right tools. That led to the next step.

### Carefully Plan

Rather than rush out to buy whatever the big box stores had on special, I carefully researched what I'd need to work efficiently from home, based on the next proverbs.

18. To the left of each attribute, write the letter of the result that goes with it (Proverbs 19:2; 21:5). Each attribute matches one unique result.

| Attribute | Result |
|---|---|
| Desire without knowledge | A. Is not good |
| Diligent plans | B. Miss the way |
| Haste | C. Lead to profit |
| Hasty feet | D. Leads to poverty |

We might *desire* success, but if we're *hasty* and proceed without the *knowledge* necessary, we'll *miss the way*. The *diligent* make solid *plans* instead of moving in *haste*.

After researching products, we invested in a quality computer, an excellent laser printer, and the best software. I set up an inexpensive oak desk, filing cabinet, and folding table in a spare bedroom. I was ready to go.

### Be Diligent

Proverbs links wealth to diligence and poverty to laziness. This was particularly true in an agrarian society where the whole family pitched in to raise crops and shepherd sheep, but it still applies today.

**19.** To the far left of the people found in the Proverbs verses cited below, write the letter of their actions. To the right of the people, circle "D" if they're diligent or "L" if they're lazy. People match to one unique action.

| Verse | People | D or L | | Their Actions |
|---|---|---|---|---|
| 10:5 | Disgraceful sons | D | L | A. Crave for more |
| | Prudent sons | D | L | B. Don't roast game |
| 12:27 | The diligent | D | L | C. Feed on riches of hunt |
| | The lazy | D | L | D. Gather crops in summer |
| 21:25-26 | The righteous | D | L | E. Give without sparing |
| | Sluggards | D | L | F. Sleep during harvest |

The *disgraceful son* shamed his parents by not caring for and working toward the family's well-being. *The lazy* don't bother to cook the *game* they hunted; in other words, they start but don't finish endeavors.

**20.** Compare what diligence and laziness lead to (10:4; 12:24; 13:4; 20:4).

| Diligence Leads To | Laziness Leads To |
|---|---|
| | |

Kings used *forced labor* for building projects; the modern equivalent could be bottom-rung jobs meant to lead to advancement. The *sluggard's appetite is never filled* because they don't do the work needed to reach their dreams. Because *sluggards* don't work at the proper time, payday brings *nothing*.

Of course, laziness is not the only cause of poverty. The Old Testament lists oppression, famine, and war as causes. But all other things being equal, the diligent will gain far more wealth than the lazy.

## Don't Procrastinate

Sometimes fear and insecurity cause me to put off scarier tasks. What about you? Does fear keep you from moving forward? Do you talk about goals without working on them? Is the way to what you want obstacle-filled? Do you start but not finish many tasks? The next group of proverbs addresses these.

21. Underline actions these proverbs commend and circle their benefits. Wavy-underline what people do instead of work, and wavy-circle the drawbacks.

    12:11 Those who work their land will have abundant food,
    but those who chase fantasies have no sense.

    14:23 All hard work brings a profit,
    but mere talk leads only to poverty.

    19:15 Laziness brings on deep sleep,
    and the shiftless go hungry.

    20:13 Do not love sleep or you will grow poor;
    stay awake and you will have food to spare.

    28:19 Those who work their land will have abundant food,
    but those who chase fantasies will have their fill of poverty.

If Solomon were writing today, he might add, "*Do not love TV, video games, or social media, or you will grow poor. Keep working, and you will have food to spare.*"

22. To the left of people types below, write the letter of the effect hunger has on their actions (Proverbs 16:26; 19:24). Each people type matches to one unique effect. One effect has no match.

| | People | Hunger's Effect on Their Actions |
|---|---|---|
| | Laborers | A. Drives them on |
| | Sluggards | B. No effect |
| | | C. Sends them begging |

People *hunger* for many things. Keeping the goals we hunger for in sight defeats procrastination and helps us finish what we start.

23. In the proverbs below, wavy-underline excuses the sluggard uses to avoid work

    15:19 The way of the sluggard is blocked with thorns,
    but the path of the upright is a highway.

    22:13 The sluggard says, "There's a lion outside!
    I'll be killed in the public square!"

*The sluggard* claims too many obstacles or dangers exist for them to work. The diligent meet obstacles, too, but they persevere with prayer and hard work to overcome them.

24. Read Proverbs 26:13-16 below. Write "Excuse" next to the sluggard's excuse not to work. Write "Lazy" next to descriptions of a sluggard's actions and inactions. Wavy-underline the reason the sluggard stays lazy.

    26:13 A sluggard says, "There's a lion in the road,
    a fierce lion roaming the streets!"

### The Little Details
#### *2 Thessalonians 3:6-12 on Hunger and Work:*

In the name of the Lord Jesus Christ, we command you, brothers and sisters, to keep away from every believer who is idle and disruptive and does not live according to the teaching you received from us. For you yourselves know how you ought to follow our example. We were not idle when we were with you, nor did we eat anyone's food without paying for it. On the contrary, we worked night and day, laboring and toiling so that we would not be a burden to any of you. We did this, not because we do not have the right to such help, but in order to offer ourselves as a model for you to imitate. For even when we were with you, we gave you this rule: "The one who is unwilling to work shall not eat."

We hear that some among you are idle and disruptive. They are not busy; they are busybodies. Such people we command and urge in the Lord Jesus Christ to settle down and earn the food they eat.

## The Little Details

### How God Commanded Israel to Care for the Poor

God commanded farmers not to reap to the edges of the fields but to leave food for the poor to gather (Leviticus 19:9-10; Deuteronomy 24:19-22). The hardworking poor could glean the food they needed.

The Law provided for all to own land. If someone became poor and sold the land, the nearest capable relative should redeem the land. All sold land had to be returned to the original owner in the Year of Jubilee (Leviticus 25:25-28).

God commanded the Israelites to help the poor, give them no-interest loans, and sell them food at cost. If an Israelite became their indentured servant to work off debt, they were to treat the servant like a hired worker, not like a slave (Leviticus 25:39-43).

Additionally, God commanded people to generously lend to the poor (Deuteronomy 15:7-11). If a poor person gave a cloak as security for a loan, the lender had to return it before sunset so the poor could sleep in it (Exodus 22:26-25). They were to pay a poor person's wages daily before sunset, not making them wait (Deuteronomy 24:14-15).

---

> 14  As a door turns on its hinges,
>        so a sluggard turns on his bed.
> 15  A sluggard buries his hand in the dish;
>        he is too lazy to bring it back to his mouth.
> 16  A sluggard is wiser in his own eyes
>        than seven people who answer discreetly.

One of my foster girls asked for help with homework on the computer. When I showed her how to set up her document, she told me it was too hard. I said, "Oh, here. I'll set it up for you." When I finished, she said, "Mom, guess what word we learned today? *Manipulate*." She had me. The assurance that someone will take up one's slack is one of the reasons sluggards think they're *wiser* than others.

## Develop Value

The people at the company that laid me off knew my skill set, but when I wanted to submit proposals to other companies, I needed proof that I could handle the work. So I studied and earned certifications from Microsoft, Adobe, and other companies so potential clients could trust me. Developing value that clients or employers want to reward is what the next proverbs are about.

---

**25.** Underline the assets employers value.

> 14:35  A king delights in a wise servant,
>        but a shameful servant arouses his fury.
> 22:29  Do you see someone skilled in their work?
>        They will serve before kings;
>        they will not serve before officials of low rank.
> 25:13  Like a snow-cooled drink at harvest time
>        is a trustworthy messenger to the one who sends him;
>        he refreshes the spirit of his master.
> 27:18  The one who guards a fig tree will eat its fruit,
>        and whoever protects their master will be honored.

---

Skill, trustworthiness, and guarding someone's possessions and reputation are all traits employers and clients value.

Another way to develop value is to cultivate leadership qualities by volunteering to lead projects. Many proverbs about kings apply to most leadership roles. Let's look at some and see what they tell us about leadership qualities.

---

**26.** Think of your various leadership roles: parent, boss, facilitator, and so on. To the left of each Proverbs passage, write the letter of the leadership quality that goes with it. Each passage has one unique match. Think of how the kings needed each quality, and then think about how you need them in your leadership roles. For those you particularly need, write the role in the column to the right of the passage.

| Proverbs Passages | My Leadership Role | Leadership Quality |
|---|---|---|
| 16:10 | | A. Detests wrongdoing |
| 16:12 | | B. Hates ill-gotten gain |
| 20:26 | | C. Removes wicked officials |

Chart continues on the next page.

| | | |
|---|---|---|
| 25:2-3 | | D. Searches out matters |
| 25:4-5 | | E. Stabilizes leadership by justice |
| 28:16 | | F. Winnows out the wicked |
| 29:4 | | G. Words don't betray justice |

*A king* speaking in his official capacity must speak righteous and just words. *Kings* in Israel had to *detest wrongdoing* because God overthrew the unrighteous. Just as a *threshing wheel* separated the grain from the chaff, so must a *wise king* separate the good from the *wicked*. Assassins often shortened the *reign* of a *tyrannical ruler*. *Justice* and *bribes* do not go together.

I've shared how many of these proverbs helped me, or would have helped me had I better understood them. Now it's your turn.

27. ♥ (a) How have the principles in the proverbs we read today helped you? (b) How might one proverb have helped you more if you'd better understood its principle and applied it? (c) What's your favorite method for beating procrastination?

In this lesson, we discovered wise ways to make money. We learned to invest in good tools, carefully plan, be diligent, avoid procrastination, and develop value. In the next lesson, we'll learn how to manage the money we've worked hard to get.

## Day 4

## Managing Money

As I mentioned earlier, when I bought my first car, my dad cosigned the loan. That made him legally liable if I defaulted. He was guaranteeing the loan's repayment. Since I was a teenager with no credit history, it was the only way I could buy a car to drive to work.

Proverbs has a lot to say about whether we should guarantee others' debt repayment, but it uses phrases unfamiliar to many. For example, the NIV and ESV use the phrase *put up security* to describe it. Merriam-Webster defines *security* as "something given, deposited, or pledged to make certain the fulfillment of an obligation."[4] In Old Testament times, security could be a garment or other possession, while today pawnshops might require borrowers to provide a watch or heirloom as *security* for the high-interest loans they offer. For my car, I provided the down payment, and my dad gave his signature on loan papers as security, guaranteeing repayment.

The RSV and NKJV use the phrase *become surety*. Merriam-Webster defines *surety* as "one who has become legally liable for the debt, default, or failure in duty of another."[5] In my case, my dad became surety for my debt when he cosigned my loan.

### Don't Risk What You Can't Afford to Lose

Cosigning isn't the only way we guarantee payment. When I first started my business, I didn't realize that proverbs about putting up security applied to more than just cosigning. Initially, I didn't offer my clients contracts because I thought they'd think I didn't trust

Proverbs has a lot to say about whether we should guarantee others' debt repayment.

## The Little Details

### 1 Timothy 5:4-8 on Providing for Family:

If a widow has children or grandchildren, these should learn first of all to put their religion into practice by caring for their own family and so repaying their parents and grandparents, for this is pleasing to God. The widow who is really in need and left all alone puts her hope in God and continues night and day to pray and to ask God for help. But the widow who lives for pleasure is dead even while she lives. Give the people these instructions, so that no one may be open to blame. Anyone who does not provide for their relatives, and especially for their own household, has denied the faith and is worse than an unbeliever.

them. My failure to do so was due to my not fully understanding the principle behind the verses we're about to read: Don't risk money on strangers. Without a contract, I was taking a risk that clients might not pay for completed work.

> 28. In the proverbs below, draw a box around those for whom you shouldn't cosign (put up security). Wavy-underline the reasons.
>
> 11:15　Whoever puts up security for a stranger will surely suffer,
> 　　　　but whoever refuses to shake hands in pledge is safe.
> 17:18　One who has no sense shakes hands in pledge
> 　　　　and puts up security for a neighbor.

A *stranger* is a non-relative who isn't known well. A *neighbor* is an acquaintance or friend. When I didn't require a contract from my first clients, Proverbs 17:18 declares I was *one who has no sense*. Proverbs 11:15 advised I would *surely suffer* for it. The first time someone tried to cheat me, I was stressed! Thankfully, the client eventually paid my invoice when the friend who introduced us pressured him.

After that, I bought a book on how to write contracts. It turned out all my clients were pleased to have contracts because it gave them security too.

Helping family, though, is different. We know the person's creditworthiness, and it's natural to help loved ones. Indeed, Job 22:6 describes as wicked the one who takes essentials from family as security: "You demanded security from your relatives for no reason; you stripped people of their clothing, leaving them naked." But that doesn't mean there aren't limitations.

> 29. When shouldn't you put up security for family (Proverbs 22:26-27)?

Parents often cosign for adult children who haven't yet established credit, as my dad did. But they should never do it if they *lack the means to pay*. Sadly, *Consumer Reports* reveals that "some families are putting their own finances at risk to help their kids pay for school" and "parent default rates are rising."[6]

> 30. If someone wants to borrow from you and promises someone else will pay if they can't, what should you do (Proverbs 20:16 or 27:13)?

If someone takes responsibility for another's debt, they're responsible to pay if necessary. So get *security* from them, such as a legally binding loan contract. That's what our real estate agent advised when we sold a relative's house. The purchaser said his money was tied up in investments for a year, so he wanted to make monthly payments to us until his funds were freed and he could pay the balance. Our real estate agent drew up the paperwork using the house as security. He told us to tell him if the buyer missed even one payment so he could begin procedures for taking back the property.

## Build Wealth Wisely

In our early marriage, Clay and I had little money. When we're in that situation, doesn't it seem like a sudden windfall would be the best solution?

**31.** In the ESV Proverbs verses below, wavy-circle what happens to wealth hastily gained. Circle what happens to wealth obtained slowly and steadily.

13:11   Wealth gained hastily will dwindle,
           but whoever gathers little by little will increase it.
20:21   An inheritance gained hastily in the beginning
           will not be blessed in the end.

In both verses, the word translated *hastily* may suggest something unrighteous in how the wealth was obtained.[7] Verse 20:21 suggests both that the immature mishandle money, and that the greedy who demand an early inheritance *will not be blessed* (the prodigal son in Jesus's parable was both immature and greedy—see sidebar).

The idea behind both verses is that wealth gained quickly can be lost quickly. Indeed, *Reader's Digest* reports that 70 percent of lottery winners lose or spend their winnings within five years.[8] But wealth obtained *little by little* through disciplined work and methodical saving *will increase*.

Let's look at a few unwise methods for increasing wealth fast.

**32.** List wrong ways of building and using wealth (Proverbs 20:17; 22:16; 23:4-5).

1                          3

2                          4

*Food gained by fraud* means anything gained dishonestly. One's conscience and fears of being found out torment unless one justifies the fraud. Even if the community doesn't uncover and condemn the fraud, the fraudster will have to face the final judgment. God will punish *one who oppresses the poor*. Giving *gifts to the rich* wastes money. It's foolish to *wear yourself out* for something you can't guarantee will last on earth and certainly can't be taken to eternity.

## Give Generously to the Poor

Jesus said, "Sell your possessions and give to the poor. Provide purses for yourselves that will not wear out, a treasure in heaven that will never fail, where no thief comes near and no moth destroys" (Luke 12:33). That's the perfect segue to what Proverbs teaches about giving.

**33.** To the left of each action below, write the letter of the result that goes with it (Proverbs 11:24-26; 14:31). Each verse has two actions. Each action matches one unique result.

| Action | Result |
|---|---|
| Are kind to the needy | A. Blessed by people |
| Generously give | B. Come to poverty |
| Give freely | C. Cursed by people |
| Hoard grain | D. Gain more |
| Oppress the poor | E. Honor God |
| Refresh others | F. Prosper |
| Sell grain | G. Show contempt for God |
| Withhold unduly | H. Will be refreshed |

### The Little Details
***Jesus in Luke 15:11-20 on Squandering an Inheritance:***

There was a man who had two sons. The younger one said to his father, "Father, give me my share of the estate." So he divided his property between them.

Not long after that, the younger son got together all he had, set off for a distant country and there squandered his wealth in wild living. After he had spent everything, there was a severe famine in that whole country, and he began to be in need. So he went and hired himself out to a citizen of that country, who sent him to his fields to feed pigs. He longed to fill his stomach with the pods that the pigs were eating, but no one gave him anything.

When he came to his senses, he said, "How many of my father's hired servants have food to spare, and here I am starving to death! I will set out and go back to my father and say to him: Father, I have sinned against heaven and against you. I am no longer worthy to be called your son; make me like one of your hired servants." So he got up and went to his father.

**The Little Details**

*2 Corinthians 9:6-8 on Generosity:*

Remember this: Whoever sows sparingly will also reap sparingly, and whoever sows generously will also reap generously. Each of you should give what you have decided in your heart to give, not reluctantly or under compulsion, for God loves a cheerful giver. And God is able to bless you abundantly, so that in all things at all times, having all that you need, you will abound in every good work.

The *one who hoards grain* is either the merchant who hoards food to raise prices or the rich farmer who refuses to sell seed to the starving because he wishes to sow it later for bigger profit. One who *oppresses the poor shows contempt for their Maker* both because the oppressor disobeys God's commands and because the poor are made in God's image. The *poor* are those in need of essentials, not the person who bought new skis and now wants a handout so he doesn't have to sell them.

34. List what happens to the generous and stingy (Proverbs 21:13; 22:9; 28:8, 27).

| Generous | Stingy |
|---|---|
|  |  |

God cares for the poor and commanded this in Exodus 22:25-27 (ESV):

> If you lend money to any of my people with you who is poor, you shall not be like a moneylender to him, and you shall not exact interest from him. If ever you take your neighbor's cloak in pledge, you shall return it to him before the sun goes down, for that is his only covering, and it is his cloak for his body; in what else shall he sleep? And if he cries to me, I will hear, for I am compassionate.

That's the basis for proverbs about generosity to the poor.

35. In Proverbs 13:23 (ESV) below, box the people about whom God is concerned. Circle what the land would produce. Wavy-circle what sweeps away food.

    13:23  The fallow ground of the poor would yield much food,
           but it is swept away through injustice.

*Food...is swept away through injustice* when landowners mistreat sharecroppers, as in Amos 5:11 (ESV), which condemns those who "exact taxes of grain from" the poor. In Israel, God commanded farmers not to harvest the edges of their fields or gather fallen fruit, for that food belonged to the poor (Leviticus 19:9-10). Disobeying was *injustice*.

36. ♥ (a) How have the principles in the proverbs we read today helped you? (b) How might one proverb have helped you more if you'd better understood its principle and applied it?

In this lesson, we discovered how to manage money well by not risking funds we can't afford to lose, building wealth steadily, and giving generously to the poor. In the next lesson we'll look at wise ways to spend money.

## Day 5

# Spending Money

Now that we've discovered godly ways to prioritize, make, and manage money, let's look at what Proverbs tells us about spending money.

## Know Your Financial Condition

> **37.** Read Proverbs 27:23-27. (a) Why did shepherds need to know the condition of their flocks and herds (24)? (b) What would lambs and goats provide (26-27)?

Solomon writes to well-to-do young men being trained for government work. He tells them not to depend solely on an inheritance or whatever income they're currently receiving. Instead, they should also take care of herds and lands. The takeaway is that we need to care for our livelihoods and not put all our eggs in one basket.

In practical terms, that means we should know the condition of our finances and the condition of the industry in which we work. For example, I use accounting software that shows me the condition of both my personal and business finances.[9] I can see at once what I can afford, what expenses are upcoming, and what my projected balances are. I also subscribe to journals that tell me the condition of the industries in which I work (they're a deductible business expense!).

> **38.** ♥ How do you track the condition of your finances? What helpful tips can you share?

## Choose Helpers Carefully

At times we must hire others to do work we can't do ourselves either because we're too busy or don't have the skills. Shopping around is wise. Here's why.

> **39.** How might trusting strangers mislead you (Proverbs 20:14)?

A dishonest *buyer* tells a seller the product is *no good* and then *boasts about* the exceptional deal he got. This is more than just haggling at a bazaar; it's taking advantage of others.

Here's another person to watch out for.

> **40.** In these proverbs, box the types of people we should avoid relying on.
>
> 10:26  As vinegar to the teeth and smoke to the eyes,
>            so are sluggards to those who send them.
> 18:9  One who is slack in his work
>            is brother to one who destroys.

We need to care for our livelihoods and not put all our eggs in one basket.

Depending on sluggards irritates like *smoke to the eyes*. The slacker produces shoddy work that may need redoing, causing damage like *one who destroys*. For example, the builders of our housing development went bankrupt over poorly installed windows.

If relying on sluggards is bad, how can we recognize them?

> **41.** Read Proverbs 24:30-34. (a) What was the vineyard owner like (30)? (b) What three things were in the vineyard that shouldn't have been (31)? (c) What's the lesson (33-34)?

Seeing the condition of a business or home tells us a lot. Asking for referrals and references is another way to avoid hiring *a sluggard*.

In this lesson, we looked at principles behind spending money well, such as know your financial condition, don't trust naively, and avoid sluggards.

### Wisdom's Worth

> **42.** ♥ In what way did you apply wisdom from Proverbs to your life this week?

In this chapter, we discovered how to wisely prioritize, make, manage, and spend money. In the next chapter we'll discover wisdom over a range of topics.

### *Wisdom Worship*

Find a quiet place and prepare your heart for grateful worship. In Proverbs 119:113, "To 'hate' includes the idea of rejecting, and 'love' the idea of choosing."[10]

> Turn to Psalm 119:113-128 in your Bible and pray the passage aloud.

## Karla's Creative Connection

*The plans of the diligent lead to profit as surely as haste leads to poverty.*

Proverbs 21:5

My daughter still reminds me of how, when she was young, I would always say, "We may not have a lot of money, but we're rich in love." When Michelle was just a toddler, my husband, Michael, and I decided I would be a stay-at-home mom, which meant we couldn't afford the same luxuries two-income families could. So sometimes she would see her friends with things we couldn't buy for her. I know this wasn't always easy for Michelle, but we were truly "rich in love." And that was because I had decided to diligently follow Jesus because of what he'd done for me.

We chose to live on one income for 15 years and then moved to the city, where it took two incomes just to keep the bills paid. We weren't the brightest kids on the block when it came to money, so no matter how hard we tried on our own, we never gained financial prosperity.

The financial wisdom Jean has shared with us this week from Proverbs is invaluable, and I wish Michael and I had learned these truths at a younger age. I'm so thankful, however, that the wisdom of this week's key verse can be applied to our spiritual lives as well as to our financial lives.

The truth is if we're diligent in seeking God and intentionally planning our days to invest time with him, our souls will prosper, and we will become rich in the blessings of the Lord. And if we're regularly investing our time and talents in his kingdom with the purpose of bringing him glory and blessing others, we'll gain riches that unforeseen expenses, inflation, or the stock market can't steal from us. But sadly, the reverse is also true in regard to haste. If we're always too busy for God, seeking him haphazardly or seeking worldly wealth instead of him, our souls are bound to suffer. We will always long for what we do not have.

Interestingly, the Hebrew word translated *plan* also means "thought," "purpose," or—wait for it—"imagination"! So this week, using your imagination, try creatively connecting with God by asking him to help you design a spiritual-life budget. Set up accounts that represent where you want to become spiritually rich such as in love, joy, or peace, or in actions such as giving, caring, or sharing. Then in order to see a profit, decide on the types of investment you'll need, such as Bible study, prayer, or Scripture memorization and how much time you're willing and able to invest in each one.

Maybe seeing your spiritual life investments from a financial perspective will help you become richer in the blessings God has for you!

*Karla*

THE PLANS of the DILIGENT LEAD to PROFIT AS · SURELY · AS HASTE LEADS to POVERTY.

PROVERBS 21:5

## Chapter 8

# Proverbs 22:17–25:14
## Assorted Words to the Wise

How can we be wise in all matters of life?

**Day 1**

## Neighbors Helping Neighbors

Loud barks and a woman's screams cut through the quiet, seeming to come from our front yard. Clay and I darted outside. On the sidewalk in front of our house, a slender middle-aged woman was straining against the thick leashes of two German shepherds, shouting, "Drop it! Drop it!" to the male, who was ferociously shaking a small animal with a fluffy white tail. A petite woman we knew lived with five white Pomeranians a few doors down lay in the street wailing. Neighbors poured out of their houses to help.

My husband quickly grabbed our garden hose, turned on the water full force, and sprayed the German shepherd until he dropped the creature. Clay shouted for me to take the hose and threw it down, then reached toward the leashes and said to the woman, "Here, let me help." She passed him the female German shepherd's leash, and together they pulled both her dogs out of the street. The small animal—a Pomeranian—lay still on the black asphalt. I quickly retrieved the hose and turned off the water.

A younger woman cautiously approached with a towel. With one eye on the German shepherds, she gently wrapped the injured little dog in the towel, gathered it in her arms, and then turned and ran down the street. She laid it behind a low wall, where several neighbors checked its condition.

Suddenly, a second Pomeranian charged the female German shepherd. Clay pulled the larger dog out of the smaller dog's reach just as the German shepherd snapped at it. The snarling white dog dashed into the street, and two men tried to corral it away from the German shepherds. The woman who had hidden the injured dog rushed to its owner, knelt, lightly touched her shoulder, and spoke softly to her. The crying woman jerked up, mouth agape. She stood and ran home, her uninjured dog disappearing with her.

A man approached us and said gently, "We've called animal control."

The German shepherds' owner and I sat on the curb to wait for them. One of her dogs sat with us, panting and holding his ears alert. The other sat on the lawn at Clay's feet.

The woman explained she was staying with a friend and had been walking her dogs when she heard barking from an open garage. She crossed the street until she passed that house, hoping the white dogs would calm down. She could see them jumping against the pet gate enclosing them.

I nodded. I'd seen them do that many times.

## The Little Details
### Chew and Spit

In her book *Mama Bear Apologetics,* Hillary Morgan Ferrer cautions parents against labeling movies and books as simply safe or dangerous. That's because "kids will eventually (and perhaps accidentally) swallow a lie from something they thought was safe or Christian, or reject a truth from something they thought was dangerous or non-Christian."[1]

She advises what she calls the chew-and-spit method. If you're enjoying a great steak until you discover you're chewing on gristle, you "discreetly spit the gristle into a napkin."[2] In other words, you chew and spit.

Parents can teach their children to treat culture like one would a steak with bits of gristle. Chew on whatever culture presents, and spit out whatever is false. For example, watch a movie with your kids, then ask them to think about what was true (chew) and identify what was false and should be rejected (spit).

Since "most lies are wrapped in attractive packages," teaching children discernment is more valuable than simple labels.[3]

But as she headed for the sidewalk in front of our house, one of the penned dogs escaped and attacked her dog. The German shepherd grabbed it and wouldn't let go. Now she was afraid animal control would put her dogs down.

Before we return to this story, let's prepare to read the next few chapters of Proverbs. This chapter looks at miscellaneous topics Proverbs treats with just a few passages. The first two lessons are about community life, which involves neighbors helping neighbors, as happened that afternoon in front of our house.

> 1. ♥ (a) How has a neighbor or nearby relative helped you? (b) How have you helped a neighbor?

## God's Word to Us in Proverbs

For the next question, we'll read all of Collection III and Collection IV, plus a small portion of Collection V. **Collection III: Thirty Sayings of the Wise** is found in Proverbs 22:17–24:22; **Collection IV: Further Sayings of the Wise** is in 24:23-34; and **Collection V: More Proverbs of Solomon** is in 25:1–29:27 (we'll read just part of this one).

Collection III trained young court officials. It contains "the words of the wise" presented as "thirty sayings of counsel and knowledge" (Proverbs 22:17, 20 ESV). That's why it's often called Thirty Sayings of the Wise. "The wise" suggests Solomon collected proverbs from wise people and adapted them for religious life in Israel.

We do the same when we use popular proverbs we know fit with biblical teaching, such as "A penny saved is a penny earned" and "Wise men learn more from fools than fools from wise men." We must take care, though, not to Christianize sayings that aren't biblical, such as the ancient Greek proverb, "The gods help them who help themselves." Some convert that to "God helps those who help themselves," which isn't in the Bible. As we've seen, though, while the Lord doesn't want us to be lazy, we can always ask for his help.

Collection IV begins with this heading: "These also are sayings of the wise" (Proverbs 24:23). This small collection alternates between two topics:

    A    Honest justice in the court (verses 23-26)
        B    Wise economy in the field (verse 27)
    A'   Honest justice in the court (verses 28-29)
        B'   Wise economy in the field (verses 30-34)[4]

Collection V has a heading too: "These also are proverbs of Solomon which the men of Hezekiah king of Judah copied" (Proverbs 25:1 ESV). King Hezekiah was a godly king who lived many years after Solomon and brought an apostate nation back to worshiping God. The heading tells us he arranged for his men to select and add more of Solomon's three thousand[5] proverbs to the book of Proverbs.

Take a moment to pray for insight as you read God's Word.

2. ♥ Read Proverbs 22:17–25:14 (note that we're reading only half of chapter 25). (a) What stood out to you in your reading? Why? (b) How can you apply that insight to your life this week?

## A Time of Trouble

I began this chapter relating how my community helped two women and four of their dogs. This chapter's key verse, Proverbs 24:10, comes from a passage related to helping others: Proverbs 24:10-12.

3. Wavy-underline what faltering in times of trouble shows (24:10b). Underline the two commands (11ab). Underline what God does (12bd).

24:10  If you falter in a time of trouble,
        how small is your strength!
11     Rescue those being led away to death;
        hold back those staggering toward slaughter.
12     If you say, "But we knew nothing about this,"
        does not he who weighs the heart perceive it?
        Does not he who guards your life know it?
        Will he not repay everyone according to what they have done?

*A time of trouble* shows what our true *strength* is. The Lord's people should try to *rescue* those in danger. In my neighborhood, people tried to protect both the women and their dogs. When we share the gospel, we're working with the Lord toward his rescuing others from eternal *death*. (The NIV, NRSVUE, and ESV consider Proverbs 24:10 as part of the same saying as verses 11 and 12, while the NASB and NKJV interpret it as a separate saying.)

In this lesson, we discovered how secular wisdom and godly wisdom occasionally overlap. We also considered the importance of helping neighbors in need. Next we'll continue the canine saga while discovering how to live well in community with others.

# Pam's Simply Beautiful Wisdom

*Whoever pursues righteousness and love finds life, prosperity and honor.*

Proverbs 21:21

Life, prosperity, and honor. Sound like good goals? All God asks is a pursuit of righteousness. *Pursue* means to "chase" or "hunt," which is very intentional. Three simple skills of decision-making can help you live in a way God will honor you with wisdom and clarity for the path ahead.

## Predecide and Automate Choices

Have you ever stood beside a child trying to decide which of the thirty-one flavors of ice cream to order? It can be a painful wait as they keep second-guessing themselves. You might be tempted to impatiently and firmly nudge, "Decide already!" or "There are no wrong choices with ice cream, sweetie."

To save time, energy, and effort, you can predecide some decisions:

- How you take your coffee or tea
- What speed to set your car's cruise control
- Your morning alarm and start-your-day routine
- Your nighttime wind-down ritual and bedtime

I heard Dr. Mehmet Oz share what he considers the same two breakfast options every day: Greek yogurt, granola, and blueberries, or steel cut oats and blueberries. He established those choices after evaluating what morning foods kept him energetic for surgeries. By predeciding, you can devote your thinking to more vital causes.

I have automatic answers for various requests that come into our ministry. For example, if any pro-life pregnancy center asks for a donation of my books for fundraising, I always give them an enthusiastic yes!

As a mom, I predecided to break the pattern of yelling from my family of origin. Instead of screaming, I would first pray, then walk to my child, bend down, turn him to face me, and whisper my instructions or correction.

I automatically kiss Bill as he leaves and reenters our home. We both automatically say, "I love you" when we end our phone conversations.

## Practice the Wisdom Test

The smartphones we use every day are computers more powerful than the one that first put men on the moon! Yes, we have access to vast amounts of knowledge. Wisdom, however, is much more than knowledge.

- Knowledge is the *what*
- Wisdom is the *how* and *why*

In chapter 1, I explained the Obvious Test. If the decision isn't clear, move to the **Wisdom Test**:

- Does this decision line up with my convictions?
- Will the people I respect most agree with this decision? Have I asked them?
- Is this decision based on healthy boundaries that will produce self-respect?
- Will this decision cause personal growth in my life?
- Would I encourage my best friends or child, sibling, or parent to make this same decision?

## Practice the Priorities Test

Some decisions in life require more effort to figure out. You've gone through the Obvious Test and the Wisdom Test, but you still need more evidence for making the best decision. This happens when...

- The Bible doesn't specifically address the decision before you.
- You have many options to choose from.
- Your two best options are equally attractive to you.
- The decision will affect your life for a long time to come.
- People you respect have differing opinions on how you should proceed.

When this occurs, do the ***Priorities Test***, taking some simple and practical steps, in this order:

***First, write out your decision in a positive way.*** Describe what will happen if you say yes to this decision. For instance, *I'm considering moving my family to Colorado to work for a company there, resulting in a pay increase.* This wording encourages you to think about momentum in your life.

***Second, make a pro/con list.*** Create two columns on a sheet of paper. In one column, write the reasons you ought to take this course of action. In the other column, write the reasons this course of action is not a promising idea.

***Third, prioritize your reasons.*** The Bible clearly teaches that priorities lead to progress. Psalm 90:12 challenges us, "Teach us to number our days, that we may gain a heart of wisdom." I prefer to use an ABC system to prioritize my lists. This means I assign an A to the vital reasons. The supportive reasons get a B. I reserve a C for reasons that are creative but don't really impact the decision.

***Fourth, compare the high-priority reasons from both lists.*** Evaluate both the A reasons for saying yes and the A reasons for choosing no. If it's a tie, move to the B reasons to see if the decision becomes clear. Don't be fooled by quantity; it's quite possible that one list will have more reasons, but quantity is no substitute for quality. The way to build clarity is to deliberately prioritize the evidence and discipline yourself to focus on the A reasons.[6]

A quick example: When all our sons had left home, we used this process and decided to stay put in our house in San Diego. Several years later, however, one night Bill arrived home at midnight after commuting seven hours each way to care for his aging parents. This was an arduous trip he'd made numerous times over the past few months. I looked at my weary husband and said, "Oh, sweetheart, seems like keeping your parents alive is killing you! Do we need to move?" The ***Priorities Test*** gave clear indication it was time to downsize and relocate near his folks.

P.S.: I have provided the Priorities Test worksheet we use for our decisions in the extras section for this chapter on DiscoveringTheBibleSeries.com.

*Pam*

## Experiencing Scripture Creatively (Optional)

If you have extra time, consider these suggestions for creatively engaging with verses from this week's reading. The appendix has even more ideas.

- Using photo editing software, place your favorite verse from Day 4's lesson on divine revelation on a photo of God's magnificent creation.
- Choose one proverb that addresses an area you want to change. Write it on a card and copy Karla's art around it. Place it somewhere you'll see it often. When you do, pray for God's help in making this change.
- Follow Karla's instructions at the end of this chapter for creatively imagining yourself in a boxing ring.

## The Little Details
### *For Budding Poets*

Psalm 119 contains stanzas of eight poetic lines, each of which consists of two line segments.

To create your own psalm based on Psalm 119, first list reasons you love God's Word and instructions. Next list ways you'd like God's help with understanding the Bible and following his commands. From the two lists, select up to eight items and write a short wisdom psalm structured like Psalm 119's stanzas. Add a title and verse numbers.

- Color Karla's full-page illustration at the end of the chapter while repeating the words of the verse aloud.

- Create a poem from one or more proverbs. See examples in other chapters' Day 1 lesson.

- You've been reading Psalm 119 at the end of every chapter. Our Day 4 lesson examines how we need God's Word, so write a wisdom psalm that expresses your need for Scripture. Here's an example:

*A psalm of Jean concerning the Word of God.*

1      Your words show the path to eternal life
         and the way to your everlasting realm.
2      The Bible's pages reveal your plan of salvation
         formed before the beginning of time.
3      Scripture displays your loving-kindness
         and shines forth your justice and mercy.
4      The Gospels unveiled Jesus as Savior to me
         and exposed the falsehoods I had believed.
5      Your commands teach me how to love others
         with patience, kindness, and grace.
6      Your instructions show me how to live
         in ways that bring blessing and reward.
7      Your wisdom displayed throughout your Word
         helps me discard foolish and sinful habits.
8      Help me to know and understand your words
         that I may be molded by them.

## Day 2

# Community Life

"He says your coding is poor and we should fire you and give him your work," my client said. I was stunned. She'd hired the other consultant and me to work together to connect a program I'd coded with another platform I didn't know well. Now she didn't know whom to believe.

She asked me to implement a security change the other consultant suggested. I made the change, but that resulted in only one person being able to log into the program at a time. When I walked the client through the code so she could see how the change worked, she had me reverse it.

Later, the other consultant implemented changes in his code that weren't according to specifications. When I asked him about it over speakerphone, he said that, of course, I was right, and he would have completed the work according to specs, but the client had insisted on the change.

He forgot she was standing next to me, and she blurted, "What?"

He quickly injected, "Let's not assign blame."

Shortly after, the client's director asked me if I knew the other consultant's platform well enough to take over. I did. She fired him and gave me the rest of his work.

> **4.** What happens to those who intend to harm others (Proverbs 26:27)?

What happened with the conniving consultant is an example of how God can cause *a stone* with which wrongdoers intend to hurt others to inflict them instead.

## Community Crimes

Let's look at what else damages community.

> **5.** What belongs to the Lord (Proverbs 16:11)?

The dishonest kept light and heavy *weights in* their *bag* so they could cheat others.

> **6.** What happens to those who fraudulently take land (Proverbs 23:10-11; 22:28 is similar)?

Under Joshua, God gave the Jews' *ancestors* land allotments meant to stay in the family. *The fatherless* had no human to stand up for their rights, making them vulnerable.

## Community Leadership

In the USA, we elect civic leaders and association boards to ensure people live together well in their communities. We also elect government leaders we expect to pass laws that reflect our values. Proverbs has much to say about leadership. In fact, as mentioned earlier, the principles behind some proverbs about kings apply to all leaders. But even those that apply to just Israel's and Judah's kings teach us God's values.

> **7.** To the left of each attribute, write the letter of what it brings (Proverbs 11:14; 14:28; 20:28). Each attribute has one unique match.
>
> | | Attribute | Brings |
> |---|---|---|
> | | A large population | A. Glory |
> | | Love and faithfulness | B. Safety |
> | | Many advisors | C. Victory |

The leaders of *a nation* need wise *guidance*. Kings value *a large population* partly because *subjects* flee countries with corrupt governments, leaving the ruler *ruined*. (Likewise, in businesses, employees transfer out of poorly run departments.) As I write, Russia is invading Ukraine to regain what Putin considers the *glory* of the former Union of Soviet Socialist Republics. God promised *love and faithfulness* to the kings descended from David. He kept their *throne secure* if they were faithful to him.

God can cause *a stone* with which wrongdoers intend to hurt others to inflict them instead.

**8.** To the left of each type of ruler, write the letter of the result that goes with it (Proverbs 28:2, 3; 29:2, 12, 14). Each verse has one type of ruler and one unique result.

| | Rulers | Result |
|---|---|---|
| | Who are wicked | A. Are like crop-destroying rains |
| | Who have discernment | B. Cause people to groan |
| | Who listen to lies | C. Maintain order |
| | Who judge the poor fairly | D. Will be established |
| | Who oppress the poor | E. Will have wicked officials |

The northern kingdom of Israel was *rebellious* from the start and had nearly twice as *many rulers* as Judah in the same time frame due to frequent assassinations.[7] The NASB, ESV, and NKJV translate verse 28:3 as a *poor man who oppresses* the poor, while the NIV has *a ruler* as the oppressor. A *ruler* needs *officials* who tell the truth even if it's not what they want to hear, but many kings persecuted true prophets and heeded false ones. The *poor* are the most vulnerable and the most in need of *fairness*.

### Living Under Community Leaders

Proverbs also instructs us about living and working under good and bad leaders. Let's look first at reasons we should show leaders respect.

**9.** Compare what a leader's favor and wrath are like (Proverbs 16:14-15; 19:12; 20:2).

| Favor | Wrath |
|---|---|
| | |

Solomon's *wrath* brought death to rebels, while *the wise* knew how to *appease* anger. Israel needed *dew* between rainy seasons. Wayward rulers' *wrath* took prophets' *lives*.

**10.** In the two Proverbs passages below, underline what followers should do. Wavy-underline what they shouldn't do.

> 24:21 Fear the LORD and the king, my son,
> and do not join with rebellious officials,
> 22 for those two will send sudden destruction on them,
> and who knows what calamities they can bring?
> 25:6 Do not exalt yourself in the king's presence,
> and do not claim a place among his great men;
> 7 it is better for him to say to you, "Come up here,"
> than for him to humiliate you before his nobles.

The principle behind Proverbs 24:21 applies to all leaders. Many an employee has lost a job over ignoring a boss. Jesus applied Proverbs 25:6-7 to people snagging honorable seats at a wedding, showing us how to apply its principle to all of life (Luke 14:7-10).

---

Jesus applied Proverbs 25:6-7 to people snagging honorable seats at a wedding, showing us how to apply its principle to all of life (Luke 14:7-10).

---

## Righting Wrongs

Everyone eventually suffers from others' wrongdoing. Proverbs gives us useful principles for when that happens.

### Appeal to Proper Authorities

When serious troubles arise between neighbors, we must appeal to the proper authority. Today that might be an association board, the judicial system, police, or animal control. In ancient Israel, the ultimate authority was the king.

> **11.** (a) What was one of the king's duties in ancient Israel (Proverbs 20:8)? (b) How should he perform this duty?

In ancient times, a *king* was also a *judge*. He was like one who *winnows*. After a farmer harvested grain and threshed it, he tossed it in the air with a winnowing fork so the wind would blow away the lighter chaff and what was good to eat would fall back on the floor. *Evil* is like chaff, and the king's *eyes* are like the winnowing fork. In a broader sense, all leaders must judge good and evil.

### Appeal to Justice

As I sat with the tearful owner of the two German shepherds, I pondered how unjust it would be if animal control put her dogs down when she hadn't done anything wrong. It wasn't fair that my neighbor's dog was injured, either, but her pet gate hadn't stopped her dogs from getting out. We didn't know what would happen.

Proverbs offers insights into what *should* happen if just laws apply.

> **12.** In these verse, box descriptions of people. Wavy-underline what's bad. Underline what's good.
>
> 17:26 If imposing a fine on the innocent is not good,
>    surely to flog honest officials is not right.
> 18:5 It is not good to be partial to the wicked
>    and so deprive the innocent of justice.
> 24:23 To show partiality in judging is not good:
> 24 Whoever says to the guilty, "You are innocent,"
>    will be cursed by peoples and denounced by nations.
> 25 But it will go well with those who convict the guilty,
>    and rich blessing will come on them.

Punishing *the innocent* destroys a society. *To be partial to the* powerful and influential *wicked* is sinful. *Partiality* in 24:23 means clearing *the guilty*.

> **13.** Why do courts punish (Proverbs 20:30)?

Traffic tickets reduce speeding. A broken foot makes one more cautious. More importantly, the wounds our Savior suffered cleanses our *evil*:

But He was wounded for our transgressions,
He was bruised for our iniquities;
The chastisement for our peace was upon Him,
And by His stripes we are healed" (Isaiah 53:5 NKJV).

14. ♥ Describe a time you appealed to an authority for justice. Were you satisfied with the result?

While perfect justice doesn't always come on earth, it will arrive at the final judgment.

### The Authorities' Verdict

When the animal control truck arrived, a burly man and a slender woman with a blond ponytail stepped out. After hearing the basics, the man retrieved a metal clipboard and interviewed us individually. Someone told him the owner of the injured dog had taken it to the veterinarian. He said he'd interview her later.

Then both the animal control workers approached the German shepherds' owner. "Ma'am, were your dogs leashed the entire time?"

"Yes," she replied.

"Were the other dogs leashed?"

"No, they escaped from the garage over there." Her voice trembled as she pointed. "Are-are you going to take my dogs?"

"Ma'am, you have nothing to worry about. Your dogs protected you, just as they're supposed to. The other dogs were unleashed outside of their owner's property, and that's against city leash laws. You should have your dogs checked for injuries by a vet, and you can require the other dogs' owner to pay the costs."

The blonde smiled and said, "Your dogs are good dogs. You should be proud."

Justice prevailed for this neighbor.

In this lesson, we saw how to live well in community with others. Next, we'll find what Proverbs tells us about the heart's emotions, attitudes, longings, and appetites.

*Day 3*

## The Heart Within

I was sad to learn that the injured Pomeranian died later that day, bringing heartache to its owner. The passing of beloved pets not only grieves us but reminds us of our own mortality.

To the ancient Hebrews, such emotions were a part of the heart. It was not just a blood-pumping organ but "considered to be the seat of the emotions and passions and appetites...and embraced likewise the intellectual and moral faculties."[8] Other chapters have delved into the intellectual and moral aspects of the heart, but here we'll look at its emotions, attitudes, longings, and appetites.

While perfect justice doesn't always come on earth, it will arrive at the final judgment.

## The Emotions of the Heart

**15.** To the left of each heart description below, write the letter of the phrase that goes with it (Proverbs 14:10, 13; 15:13, 15). Each verse has one heart description and one phrase.

| | Heart Description | Phrase |
|---|---|---|
| | A cheerful heart has | A. A cheerful face |
| | A happy heart makes | B. A continual feast |
| | A heart knows | C. Its own bitterness |
| | A heart may ache even in | D. Laughter |

Others cannot fully know the depths of our *bitterness* and *joy*—we can only imagine the pain my neighbor with the Pomeranians expressed in wails. Emotions are often mixed, as when my joy for the owner of the German shepherds mixed with sadness for the deceased dog's owner. Happiness and *heartache* affect the *face* and *spirit*. *Oppressed* is parallel to *cheerful heart*, suggesting that the *wretched* here are inwardly oppressed.

**16.** List what does and doesn't cheer hearts (Proverbs 12:20, 25; 15:30; 25:25).

| What Cheers | What Doesn't Cheer |
|---|---|
| | |

*Those who promote peace* escape the turmoil that swirls around those who don't. In the Hebrew of Proverbs 12:25, *it* refers to *anxiety*, not *heart*.[10] Emotions affect our body language, including the expression of our *eyes* and the erectness of our posture. Before telephones and telegrams, one waited a long time for *news from a distant land*.

## The Attitudes of the Heart

The heart's attitudes not only affect our emotions but show who we are.

**17.** Underline what reflects a person in Proverbs 27:19 (ESV) below.

> 27:19  As in water face reflects face,
> so the heart of man reflects the man.

This proverb is difficult to translate because the Hebrew has no verbs. Ross writes, "The simplest way to take the verse is to say that as clear water gives a reflection of the face, so the heart reflects the true nature of the man...The point seems to be that through looking at our attitudes of heart we come to true self-awareness."[11]

## The Longings of the Heart

When Clay and I first married, we dreamed of many wonderful things for our future. Many came to be, but some didn't. For example, I couldn't have children. (Find a link to my story on DiscoveringTheBibleSeries.com.)

### The Little Details
***John Wesley on Despair:***

In his booklet *An Earnest Appeal to Men of Reason and Religion*, John Wesley tells of a man he once met who had fallen into deep despair and unbelief. Out of the bitterness of his soul, the man said to Wesley, "All is dark; my thought is lost. But I hear... you preach to a great number of people every night and morning. Pray, what would you do with them? Whither would you lead them? What religion do you preach? What is it good for?"

Wesley answered, "You ask 'what I would do with them': I would make them virtuous and happy, easy in themselves and useful to others. 'Whither would I lead them?' To heaven; to God the Judge, the lover of all; and to Jesus the Mediator of the new covenant. 'What religion do I preach?' The religion of love: the law of kindness brought to light by the gospel. 'What is this good for?' To make all who receive it enjoy God and themselves: To make them like God; lovers of all; contented in their lives; and crying out at their death in calm assurance, 'O grave, where is thy victory! Thanks be unto God, who giveth *me* the victory through my Lord Jesus Christ.'"[9]

## The Little Details
## Times of London *on Jealousy:*

There is no vice of which a man can be guilty, no meanness, no shabbiness, no unkindness, which excites so much indignation among his contemporaries, friends, and neighbors, as his success. This is the one unpardonable crime, which reason cannot defend, nor humility mitigate. "When heaven with such parts blest him, have I not reason to detest him?" is a genuine and natural expression of the vulgar human mind. The man who writes as we cannot write, who speaks as we cannot speak, labours as we cannot labour, thrives as we cannot thrive, has accumulated on his own person all the offenses of which man can be guilty. Down with him! Why cumbereth he the ground?[13]

18.  ♥ (a) What's something you hoped for but didn't receive? (b) What's a longing that's been fulfilled?

Let's look at what Proverbs has to say about the yearnings of the heart.

19.  What do all these have in common: death, destruction, human eyes, leeches, graves, barren wombs, land, and fire (Proverbs 27:20; 30:15-16)?

*Death* (Sheol) is the grave, death, extreme danger, or the realm of the dead who "are cut off from fellowship with God,"[12] while *Destruction* (Abaddon) is the name of the angel of the bottomless pit (Revelation 9:11). Likening them to *human eyes* is sobering. *Two daughters* describes the two suckers *the leech* has. *Grave* in 30:16 is also Sheol.

20.  What is harder to stand against than anger (Proverbs 27:4)?

Its presence destroys love, causes sin, and leads to foolish behavior, as the next verse shows.

21.  In Proverbs 12:9 (ESV) below, underline what's better, and wavy-underline what isn't.

> 12:9    Better to be lowly and have a servant
>            than to play the great man and lack bread.

Wanting to be seen as *the great man* can lead to status symbol purchases causing lack.

## The Appetites of the Heart

I love trying new foods. My mother was Hispanic, so whenever I sorted pinto beans, I knew we'd have bean soup that night, *chili verde* the next, and burritos from the leftovers after that. My grandmother bought us pickled pig's feet and colorful *pan dulce* (sweet pastries) from her Mexican market. Before I developed food allergies, I savored trying most anything once. Proverbs says much about eating and drinking.

22.  How can we help children eat veggies (Proverbs 27:7)?

Based on this proverb, we told our foster children they never had to eat anything they didn't like, but they could have ice cream only if they finished their meals. The child with the biggest sweet tooth missed dessert only once.

23.  When should we take particular care not to eat too much (Proverbs 23:1-3, 6-8; 25:16)?

☐ Dining alone                    ☐ Dining with a begrudging host

□ Dining with a ruler    □ Dining with the poor
□ Eating meat            □ Eating sweets

Manners count at meals. So do companions. And there can be too much of a good thing. Here's a similar proverb, Proverbs 25:27 (NRSVUE).

24. Wavy-underline what one shouldn't seek too much of.

    25:27  It is not good to eat much honey
           or to seek honor on top of honor.

The second half of the verse is difficult to translate (the Hebrew is literally "The investigation of their glory is glory"[14]). An alternative is "nor is it honorable to search out matters that are too deep" (NIV), meaning that some things may be too deep for human minds to understand. For what we don't understand, we trust our loving God.

25. What overindulgence leads people astray and causes woes (Proverbs 20:1; 23:29-35)?

Hubbard writes of Proverbs 20:1, "The specific point of the final line is not that it is unwise to drink but that drink, when we are in its grips, renders us unwise."[15]

In this lesson, we looked at the heart's emotions, attitudes, longings, and appetites. Next, we'll discover two kinds of divine revelation and why we need them both.

 Day 4

# Divine Revelation

Math and science always fascinated me. I even checked out books from the library on them to read in my free time. (Yes, I was a nerdy kid. My husband says I'm still a nerd.) So even though my dad told me God didn't exist, the complexity and vastness of the universe suggested to me that he did.

## General Revelation: What Creation Teaches

What creation tells us about God is called *general revelation*. God revealed much about his power, character, and ways in creation. Romans 1:20 (NRSVUE) explains, "Ever since the creation of the world God's eternal power and divine nature, invisible though they are, have been seen and understood through the things God has made."

Proverbs shows us that God also teaches us about ourselves via nature.

26. To the left of each animal, write the letter of the person who is like it (Proverbs 11:22; 17:12; 28:15). Each verse matches one animal and one person.

| Animal | Person |
|---|---|
| Bear robbed of her cubs | A. Beautiful woman lacking discretion |
| Pig with gold ring in its snout | B. Fool bent on folly |
| Roaring lion or charging bear | C. Wicked ruler |

The Little Details
*Psalm 19:1-4 (ESV) on General Revelation:*

The heavens declare the glory of God, and the sky above proclaims his handiwork. Day to day pours out speech, and night to night reveals knowledge. There is no speech, nor are there words, whose voice is not heard. Their voice goes out through all the earth, and their words to the end of the world. In them he has set a tent for the sun.

## The Little Details
### Examples of Proverbs 30:21-23

***Jeroboam*** was a servant who became king and, in his fear of losing his newly gained power, built new temples, installed golden calves as the gods to worship, and replaced both the priesthood and God's assigned festivals (1 Kings 12:25-33).

***Nabal*** was a wealthy fool who treated David with contempt and refused to share food from a feast with David's men, who had protected Nabal's flocks (1 Samuel 25). His wife Abigail rushed food to David, saving Nabal's life. But God smote Nabal, and he died shortly after.

***Leah***'s father tricked Jacob at his wedding by having her pretend to be the woman he loved: her sister Rachel. Jacob married Rachel, too, and Leah suffered from knowing she did not have his heart as Rachel did (Genesis 29:21-32).

***Hagar*** was Sarai's servant. When Sarai couldn't conceive, she asked her husband, Abram, to give her a child through Hagar (a common ancient practice). Then when Hagar became pregnant, she treated Sarai with contempt (Genesis 16:4).

According to Ross, *discretion* can be physical taste, intellectual discretion, or ethical judgment.[16] A *fool* is often dangerous. In ancient times, a *dog* was a wild scavenger, not a pet. Examples of a *wicked ruler* include Shallum (Jeremiah 22:11-17), Nero (who killed the apostles Paul and Peter), and Hitler.

We read one of the "four things" passages in the last lesson. Here are more, all based on nature.

27. To the left of each creature/thing below, write the letter of the description that goes with it (Proverbs 30:18-19, 21-23, 24-28, 29-31). Each verse has four creatures and one description.

| Creature/Thing | Description |
|---|---|
| Ant | A. Makes the earth tremble |
| Contemptible woman who marries | B. Small but wise |
| Eagle in the sky | C. Stately |
| Godless fool who eats plenty | D. Too amazing to understand |
| He-goat | |
| Hyrax (badger) | |
| Lion | |
| Lizard | |
| Locust | |
| Man with a young woman | |
| Secure king | |
| Servant who becomes king | |
| Servant who displaces her mistress | |
| Ship on high seas | |
| Snake on a rock | |
| Strutting rooster (NKJV, greyhound) | |

The mysteries of Proverbs 30:18-19 build to a climax in the last line. Proverbs 30:21-23 humorously describes people suddenly elevated to positions they're unprepared for, so they react with hubris and contempt, intoxicated by power (see sidebar). Those who think themselves less gifted than others can take comfort from Proverbs 30:24-28. Proverbs 30:29-31 encourages leaders to act with dignity.

28. ♥ Which lesson from nature stood out to you the most? Why?

## Special Revelation: What God's Word Teaches

As a young teenager, I wanted to get ahold of a Bible. I reasoned that a good God would want to communicate how to reach him in a way that people could discover. An all-powerful God could put how to reach him in written form—such as the Bible—and preserve that message throughout centuries.

My girlfriend gave me a paperback New Testament called *Good News for Modern Man,*

and every day I rushed through my homework so I could read about how to get to heaven. When I read the Gospel of John, I discovered the good news that changed my life. (I tell the fuller story in our book *Discovering Good News in John*.)

While what God reveals through creation is called *general revelation*, what he reveals supernaturally is called *special revelation*. This includes prophecies, visions, and dreams, such as those recorded in the Bible. The Bible is also special revelation. It holds the words God inspired people to write and preserve for all generations.

The next passage we'll read refers to both general and special revelation. It follows a three-part outline: confession, questions, resolution.

> **29.** In Proverbs 30:1-6 below, box the names of people and references to God. Underline what Agur calls his writings (1a). Wavy-underline what frustrated Agur (2b, 3ab). To the right of the passage, number the six questions (4a-f). Underline the answer to Agur's initial distress (5). Wavy-underline his warning (6).
>
> 30:1 The sayings of Agur son of Jakeh—an inspired utterance.
>     This man's utterance to Ithiel:
>     "I am weary, God,
>         but I can prevail.
> 2   Surely I am only a brute, not a man;
>         I do not have human understanding.
> 3   I have not learned wisdom,
>         nor have I attained to the knowledge of the Holy One.
> 4   Who has gone up to heaven and come down?
>         Whose hands have gathered up the wind?
>     Who has wrapped up the waters in a cloak?
>         Who has established all the ends of the earth?
>     What is his name, and what is the name of his son?
>         Surely you know!
> 5   "Every word of God is flawless;
>         he is a shield to those who take refuge in him.
> 6   Do not add to his words,
>         or he will rebuke you and prove you a liar."

**Confession.** Agur seems to have converted to the Jewish faith.[17] In verses 2-3, he professes weariness over his search for wisdom. He cannot find wisdom on his own, though he knows he'll *prevail*. He confesses that he had attained neither understanding, wisdom, nor knowledge of God, the *Holy One*. This makes him feel that he's only a *brute*—an animal lacking reason.[18] The parallel between brutishness and attaining knowledge of God (see below) suggests that the way to true humanity is through knowing the Holy One.[19]

A    I am only a brute
        B    I do not have understanding
        B'   I have not learned wisdom
A'   I have not attained the knowledge of the Holy One

**Questions.** Agur poses rhetorical questions to Ithiel. The answer to the *Who* questions is "God." The answer to *What is his name?* is "I AM" and "LORD" (Exodus 3:13-15). In Solomon's day, the answer to *What is the name of his son?* would have been "Israel" or

## The Little Details
### *Jesus on Special Revelation*

*Matthew 11:27 (ESV):* All things have been handed over to me by my Father, and no one knows the Son except the Father, and no one knows the Father except the Son and anyone to whom the Son chooses to reveal him.

*John 3:12-13 (ESV):* If I have told you earthly things and you do not believe, how can you believe if I tell you heavenly things? No one has ascended into heaven except he who descended from heaven, the Son of Man.

*John 3:31-33 (ESV):* He who comes from above is above all. He who is of the earth belongs to the earth and speaks in an earthly way. He who comes from heaven is above all. He bears witness to what he has seen and heard, yet no one receives his testimony. Whoever receives his testimony sets his seal to this, that God is true.

## The Little Details

*Bruce K. Waltke on Parallels Between Proverbs 30:2-6 and Job 28:12-28:*

Job 28:12-28 develops the same argument, moving from human inability to obtain wisdom (vv. 12-19) to the LORD's finding and testing of it (vv. 20-27) to his revealing it to human beings (v. 28). Agur's four questions in 30:4a proceed along the same line of reasoning. The first question establishes the unbridgeable gap between the earthling and heaven, presumably where wisdom dwells. The last three establish that God must possess wisdom because he demonstrates it. In Job 38 the LORD asks Job similar questions to Agur's and implies the answer, "Not you, Job, but God" (Job 38:5, 25, 29, 36, 37, 41; 39:5).[21]

"Solomon," for God called the kingdom of Israel and the kings descended from David his "son" (Exodus 2:22; 2 Samuel 7:14; *son* was what great kings called subordinate kings). The later prophets and the New Testament announce that both were a type of Jesus, God's only begotten Son *who has gone up to heaven and come down*, giving the questions more poignancy now.[20] Agur challenges Ithiel to answer the questions: *Surely you know!*

***Resolution.*** Verses 5-6 resolve Agur's initial despair. Wisdom and knowledge of the Holy One come by humbly accepting God's revelation of himself through his words. The wisdom he could not attain on his own he can find in God's revelation. Verse 5 cites David in Psalm 18:30, a psalm that answers four of Agur's questions (18:9-11, 31). Verse 6a alludes to Moses's commands in Deuteronomy 4:2, which also gives God's name. Moses elsewhere answers the remaining two of Agur's questions (Genesis 1:1; Exodus 4:22) and states that people do not need to ascend to heaven to get God's words, for he has revealed them and they are near (Deuteronomy 30:12-14).

There's a New Testament application to verses 5-6. When the Pharisees accused Jesus of wrongdoing, it wasn't over breaking the law of Moses. Rather, he broke the oral traditions the Pharisees added to the law. Jesus rebuked them, saying, "You have let go of the commands of God and are holding on to human traditions" (Mark 7:8).

---

**30.** In the proverb below, wavy-underline what happens without revelation. Circle "blessed." Underline what the blessed person does.

> 29:18  Where there is no revelation, people cast off restraint;
> but blessed is the one who heeds wisdom's instruction.

---

Without divine *revelation*, people make up their own morality. When they hear God's words, they reject their divine nature and instead *cast off* what they see as *restraint*.

---

**31.** What are the prayers of those who don't heed instruction (Proverbs 28:9)?

---

Of course, *prayers* of repentance reverse the sorry state. The next proverb reveals who needs such prayers.

---

**32.** What can no one say accurately, according to Proverbs 20:9? Check all that apply.

☐ I am clean and without sin.

☐ I don't need divine revelation to know right from wrong.

☐ I don't need to repent.

☐ I have kept my heart pure.

---

Praise be to God that "righteousness is given through faith in Jesus Christ to all who believe...for all have sinned and fall short of the glory of God, and all are justified freely by his grace through the redemption that came by Christ Jesus" (Romans 3:22-24). Jesus is the Word of God that became flesh (John 1:1, 14). He is the ultimate revelation of the Lord, "the image of the invisible God" (Colossians 1:15).

In this lesson we discovered that God gives general revelation about himself through nature. He also gives special revelation through prophecy, dreams, the Bible, and—most importantly—his Son, Jesus Christ. In our next lesson we'll look at some fun differences between people.

## Day 5

# Social Life

A wonderful team of women time the lessons in the Discovering the Bible series so I'll be sure they can be completed in 20 to 25 minutes. I also ask them to be transparent and honest if they find anything confusing or difficult.

*Discovering Wisdom in Proverbs* covers 31 Bible chapters—the most yet. So I needed to find ways to shorten the time it takes to answer questions. I experimented with asking readers to draw what I thought were simple shapes so readers could more quickly and easily trace themes. While the first reader who met this experiment enjoyed the exercise, another found it challenging:

> *I found the instructions to draw "simple" items to be a cause of anxiety and distraction! I do not enjoy drawing (never learned how, even basic shapes—I took Art History to avoid taking art classes)...This is such a stumbling block for me that it became a mental battle; I had to re-shape my anxiety over not being able to "do a simple task" into "what is God teaching me here?"*

So I changed the questions to offer options that would suit a broader range of people—including this dear friend (who loves coloring Karla's illustrations, by the way).

The Lord who made hummingbirds and hippos and flowers and forests has designed each of us uniquely. When we don't realize that not everyone thinks just as we do, likes what we like, and enjoys what we enjoy, we can end up in amusing situations.

Which is why we need to ask questions and find out more about people.

---

**33.** ♥ Describe a time you wrongly assumed someone was like you in some way.

---

Proverbs has some interesting observations about various people. Some may be like you, most probably aren't. But knowing about different people helps us know how to navigate in new social situations.

**The Little Details**
*Bruce K. Waltke on Proverbs 30:4:*

The answer to "What is the name of his son?" must be based on the lexical foundation that in Proverbs "son" always elsewhere refers to the son whom the father teaches (see 1:8). In the Old Testament, the LORD brought Israel into existence and named his firstborn (cf. Exod. 4:22; Deut. 14:1; 32:5-6, 18-19; Isa. 43:6; 45:11; 63:16; 64:8[7]; Jer. 3:4, 19; 31:20; Hos. 11:1)...

In the New Testament Jesus Christ fulfills typical Israel, for a Gentile tyrant threatened his life at birth; he, too, returned from exile in Egypt, suffered in the wilderness, and taught on a mountain. Unlike Israel, he perfectly obeyed his Father (Matt. 2:15; Heb. 5:7-10). But he is more than a son...He identifies himself as the Son of Man who comes on the clouds, the biblical symbol of divine transcendence. In Luke he is the incarnate Son of God by the virgin birth (Luke 1:29-33), and in John he is the eternal Son of God (John 17). [22]

**34.** In the left column below, write the letter of the people's state (Proverbs 11:16; 19:19; 28:17; 29:21, 24). Verse 11:16 has two people descriptions while the rest have one. Each people description has one unique match.

| People | Their State |
|---|---|
| Accomplices of thieves | A. Are honored |
| Hot-tempered people | B. Are insolent |
| Kindhearted women | C. Are their own enemies |
| Pampered youths | D. Are wealthy |
| Ruthless men | E. Must pay the penalty |
| Tormented murderers | F. Seek refuge in the grave |

Almost anyone can achieve *wealth* (think Mafia) but not so *honor*. It's useless to *pay the* legal *penalty* for people who won't change unless they suffer consequences. The law of Moses called for the death penalty (*grave*) for some offenses. A *pampered youth* won't obey a boss later. The law condemned those who "do not speak up when they hear a public charge to testify" (Leviticus 5:1).

Some things change as we enter different life stages.

**35.** To the left of each attribute below, write the letter of the description that goes with it (Proverbs 16:31; 20:11, 29). Each attribute has one unique match.

| Attribute | Description |
|---|---|
| Actions | A. Are a crown of splendor |
| Gray hairs | B. Are the glory of young men |
| Strengths | C. Reveal children's character |

Long life for those who walk in *righteousness* is the ideal. The heart shows forth in *actions*. *Splendor* refers to earned honor.

In this lesson, we looked at Proverbs' observations about people and their differences.

### Wisdom's Worth

**36.** ♥ In what way did you apply wisdom from Proverbs to your life this week?

In this chapter, we looked at proverbs on a variety of topics. We discovered how secular wisdom and godly wisdom overlap and differ. We considered the importance of helping neighbors. We studied how to live well in community with others. We looked at the heart's emotions, attitudes, longings, and appetites. We learned that God gives general revelation about himself through nature. He also gives special revelation through prophecy, dreams, the Bible, and—most importantly—his Son, Jesus Christ. Finally, we saw fun differences between people.

Our next chapter is all about speech. In it, we'll examine words that harm and words that heal.

### *Wisdom Worship*

Find a quiet place and prepare your heart for grateful worship.

 Turn to Psalm 119:129-144 in your Bible and pray the passage aloud.

## Karla's Creative Connection

*If you falter in a time of trouble, how small is your strength!*

Proverbs 24:10

I spent my first few years of walking with God in Alaska. His presence with me was so real, and our relationship was so close. His words jumped off the pages of my Bible, and I wrote them on the tablets of my heart, clinging to his promises and devoting myself to prayer. Before knowing him, I said I would never go to church. Now I wanted to be there whenever the doors were open. I learned a few praise songs on my guitar and couldn't stop singing. My life wasn't perfect, but I knew my Jesus, and he knew me, and that's all that mattered. My faith was rock solid...or so I thought.

Then we moved back to the lower 48, and my entire life fell apart. I had brought with us a girl whose parents said they didn't want her. But I didn't know her well enough, and within one year, she almost destroyed my relationships with my daughter, my husband, and God. It was the most traumatic and painful year I'd experienced since my mother legally disowned me.

I was devastated. At that time, I honestly didn't believe that God would allow something as painful as this to happen to one of his children. I'd heard he wouldn't give you more than you could handle, but I was sinking into a deep depression and felt close to the edge of giving up. My rock-solid faith was shattering into a million heartbreaking shards, but where else was I to go? To whom else could I run?

No one wants to hear that their strength is weak or their faith is puny. And no one wants to admit that they've lost courage during times of adversity. But the reality is that sometimes we're so hard hit by the battles we face that we do get knocked down. And maybe that's you today.

If so, imagine yourself in a boxing ring with the enemy of your soul. He's hitting you with one struggle after another, and you're so hurt and tired that you just can't take another blow. You feel yourself going down, and then you hear the referee standing over you counting—10...9...8...7...You've been hurt, and you can't get up.

But then you hear Jesus. He's cheering you on! You reach up and take his hand, and he pulls you to your feet. You look down and see that you're not standing on your rock-solid faith but on the rock-solid promises of God. He didn't give you more than you could handle *with his help*. Holding on to Jesus, you find the strength to finish the fight and win the victory, for God has already declared you an overcomer in Christ!

*Karla*

## Chapter 9

# Proverbs 25:15–28:28
## Words That Harm and Words That Heal

How can I speak healing words?

WITHOUT WOOD A FIRE GOES OUT; WITHOUT A GOSSIP A QUARREL DIES DOWN.

PROVERBS 26:20

## Day 1

### Too Early in the Morning

I'm a morning person, and my husband is a night person. Our first day back from our honeymoon, I bounded up from bed and waited for Clay to open his eyes. As soon as he did, I cheerily called out, "Good morning!"

He covered his head with the bedsheet.

Later, he explained he's groggy in the morning, and he asked me to wait to talk until he spoke first. So the next day, I waited until he said something before again calling out, "Good morning!"

He covered his head with his pillow.

Later, he asked if I could speak more quietly until after he'd had his bowl of Wheaties with honey and was no longer groggy.

From this exchange I learned that not everyone appreciates loud, cheery greetings in the morning. In fact, many find them annoying. (And as we'll soon see, there's a proverb about this.)

Now I wake Clay each morning by turning on a dim light, turning off the fan, and kissing his forehead. In other words, I had to learn how to speak in a way that blessed him.

I'm not alone. Clay discovered that trying to engage me in deep conversations near bedtime wasn't worth the effort. Extroverted people who are used to rescuing shy people in stalled conversations discover that, in small group discussions, those with prepared answers want to share too. Introverted people accustomed to keeping mum learn that good relationships require vulnerable sharing. Those who grew up in talkative families come to realize most people don't like constant interruptions. Those who grew up in quiet families must figure out how to interject. Speech coaches reveal talking tics and distracting mannerisms. Whew! It's a lot.

Thankfully, Proverbs guides us on communicating graciously.

1. ♥ What's a speech habit you moderated because others weren't blessed by it?

## The Little Details
### For Budding Poets

This lesson's ending poem uses **syllabic verse**. That means the number of syllables per line in the first stanza must be matched in the following stanzas. The example uses this form:

- Line 1: one syllable
- Line 2: three syllables
- Line 3: eight syllables
- Line 4: seven syllables
- Line 5: five syllables
- Line 6: three syllables

After you're satisfied with the poem's lines, use indents to flow the lines in a manner that pleases your eye.

## God's Word to Us in Proverbs

Today's reading looks at more proverbs of Solomon collected by Hezekiah's men.

> 🗨 Take a moment to pray for insight as you read God's Word.

2. ♥ Read Proverbs 25:15–28:28. (a) What stood out to you in your reading? Why? (b) How can you apply that insight to your life this week?

## Like Flies at a Picnic

This chapter will uncover good and bad speech habits. We'll start by looking at practices that aren't necessarily sinful but can be as annoying to others as flies buzzing around their picnic potato salad. So let's look at a few irritations Proverbs pinpoints.

3. In these proverbs, wavy-underline three annoying types of communication.

> 25:20 Like one who takes away a garment on a cold day,
> or like vinegar poured on a wound,
> is one who sings songs to a heavy heart.
> 27:2 Let someone else praise you, and not your own mouth;
> an outsider, and not your own lips.
> 27:14 If anyone loudly blesses their neighbor early in the morning,
> it will be taken as a curse.

Happy *songs* or saying, "Smile! It can't be that bad," are both insensitive and inappropriate. (*Wound* can also be translated *soda*. Mixing vinegar and soda makes both useless because they bubble until only salty water is left, neutralizing each other.)

Boasting attempts to boost one's reputation but makes the boaster appear needy or arrogant. The praise of an *outsider* carries more value than that of one's mama.

The phone ringing before one has arisen from bed is even more unwelcome than a morning person's talkativeness to a night person (like my cheery greetings to Clay).

As we see in Proverbs 26:2, another type of speech that's annoying to hear is cursing.

4. Underline what we should remember if someone curses at us.

> 26:2 Like a fluttering sparrow or a darting swallow,
> an undeserved curse does not come to rest.

Only God's words are powerful enough to effectually *curse*. Nonetheless, James 3:10 exhorts us, "Out of the same mouth come praise and cursing. My brothers and sisters, this should not be."

That's it for today. In this lesson, we discovered pesky habits we can start to break. In our next lesson, we'll see what Proverbs says about honesty.

## Pam's Simply Beautiful Wisdom

*Gracious words are a honeycomb, sweet to the soul and healing to the bones.*

Proverbs 16:24

God's Spirit works in connection with God's Word and your heart. Often, something in the Bible will be exactly what you need to gain access to the next step. When God sends these gracious words, they result in *healing*: a pleasant, soothing, tranquil remedy.

During a significant career change, Bill and I found ourselves off rhythm with each other. He had transitioned from senior staff at a megachurch to full-time ministry leadership with me at Love-Wise. I was excited to have him, his valuable skill set, and his incredible talents at the helm as we shifted to being co-directors of our ministry. But it was an emotional transition for Bill; he'd loved his years serving on staff with some of the best and brightest in church ministry.

Just the same, I was thrilled to team with him full-time, and I feverously began jotting down responsibilities and tasks for him to manage. Basically, my first error was welcoming him with a long "Honey, Please Do" list. His movement on the list was less than enthusiastic. I knew that, with his pastor's heart, Bill was grieving church ministry, but I found myself frustrated by the many tasks remaining on his to-do list.

Under the surface, old baggage from my upbringing fueled the unfounded fear that Bill might let me down. Bill was frustrated by what seemed to him unrealistic expectations. His old baggage stoked an unsubstantiated concern that he would never be able to live up to my growing demands.

With an underlying cooling of the temperature of our relationship, I prayed that God would show me who needed to change and own the issue. I secretly hoped it would be Bill, so I'd get a heartfelt apology. I could then valiantly forgive him, and I wouldn't have to change my to-do list for him!

Then I went to the gym, and some wonderfully irritating insight came as I was listening to the *New Testament Experience* piped into my headphones: "As a prisoner for the Lord, then, I urge you to live a life worthy of the calling you have received. Be completely humble and gentle; be patient, bearing with one another in love. Make every effort to keep the unity of the Spirit through the bond of peace" (Ephesians 4:1-3).

God's Spirit gently asked me, *Have you been humble toward Bill? Or have you already decided this has to be his fault? Have you been gentle? Patient? Have you been bearing with him and the pile of responsibilities on his list coming from all different directions? When was the last time you said "Thank you" instead of emailing him requests? Pam, have you made every effort to bless your husband? Every effort to encourage him? Every effort to lower his stress? Every effort to meet his emotional needs? You are a relationship specialist, so, Pam, pause for a moment, right here in this gym, and pray. Ask me what you can do for Bill that will help him feel my love, my plan, my hope. The way to your hope, Pam, is to give Bill hope.*

I went home, wrapped my arms around my husband, and with compassion said, "I'm so sorry for pressing you, being so demanding and abrupt in our work conversations. I trust you and God to handle the work priorities your way, in your timing. I love you."[1]

Bill explains what happened soon after my apology to him:

> Ephesians 6:17 tells us that the word of God is "the sword of the Spirit." The Holy Spirit utilizes the words of the Bible to guide our steps. As you spend time reading and hearing the Bible, you will notice that some verses seem to jump off the page: some help you feel better about yourself and about life while

others disturb you and make you aware of some area of your life that God wants to change. As you pay attention to these verses, God interactively leads you toward His best plan for you.

For instance, the significant career transition above, was one of the hardest transitions in my life because I was good at what I did and loved church ministry. I also love what Pam and I do together in Love-Wise but it required new skills and a new learning curve. I was anxious about the process and was seeking confirmation from God. During this search, I read Psalm 32:8-9: "I will instruct you and teach you in the way you should go; I will counsel you with my loving eye on you. Do not be like the horse or the mule, which have no understanding but must be controlled by bit and bridle or they will not come to you."

As soon as I read it, two thoughts flooded my mind. The first was, Jesus has taken a personal interest in leading me through this transition in my life (*Wow!*). The second was, I am stubborn and I need to change (*Ouch!*). I was faced with the choice: cooperate with God and gain a blessing or fight the change and experience a long hard journey.[2]

Bill then practiced what he preaches, owned his issue, and apologized to me for his stubbornness. Through the Spirit's prompting and pointing out needed growth in each of our lives, healing came to our relationship.

### Experiencing Scripture Creatively (Optional)

Consider these suggestions for creatively engaging with Scripture.

- Follow Karla's steps at the chapter's end for creatively avoiding gossip.
- Form an answer into syllabic verse. This example is from question 27:

*Syllabic verse by Jean concerning Proverbs 11:12; 17:14; 20:3; 26:17.*
Sense
  the fool lacks
    when his neighbor he derides or
    he's quick to quarrel and fight,
      starting arguments
  on the fly.

Sense
  the wise has
    and honor when avoiding strife;
    understanding holds his tongue
      and he is quick to
  drop matters.

Sense
  meddlers spurn
    when they plunge unheeding into
    quarrels they don't belong in—
      like grabbing stray dogs
  by the ears.

## Day 2

## To Tell the Truth

"Don't ever talk about Jesus again!" my grandmother commanded, her blue eyes sharp. Knowing she and Grandpa were atheists, I'd begun to share the gospel with them. Grandma could be gruff, so I prayed that I'd get a chance to talk to Grandpa alone sometime. He was quiet and soft-spoken, so I thought he might listen.

Many years later I learned they hadn't always been atheists. They and Grandpa's brother Lowell and Grandma's sister Vera (who were married to each other) had all attended church together. But one day church funds went missing, and the pastor blamed Lowell, who was the church treasurer. The truth eventually came out; the pastor had stolen the money. But my grandparents abandoned church and belief in God.

### God's Heart on Honesty

The ninth of the Ten Commandments God gave Moses reads, "You shall not give false testimony against your neighbor" (Exodus 20:16). And through Moses, God gave many further commands that expand on how to apply this one to everyday life (see sidebar). The New Testament likewise exhorts us, "Do not lie to each other, since you have taken off your old self with its practices" (Colossians 3:9). In other words, God highly values truthfulness. Proverbs not only reflects this but explains why.

**The Little Details**
*Leviticus 19:11-16 on the Ninth Commandment:*
Do not lie.

Do not deceive one another.

Do not swear falsely by my name and so profane the name of your God. I am the LORD…

Do not pervert justice; do not show partiality to the poor or favoritism to the great, but judge your neighbor fairly.

Do not go about spreading slander among your people.

5.  To the left of each attribute below, write the letter of the result that goes with it (Proverbs 12:19, 22). Each proverb lists two attributes. Each attribute has one unique result.

| | Attribute | Result |
|---|---|---|
| | Lying lips | A. Endure forever |
| | Lying tongues | B. Last only a moment |
| | Trustworthy people | C. The LORD delights in |
| | Truthful lips | D. The LORD detests |

### Disastrous Dishonesty

On December 4, 2016, an armed man entered the Comet Ping Pong pizza restaurant. He'd read on social media that the restaurant's owner, James Alefantis, and Hillary Clinton were running a satanic child sex abuse ring in the restaurant's basement. He shot the padlock off a closet, damaging computer equipment. But he found no captive children. Indeed, the restaurant didn't even have a basement. He surrendered to police and pled guilty to weapons and assault charges, receiving a four-year prison sentence.[3] Dubbed Pizzagate, spiteful slander hurt not just the people it named but also those who believed its lie. Proverbs explains why people invent dangerous deceptions.

6.  To the left of each type of people below, write the letter of the action that goes with it (Proverbs 10:18; 17:4; 26:18-19, 28). Each people type matches one unique action.

| | Type of People | Actions |
|---|---|---|
| | Deadly deceivers | A. Claim "I was only joking" |
| | Lying fools | B. Hate those they hurt |
| | Those with lying tongue | C. Hide hatred and spread slander |
| | Wicked liars | D. Listen to deceit and destructive speech |

## The Little Details
### *Jeremiah 9:3-8 on Dishonesty's Harm:*

"They make ready their tongue like a bow, to shoot lies; it is not by truth that they triumph in the land. They go from one sin to another; they do not acknowledge me," declares the LORD. "Beware of your friends; do not trust anyone in your clan. For every one of them is a deceiver, and every friend a slanderer. Friend deceives friend, and no one speaks the truth. They have taught their tongues to lie; they weary themselves with sinning. You live in the midst of deception; in their deceit they refuse to acknowledge me," declares the LORD.

Therefore this is what the LORD Almighty says:

"See, I will refine and test them, for what else can I do because of the sin of my people? Their tongue is a deadly arrow; it speaks deceitfully. With their mouths they all speak cordially to their neighbors, but in their hearts they set traps for them."

In 26:28, *lying tongue* is parallel to *flattering mouth*; both dupe and damage the deceived.

> 7.  Fill in the blanks from the Proverbs verses to the left.
>
>    26:23 Fervent lips with an evil heart are like _____ .
>    24   Enemies _____ themselves with their words.
>         They harbor_____ in their hearts.
>    25   Don't believe their_____ .
>    26   They conceal malice by_____ .

*Coating* cheap pottery with *silver* tricks others into believing it's valuable. Likewise, *charming speech* disguises *deceit* and *abominations*. Today, social media allows slanderers to anonymously spread malicious lies that masquerade as moral missions.

### Honesty's Value

Initially, our foster children didn't trust us. After all, they'd been lied to many times. So we let them know we would not lie to them, and that eventually gave them more security than they'd grown up with.

Security around those you trust opens doors for healing. As a child, I knew Grandma and my parents lied. Since they weren't Christians, they had to set their own standards of morality. Naturally, sometimes they thought deception was best, but catching them in lies left me never knowing what to believe. Sometimes I believed lies.

When I dated Clay, though, we were both committed to honesty. That gave me security. Trusting what he said enabled me to replace many of the lies I grew up believing with healing truth. As Jesus said, "If you hold to my teaching, you are really my disciples. Then you will know the truth, and the truth will set you free."[4]

> 8.  To the left of each state below, write the letter of the comparison that goes with it (Proverbs 19:22; 21:6; 24:26). Each state has one unique match.
>
> | | State | Comparison |
> |---|---|---|
> | | Being poor | A. Is better than being a liar |
> | | Having a fraudulently gained fortune | B. Is fleeting and a snare |
> | | Receiving an honest answer | C. Is like a kiss |

A *liar* harms the community, while faithful friends are *honest*. Gaining *riches* through fraud is a *deadly snare*, not just if the fraud is found out but also at the final judgment.

### *In the Courtroom*

For justice to be served, courts require the testimony of honest witnesses.

> 9.  Compare honest witnesses with false witnesses (Proverbs 12:17; 14:5, 25; 19:5, 9; 21:28).
>
> | Honest Witnesses | False Witnesses |
> |---|---|
> | | |

The Old Testament law reflects the importance of honest witnesses by commanding this:

"The judges must make a thorough investigation, and if the witness proves to be a liar, giving false testimony against a fellow Israelite, then do to the false witness as that witness intended to do to the other party" (Deuteronomy 19:18-19). A *truthful witness saves lives* when the innocent are freed. But a *false witness will perish* if accusing someone of something that would bring the death penalty if believed.

In chapter 8, I described two members of animal control taking witness statements. Later, we received an official report to review. I corrected an incorrect address, filled in a few missing details, signed it, and returned it.

---

**10.** Fill in the blanks using the verses from Proverbs to the left.

19:28 Corrupt witnesses _____ at justice

25:18 Givers of false testimony are like _____

---

Jesus gives this assurance to those who face persecution: "There is nothing concealed that will not be disclosed, or hidden that will not be made known" (Matthew 10:26). Sometimes corrupt witnesses are believed, but the final judgment will reveal all.

---

**11.** Use Proverbs 25:7-10 to fill in the two actions that can bring shame in lawsuits.

Don't sue _____ over what you've seen.

Don't _____ when suing.

---

Make sure you know all the facts before you head to court.

### At Work

People want to know whether those with whom they do business are trustworthy.

---

**12.** To the left of each attribute, write the letter of the result that goes with it (Proverbs 16:13; 17:7). Each verse lists two attributes. Each attribute has one unique match.

| | Attribute | Result |
|---|---|---|
| | Eloquent lips | A. Kings take pleasure in |
| | Honest lips | B. Kings value |
| | Lying lips | C. Unsuited to a godless fool |
| | Right speech | D. Unsuited to a ruler |

---

## Promises, Promises

You probably know which of your friends and relatives keep promises. Broken promises harm relationships while kept promises strengthen them.

---

**13.** Why is it important to consider before agreeing to do something (Proverbs 20:25; 25:14)?

---

Southern California needs winter and spring rains to fill reservoirs. If clouds blow in but don't deposit moisture, the following summer we'll face drought, water rationing, and fires. Those who boast of gifts they don't give are like such clouds.

### The Little Details
### *Dealing with False Witnesses in Psalms*

Some are shocked at so-called curses in the psalms, such as Psalm 109:9: "May his children be fatherless and his wife a widow." What's missing, though, is an understanding of the law of Moses.

David's prayer says that "wicked and deceitful" men have falsely accused him of something that carries the death penalty (verses 2, 31). According to Deuteronomy 19:18-19, if someone falsely accuses another, the penalty that would have befallen the victim is what the false witness must receive. David asks for the accuser to stand trial and "when he is tried, let him be found guilty" (verse 7).

Thus, "May his children be fatherless and his wife a widow" is merely a poetic way of praying that what the accuser attempted to bring upon David would fall on him instead. In other words, since he falsely accused David of something that would deserve death, may the accuser be found guilty of false testimony and punished with death.

**The Little Details**

*Hillary Morgan Ferrer on Teaching Kids to Spot Partial Truths:*

Truth is powerful, and the most potent lies are wrapped in partial truths. If a spoonful of sugar helps the medicine go down, then partial truths help the lies go down. [Telling children that books or movies are either] all safe [or all] dangerous...teaches kids that lies are easy to spot. The chew-and-spit method teaches them that most lies are wrapped in attractive packages.

Being a Mama Bear isn't limited to protecting your kids from the dangers in this world, although that is part of it. The best Mama Bears *teach their kids how to spot danger on their own* and avoid it! We here at Mama Bear Apologetics use the ROAR method. ROAR is an acronym for;

**R**ecognize the message

**O**ffer discernment (affirm the good and reject the bad)

**A**rgue for a healthier approach

**R**einforce through discussion, discipleship, and prayer[5]

14. ♥ How has honesty in your relationships helped you?

In this lesson, we saw that God delights in honesty and hates lies. Honesty gives relationships trust and security. Courtrooms and employers value honesty. Keeping promises is part of being trustworthy. Our next lesson explores speech to avoid.

## *Day 3*

# Oops—I Shouldn't Have Said That

We turn now to harmful speech. You'll recognize wicked words that have been said about you—and perhaps even by you. So as we read, let's pray for those who've hurt us and thank God for grace over times we've hurt others. Remember Jesus's words, "Forgive us our debts, as we also have forgiven our debtors" (Matthew 6:12).

### The Good and the Bad

Let's begin by comparing words that heal with words that harm.

15. Compare the effects of the words of the righteous and wicked (Proverbs 11:9, 11; 12:6).

| Words of the Righteous Do This | Words of the Wicked Do This |
| --- | --- |
|  |  |

Though the *godless destroy*, the *righteous escape through knowledge* when truth stops slander. The *mouth of the wicked* destroys through malicious gossip, scandalous slander, and outright lies. For example, the wicked King Saul falsely accused David of treason and sent soldiers to *lie in wait for blood*, but David proved his innocence when he spared Saul's life and Saul confessed in front of his soldiers that he had lied (1 Samuel 24:17). This is an example of how the *speech of the upright rescues them*.

### Sneers and Jeers

Remember junior high and all the put-downs and taunts?

16. In Proverbs 17:5 below, wavy-underline the two actions we should not take. Wavy-circle the reasons.

> 17:5 Whoever mocks the poor shows contempt for their Maker;
> whoever gloats over disaster will not go unpunished.

God does not want us mocking or gloating over people, because he made them in his image. The one who *mocks the poor* may, like Job's mistaken pals, think that poverty proves impiety.

17. In the proverb below (ESV), underline what's better. Wavy-underline what's worse.

> 19:1   Better is a poor person who walks in his integrity
>        than one who is crooked in speech and is a fool.

*Crooked in speech* refers to deception and lack of integrity. Here we see that poverty is not, therefore, a sure-fire sign of divine disfavor.

## Did You Hear?

We come now to words about which Proverbs has much to say: *gossip* and *slander*. *Gossip* is a "rumor or report of an intimate nature."[6] *Slander* is "the utterance of false charges or misrepresentations which defame and damage another's reputation."[7]

Before we read what Proverbs says about these, take a moment to reflect on how you've been affected by them.

18. ♥ Describe a time you were affected by someone's slander or gossip, trying not to use names. How were you affected? What happened to your relationship with the wrongdoer? What do you think motivated the words? Has that experience caused you to be more careful about your own words? Explain.

So what motivates gossipers and slanderers? Yesterday's lesson showed hatred as one cause.[8] But there are others, such as pursuing power and position.[9]

19. What's another reason people gossip (Proverbs 18:8)?

*Choice morsels* are delicious and desirable, and they whet the appetite for more. Gossip is delicious because hearers take pride in knowing more than others. It's desirable because the more scandalous the accusation, the more self-righteous listeners can feel. Indeed, sanctimoniousness likely accounts for the wildfire spread of vile allegations against accomplished celebrities known for niceness. Gossipers seek more gossip to replenish the fading satisfaction of superior knowledge and greater goodness. As an old saying goes, "If you want to know a woman's faults, praise her to her friends."

20. Use Proverbs 11:13 and 20:19 to fill in the blanks.

Gossips _____ .
Trustworthy people_____ .
Avoid those who_____ .

Babblers betray unintentionally. Talebearers relish being in the know. The resentful backstab for revenge. The takeaway: Don't confide in any of them.

21. Wavy-underline what's parallel to "north wind" in Proverbs 25:23 (NRSVUE) below. Wavy-circle what's parallel to "rain." Wavy-underline what we should not do in 30:10 (NRSVUE). Wavy-circle what will happen if you do.

25:23 The north wind produces rain,
      and a backbiting tongue, angry looks.
30:10 Do not slander a servant to a master,
      lest the servant curse you, and you be held guilty.

## The Little Details
### Jesus, James, and Peter on Slander and Gossip

*Mark 7:20-23:* What comes out of a person is what defiles them. For it is from within, out of a person's heart, that evil thoughts come—sexual immorality, theft, murder, adultery, greed, malice, deceit, lewdness, envy, slander, arrogance and folly. All these evils come from inside and defile a person.

*James 1:26:* Those who consider themselves religious and yet do not keep a tight rein on their tongues deceive themselves, and their religion is worthless.

*James 4:11:* Brothers and sisters, do not slander one another. Anyone who speaks against a brother or sister or judges them speaks against the law and judges it. When you judge the law, you are not keeping it, but sitting in judgment on it.

*1 Peter 2:1:* Rid yourselves of all malice and all deceit, hypocrisy, envy, and slander of every kind.

Backbiters anger those who care for the one they're maligning. Falsely accusing a servant (or employee) makes you *guilty*.

Whew. That's a lot of convicting stuff. What can we do if we realize we've been slipping up? The first step is to apologize to anyone who's aware of our hurtful words. The second is to ask God to forgive us and help us not repeat the sin.

We can also do some things to help us avoid sinful speech. The apostle Paul encourages spending more time on godly pursuits, such as raising children. He writes that women who haven't enough to do "learn to be idlers, going about from house to house, and not only idlers, but also gossips and busybodies, saying what they should not."[10] Today, the internet can take gossip into millions of homes.

What helped me control gossiping is deciding that anytime I said something unnecessarily negative about someone, I'd go to the person to whom I had spoken, confess that it was gossip I shouldn't have shared, ask for forgiveness, and then ask the person not to spread it further.

### It's a Fight!

When I read the Gospels for the first time at age 14, I thought, *That Jesus sure argues a lot. No wonder people killed him!* My view was distorted by a relative who argued with people to prove he was smarter than they were (he confided this to me much later). He wasn't using argumentation in a godly way.

### Is Arguing Okay?

According to one of Merriam-Webster's definitions, to *argue* is "to give reasons for or against something."[11] Jesus certainly gave reasons for why people should believe God sent him to save people from their sins. That was a good thing. Indeed, Scripture tells us to do likewise: "Always be prepared to give an answer to everyone who asks you to give the reason for the hope that you have. But do this with gentleness and respect" (1 Peter 3:15).

### Quarrelers, Provocateurs, and Character Attackers

On the other hand, to be *quarrelsome* means one is "apt or disposed to quarrel in an often petty manner."[12] Quarrelsome people may be trying to prove they're smart or always right more than they're trying to prove what they say they're trying to prove. In other words, they lack humility and act out of pride.

*Provocateurs* enjoy getting a rise out of people. One woman told me that when she was a child, her older brother was bigger and knew more than she did, but she could "push his buttons" until he lost his temper. She considered that proof that she was smarter than he was.

Sometimes people who fear they're losing an argument resort to attacking their opponent's character rather than answering the contentions being made. This is called an *ad hominem* attack.[13] When we hear people resort to insults, we can assume they've lost the case they're making but don't want to admit it.

**22.** Using the Proverbs verses cited below, to the far left of the people write the one unique letter matching their description.

| | Verse | People in Verse | Description |
|---|---|---|---|
| | 17:19 | Quarrel lovers | A. Lack self-control |
| | 25:28 | Easy marks for provocateurs | B. Love sin |
| | 29:9 | Fools resorting to *ad hominem* | C. Rage and scoff |

*A high gate* is probably a metaphor for arrogant bragging.[14] In ancient times, *a city whose walls are broken through* left the inhabitants defenseless against raiders. That the *fool rages and scoffs* provides background to the next pair of verses.

**23.** In Proverbs 18:6-7 (ESV) below, box the people described. Wavy-underline what their words ("lips" and "mouth") do.

> 18:6  A fool's lips walk into a fight,
>             and his mouth invites a beating.
> 7  A fool's mouth is his ruin,
>             and his lips are a snare to his soul.

A *fool's mouth invites* a parent, boss, or judge to respond with discipline.

### Offended and Defensive

We've looked at the strife the contentious cause. But what does Proverbs tell us about conflict between those who normally try to avoid it?

**24.** Wavy-circle how the brother feels in Proverbs 18:19 (ESV) below. Wavy-underline what he's like and what quarreling is like.

> 18:19  A brother offended is more unyielding than a strong city,
>             and quarreling is like the bars of a castle.

When we're *offended*, we become defensive. That makes ending a dispute harder. Those who don't forgive often seek revenge through backbiting, thereby compounding the sin of unforgiveness with additional sins (see sidebar).

**25.** Who is more likely to speak harshly (Proverbs 18:23)? ☐ The poor ☐ The rich

As we read in Proverbs 28:11, "The rich are wise in their own eyes." Arrogance can easily lead to speaking *harshly* and not seeking forgiveness. The rich may also believe they have little to lose from belligerence since so many want their favor.

### Stopping Conflict Before It Starts

Now we come to my favorite proverb. In high school, Clay and I started dating on December 15. Later, we read a chapter of Proverbs each day, matching the chapter number to the day of the month. So every monthly anniversary of our first date, the first verse I read was Proverbs 15:1.

### The Little Details
#### Forgiveness

***Matthew 6:14-15:*** If you forgive other people when they sin against you, your heavenly Father will also forgive you. But if you do not forgive others their sins, your Father will not forgive your sins.

***Luke 17:3-4:*** If your brother or sister sins against you, rebuke them; and if they repent, forgive them. Even if they sin against you seven times in a day and seven times come back to you saying "I repent," you must forgive them.

***Romans 12:19:*** Do not take revenge, my dear friends, but leave room for God's wrath, for it is written: "It is mine to avenge; I will repay," says the Lord.

***Colossians 3:13:*** Bear with each other and forgive one another if any of you has a grievance against someone. Forgive as the Lord forgave you.

**The Little Details**

*Ephesians 4:29 (NRSVUE) on Healing Words*

Let no evil talk come out of your mouths but only what is useful for building up, as there is need, so that your words may give grace to those who hear.

**26.** Fill in the blanks from Proverbs 15:1.

15:1  A _____ turns away wrath,

A _____ stirs up anger.

What a life changer this verse was! I had little experience with soft answers during potential conflicts, but I was eager to learn and began practicing. I discovered the proverb was right. Replying gently to upset people often calms them.

**27.** Compare what calms anger with what stirs it up (Proverbs 11:12; 17:14; 20:3; 26:17).

| What Calms Anger | What Stirs Up Anger |
| --- | --- |
|  |  |

People often think they're defending their *honor* when they quarrel, but what's honorable is to *avoid strife* completely. Meddling in other people's conflicts is as dangerous as grabbing *a stray dog by the ears* (another life-changing verse for me).

In this lesson, we compared words that heal with words that harm. We studied mocking, gloating, gossip, and slander. We discovered that Scripture commends arguing (giving reasons for beliefs) but condemns quarrels, provocations, and character attacks. We finished with ways to stop conflict before it starts. Next, we'll discover healing words and seven godly communication skills.

## *Day 4*

## Talk This Way

As the ambulance sped toward the ER with its sirens blaring, Grandma and Grandpa held hands. In their nineties now, they said, "This is it. We always wanted to go together." Grandma had fallen, and when Grandpa tried to help her up, he fell too.

Clay and I visited Grandpa first. His leg was broken and needed surgery. Clay asked him if he would like to pray. Grandpa scoffed and said, "No!" So much for my belief that Grandma was holding him back. Although the surgery was successful, Grandpa contracted pneumonia and passed away a few days later.

Grandma had suffered a mild stroke that left her unsteady, and she transferred to a long-term care facility. We visited her monthly. Sometimes she was sleeping, but we sang hymns to her, praying their words would reach her. Other residents gathered to listen.

Soon she welcomed our singing even when she was awake. In an unusual moment of clarity one afternoon, she looked wistful as we sang about heaven. Clay asked if she'd like to know she would go to heaven. "Oh, yes!" she replied. We prayed with her, and then she said, "I feel such peace. Now I'm ready to go." Weeks later, heaven greeted her with welcoming arms.

Healing words reversed the harm her former pastor's lie had inflicted.

## Healing Words

Healing words come from those who are righteous and wise.

> **28.** Compare the words of the righteous with those of the wicked (Proverbs 10:11, 20-21).
>
> | Righteous Words | Wicked Words |
> | --- | --- |
> | | |

The *heart* is the intent behind the words.

> **29.** Now compare the words of the wise with those of fools (Proverbs 12:18; 15:2, 7).
>
> | Wise Words | Foolish Words |
> | --- | --- |
> | | |

Godly wisdom promotes healing.

> **30.** What are the words of the wise like (16:23; 18:4)?

The *hearts of the wise* can speak prudently, and in a way that helps others receive *instruction*. *Deep waters* suggests deep wisdom that gushes forth. Hubbard writes, "In a Palestinian setting there can be no higher tribute to helpful speech than to liken it to water, deep at its source, abundant and incessant in its flow."[15]

## Godly Communication Skills

Let's discover seven communication skills that help us impart healing words.

### 1) Listen Up

> **31.** Wavy-underline faulty communication habits in these NRSVUE proverbs.
>
> 18:2 A fool takes no pleasure in understanding
>       but only in expressing personal opinion.
> 18:13 If one gives answer before hearing,
>        it is folly and shame.
> 29:20 Do you see someone who is hasty in speech?
>        There is more hope for a fool than for anyone like that.

Showing no interest in others' thoughts communicates that we don't value people. So our first key to better communication is learning to listen well.

**The Little Details**
*Talking to People About Mistakes*

When my girlfriend Virginia worked in human resources, she advised managers who had to talk to workers about mistakes to say, "Help me understand your decision" or "Help me understand what motivated that decision."

*2) Respond Thoughtfully*

**32.** Instead of answering hastily, what do the righteous do (Proverbs 15:28)?

Thoughtful *answers* tell others we value them. That's our second key.

*3) Ask Questions*

Listening and answering aren't all good communicators do. Another key is knowing how to ask good questions.

**33.** What is one of the goals of communication (Proverbs 20:5)?

People don't always disclose or even know their inner motivations, but an insightful questioner can draw out purposes to help others understand themselves and grow.

*4) Hear All Sides*

**34.** In the NRSVUE Proverbs verse below, underline what must be done when people are involved in a conflict.

18:17 The one who first states a case seems right,
    until the other comes and cross-examines.

When we're discussing something that involves another person, hearing the other side of the story can change everything. While some carefully tell the entire truth, including parts that make them look bad, others merely justify themselves at another's expense.

*5) Interpret Signs*

**35.** To the far left of each praise type in the Proverbs verses cited below, write the one unique letter matching what it reveals.

| Verse | Praise Type in Verse | What It Reveals |
|---|---|---|
| 27:21 | Praise | A. Character |
| 28:4 | Praise of the wicked | B. Speaker has forsaken instruction |
| 29:5 | Flattery | C. Speaker is trying to entrap |

Understanding what people's *praise* reveals about them gives us insights.

*6) Bring Calm*

Proverbs invites us to compare actions that stir conflict with actions that calm it.

**36.** To the far left of each action in the Proverbs verses cited below, write the one letter matching people who act that way. Put a star next to actions you want to take. People types may be repeated.

| Verse | Action Found in Verse | People |
|---|---|---|
| 10:19 | Hold their tongues | A. Fools |
| | Multiply words | B. Mockers |

Chart continues on the next page.

| | Action | | Result |
|---|---|---|---|
| 12:16 | Overlook insults | | C. Sinners |
| | Show annoyance at once | | D. The knowledgeable |
| 12:23 | Blurt out folly | | E. The prudent |
| | Keep knowledge to themselves | | F. The understanding |
| 17:27 | Are even-tempered | | G. The wise |
| | Use words with restraint | | |
| 29:8 | Stir up a city | | |
| | Turn away anger | | |
| 29:11 | Bring calm | | |
| | Give full vent to rage | | |

Knowing how to calm anger and maintain self-control is essential for bringing healing words. When we're secure in our *knowledge*, we can restrain our words and keep our temper. It's when we're insecure that we're likely to get upset and blurt *folly*.

## 7) Talk Less

We've already seen that talking too much risks revealing secrets.

**37.** To the left of each action below, write the letter matching the result that goes with it (Proverbs 13:3; 17:28; 21:23).

| Action | Result |
|---|---|
| Those who guard their lips | A. Are thought wise |
| Those who guard their mouths | B. Avoid calamity |
| Those who keep silent | C. Preserve their lives |

To *guard* what we say avoids embarrassment, hurt, and regret.

## Um, That's Not Right

A few months after we were married, Clay and I had an argument. I don't remember what I said, but I do remember Clay's reply. He quoted Proverbs 12:18: "There is one whose rash words are like sword thrusts."[17] Then he said, "That's you, Jean." And he walked out. That was quite a rebuke. Let's read what Proverbs teaches about rebukes.

**38.** In these NRSVUE Proverbs verses, underline what wise rebukes do and are like.

10:10　Whoever winks the eye causes trouble,
　　　　　but the one who rebukes boldly makes peace.
25:11　A word fitly spoken
　　　　　is like apples of gold in a setting of silver.
12　　　Like a gold ring or an ornament of gold
　　　　　is a wise rebuke to a listening ear.
27:5　　Better is open rebuke
　　　　　than hidden love.
28:23　Whoever rebukes a person will afterward find more favor
　　　　　than one who flatters with the tongue.

*Whoever winks the eye* is someone who either secretly plans malice with an accomplice or winks at another's sin instead of rebuking it. A *word fitly spoken* is like a beautiful ornament, and *listening* is like a *gold* earring on an *ear*. Those who *love* will correct loved ones.

**The Little Details**
*David A. Hubbard on Proverbs 12:23:*

In sizing up people as potential participants in the life of Fuller Seminary, whether as administrators or trustees, I carefully observed their patterns of speech. Obviously, what they said needed to make sense. But I watched for more than that. Did they wait their turn? Did they step on the lines of others? Did they have a need for the last word? Did they try to top everyone else's stories? Did they sound off in their areas of incompetence? Could they say, "I don't know"? Did they repeat themselves badly or wander aimlessly through their subject matter? Persons with these and other verbal liabilities do not usually make it to my team. They are not sensitive enough, not succinct enough, not modest enough, and not gracious enough to work well with others. They waste time, hurt feelings, and shatter morale. They, with the rest of us, need to sit longer at the wise teachers' feet and learn that restraint in communication is essential to prudent speech.[16]

Clay's rebuke stung. I didn't think it was true at first. But after praying, I thought, *If someone who loves me thinks that, then I need to change.* I asked for God's help and started thinking before I spoke when angry. There came a day when Clay said he noticed the change. I'm grateful for the rebuke. I needed it. It helped me grow.

> **39.** ♥ Describe a time when you received a rebuke for which you are now grateful.

### The Blessings of Wise Words

When we speak wisely, we bless others and ourselves. For instance, as I learned to tame my tongue, all my relationships improved. Let's look at more blessings.

> **40.** Fill in the following blanks using the Proverbs verses to the left.
>
> 10:31 From the mouth of the righteous comes the_____ .
> 32 The lips of the righteous know what finds _____ .
> 13:2 From the fruit of their lips people enjoy _____ .
> 15:4 The soothing tongue is a _____ .
> 16:22 Prudence is a _____ .

Hubbard writes, "'*Perverse*' is the opposite of acceptable. It means saying in deliberately distorted, backward, or upside-down ways. Lying, cursing, slandering, and misleading would be its most common forms."[18] The *perverse tongue* should be *silenced* (literally, "cut out"). We experience what comes of our words, whether *good things* or *violence*.

> **41.** Fill in the following blanks using the Proverbs verses to the left.
>
> 12:14 The fruit of their lips fills people with _____ .
> 15:23 Giving an apt reply brings _____ .
> 16:24 Gracious words are _____ to the soul.
> and _____ to the bones.
> 18:20 The harvest of people's lips _____ .
> 21 The tongue has the power of _____ .
> 20:15 Lips that speak knowledge are a _____ .
> 22:11 One who speaks with grace will have the king for a_____ .
> 25:15 Through patience a ruler can be _____
> and a gentle tongue can _____ .

Wise, loving speech brings the speaker *good things.* What *joy* we have when we're able to comfort and encourage. *Gracious words* help others learn and bring *healing.* Seeing others helped leaves the wise *satisfied.* By words gang members and corrupt rulers entice the unsuspecting into ways that bring *death*, but by words the godly may bring them to ways of *life.* Those who *speak* true *knowledge* are a *rare jewel* among speakers. Godly leaders value those possessing a *pure heart* and *grace. Patience* is essential for persuasion, and *gentle* speech for breaking down opposition.

In this lesson, we discovered what healing words sound like, examined seven godly communication skills, noted how rebukes can heal, and saw how developing wise speech blesses us. Next, we'll discover what to do when we're caught in conflict.

---

When we speak wisely, we bless others and ourselves.

---

# Uh-Oh: I'm in a Conflict

Sometimes conflict happens no matter how we try to avoid it. Proverbs has plenty of advice on resolving it, though.

## Resolving Conflict

### Resolving Small Disagreements

> **42.** What's a way to settle minor disputes before they become big ones (Proverbs 18:18)?

A coin toss is a quick arbiter for minor disagreements over things like at what restaurant to have dinner or who goes first in Scrabble. But what about problems in groups where a single person is mocking and causing trouble?

### Resolving Meeting Disrupters

Conflicts between group members is inevitable. If everyone seeks to love others properly, most conflicts settle easily. But not everyone responds to correction.

> **43.** What can be done when a mocker causes strife (Proverbs 22:10)?

Once when Clay was speaking to a large group on "Crusades, Slavery, and the Oppression of Women" at an apologetics conference, a Muslim man constantly interrupted. Several times Clay asked him nicely to hold his comments until the Q&A, but he kept badgering. Finally, a massive man in a bright-yellow shirt emblazoned with the word "POLICE" told him he could leave the easy way or the hard way. He sat there for a moment and then took the easy way and left. In large meetings, a security team sometimes must remove hecklers.

In small groups, if a *mocker* persists in insulting others and refuses to listen to gentle correction, group leaders can ask the person to leave.

### Resolving Conflict When We're at Fault

What if we realize we're the one who's acting inappropriately?

> **44.** In the NRSVUE Proverbs passage below, wavy-underline foolish actions (32ab, 33c). Underline the wise action (32c).
>
> 30:32  If you have been foolish, exalting yourself,
>           or if you have been devising evil,
>           put your hand on your mouth.
> 33    For as pressing milk produces curds
>           and pressing the nose produces blood,
>           so pressing anger produces strife.

If we realize pride has led us to exalt ourselves or that the plans we've been chatting about are wrong, there's an easy answer: Stop talking! Pressing on produces *strife* as surely as over-mixing cream produces butter and pressing a nose too hard produces nosebleeds. We should also apologize where needed.

If we realize pride has led us to exalt ourselves or that the plans we've been chatting about are wrong, there's an easy answer: Stop talking!

**The Little Details**
*Duplicate Proverbs*

You may have noticed that some proverbs are duplicated elsewhere. In three of the five cases, Hezekiah's men included proverbs of Solomon that were already in another collection. Solomon's main collection duplicates a single verse. And a passage from the preamble is repeated in Further Sayings of the Wise.

Here's a list of duplicate proverbs:

- 6:10-11 = 24:33-34
- 14:12 = 16:25
- 18:8 = 26:22
- 21:9 = 25:24
- 22:3 = 27:12

*Resolving Ongoing Conflict*

Earlier we saw that pride is often behind quarrelsomeness. It can also be behind refusing to end conflict. The prideful deny their failures and exaggerate others' faults.

**45.** What would end many serious quarrels (Proverbs 24:28-29)?

We *mislead* with our *lips* when we portray a conflict in a way that excuses our own failings and exaggerates another's shortcomings. Verse 29 explains that verse 28's testimony *without cause* was motivated by revenge. God doesn't give us the go-ahead to *mislead* others about someone, even if that person has lied about us. In fact, he doesn't permit wronging those who have wronged us.

Instead, Jesus commands this: "Love your enemies and pray for those who persecute you, that you may be children of your Father in heaven" (Matthew 5:44-45). If Christians wrong us, we should show them their fault *after* we've forgiven them. Leave revenge to God. He's the only one who knows the heart.

**46.** What else can be done to end a serious conflict (Proverbs 26:20-22)?

The most common revenge is gossip. The bitter tell all what the person with whom they're angry did wrong. They shade the truth here and there, painting the target as an ogre and themselves as innocent, adding slander to the gossip. Their goal is demeaning their foe in others' eyes. But Jesus forbids this in Matthew 18:15-17:

> If your brother or sister sins, go and point out their fault, just between the two of you. If they listen to you, you have won them over. But if they will not listen, take one or two others along, so that 'every matter may be established by the testimony of two or three witnesses.' If they still refuse to listen, tell it to the church; and if they refuse to listen even to the church, treat them as you would a pagan or a tax collector.

Notice he says to tell the church about unrepentant sin. Sometimes Christians try to avoid gossip by warning others away from someone who did something bad, but they don't say what it was. That's not what Jesus calls for. If the person repented, then nothing should be said. If they didn't repent, then the misdeed should be explained. We can't make good decisions if we know only that someone failed in a way the speaker considers worthy of church discipline.

**47.** Underline what we must do when someone apologizes (Proverbs 17:9a). Wavy-underline what we should not do (9b).

> 17:9 Whoever would foster love covers over an offense,
> but whoever repeats the matter separates close friends.

The *matter* shouldn't be repeated to others—that would be gossip—and it should not be repeated to the person: "You always do this." Those who truly forgive *foster love.*

In this lesson we looked at ways to resolve conflict, whether it's small disagreements, disruptions in meetings, tensions we've caused, or ongoing disputes.

## Wisdom's Worth

**48.** ♥ In what way did you apply wisdom from Proverbs to your life this week?

In this chapter we looked at godly speech. We discovered annoying habits, the importance of honesty, words that harm, words that heal, and ways to resolve conflict. In our next chapter we'll see how to improve relationships.

### *Wisdom Worship*

Find a quiet place and prepare your heart for grateful worship. When reading, "for they do not obey your word" (Psalm 119:158), consider the speaker's loathing as being for his foes' abandonment of God's ways.

 Turn to Psalm 119:145-160 in your Bible and pray the passage aloud.

## Karla's Creative Connection

*Without wood a fire goes out; without a gossip a quarrel dies down.*

Proverbs 26:20

For several years we heated our home with only a wood stove, so the truth of this week's key verse brought back a few very real memories. On more than one occasion, we either forgot to add wood to the stove or didn't add enough, and the fire went out. Especially while living in Alaska, with temps dropping well below zero, we definitely suffered the consequences when we didn't stoke the fire.

For us, fire was a necessity and a blessing. But fire can also be incredibly destructive, as we know from all the devastating forest fires we've seen in recent years, destroying both property and people's lives as they burned out of control.

Just as a wood-stoked fire can be a means of blessing or destruction, the words we speak have the power to give life or destroy it, to build others up or tear them down. When we gossip or talk about others behind their backs, sharing secrets or other private information—whether true or not—it can be as devastating to a person's life as an out-of-control forest fire.

I had no idea how horrible gossip could be until I was the object of a malicious talebearer years ago. What shocked me most was how people listened to her gossip and judged me without even knowing me or seeking the truth.

That's why there's so much wisdom in this week's key verse. Solomon's actually telling us not to even listen to the gossiper. If we stop the gossip before we hear it, we save ourselves from being lured into judging unjustly or, even worse, from becoming the next person to spread it. But even more important, if the gossiper has no one who will listen, the gossip ends with them, and the "quarrel" or discord dies.

None of us are spared from hearing gossip these days, but I'm sure you've heard the saying, "If you don't have anything nice to say about a person, don't say anything at all." The apostle Paul says it this way: "Do not let any unwholesome talk come out of your mouths, but only what is helpful for building others up according to their needs, that it may benefit those who listen" (Ephesians 4:29).

So this week I encourage you to creatively connect with God by asking him to show you if you've either heard or spread gossip about someone. However you've participated, first ask God to forgive you, then ask him to help you see that person through his eyes and not your own. Thank God for that person's character qualities that reflect his nature, speaking words of blessing over them, and then pray for them as the Lord leads. You may be surprised at how your attitude toward that person changes.

*Karla*

## Chapter 10

# Proverbs 29:1–31:31
## Neighbors, Friends, and Family

How can we improve our relationships?

### Day 1

## Loving Neighbors

"Can I have candy?" the nine-year-old I'll call Olivia asked. The breeze lifted her straight blond hair and spilled it across her face as we walked through the park.

"No, Olivia," one of us replied. "We're having dinner soon."

"But I want candy *now*!"

"It's not good for you to have candy before dinner. It'll spoil your appetite."

Clay and I were applying a proverb we read in chapter 8: "When you are full, you will refuse honey, but when you are hungry, even bitter food tastes sweet" (Proverbs 27:7 GNT).

"I don't eat vegetables." Olivia scowled, her pale-blue eyes hard like steel and her hands clenched into fists. The counselor at her group home, where they cared for children who couldn't be placed in foster care, had already warned us she didn't eat anything green. We'd been taking her and another girl on weekly outings, and this would be our first dinner together.

"You don't have to eat anything you don't like, Olivia," I said. "But if you do finish your dinner, you may have ice cream afterward."

Her eyes shifted as she considered. "What if I don't finish dinner?"

"Then no ice cream."

She tried a few more times to get us to give in, but we repeated what we'd already said.

She finished her dinner, and we gave her ice cream.

When asked what the greatest commandment was, Jesus replied, "'Love the Lord your God with all your heart and with all your soul and with all your mind.' This is the first and greatest commandment. And the second is like it: 'Love your neighbor as yourself'" (Matthew 22:37-40). But when asked who one's neighbor is, he told the parable of the good Samaritan, showing us a neighbor is anyone, no matter who they are or where they come from, who either helps or needs help (Luke 10:30–37).

195

## The Little Details
### Proverbs 30:1

Translations present the heading to Proverbs 30 differently because ancient Hebrew texts divide the words differently. Most translations provide text notes with alternate interpretations. Bruce K. Waltke writes, "There is little consensus about the meaning of ʾukkāl.[2] Thus, some translate it as a name and others as *worn out* or *prevail*. Here are how the major English-language translations handle it.

***ESV:*** The words of Agur son of Jakeh. The oracle. The man declares, I am weary, O God; I am weary, O God, and worn out.

***NASB:*** The words of Agur the son of Jakeh, the oracle. The man declares to Ithiel, to Ithiel and Ucal.

***NIV:*** The sayings of Agur son of Jakeh—an inspired utterance. This man's utterance to Ithiel: "I am weary, God, but I can prevail."

***NKJV:*** The words of Agur the son of Jakeh, his utterance. This man declared to Ithiel—to Ithel and Ucal:

***NRSVUE:*** The words of Agur son of Jakeh. An oracle. Thus says the man: I am weary, O God, I am weary, O God, and am wasting away.

I admit I'm not the best at meeting and serving neighbors. But caring for children without suitable parents was one way we tried to love our neighbor as ourselves. Since we couldn't have children of our own and did have a stable marriage, this seemed like something we could do that not everyone could.

Our friends have cared for neighbors in other ways, according to their situations and gifts. Families serve meals to the poor. Couples operate food pantries. Men—and women—volunteer as handymen to help widows and the elderly. Both women and men visit the homebound, volunteer to help children read, and serve at pregnancy resource centers.[1] My elderly father-in-law's neighbors invited him to come over anytime, helped him when he couldn't get the television to work, and offered him hot cocoa on cold evenings.

1.  ♥ (a) What's one way you've cared for a neighbor? (b) What's one way a neighbor has cared for you?

We've discovered so much wisdom in the book of Proverbs already. This is our concluding chapter, and in it we'll look at our relationships with neighbors, friends, and family. First, though, we'll read the final three chapters in Proverbs. They're filled with relationship advice.

### God's Word to Us in Proverbs

In today's reading, we'll finish Collection V, which holds the proverbs of Solomon that King Hezekiah's men collected. Then in Proverbs 30 we'll read ***Collection VI: Sayings of Agur***. Here's how the NASB translates this collection's first verse: "The words of Agur the son of Jakeh, the oracle. The man declares to Ithiel, to Ithiel and Ucal" (Proverbs 30:1 NASB). Nothing more is known about Agur or his father. Ithiel and Ucal are his sons or disciples (but see the sidebar).

Proverbs 31 holds ***Collection VII: Sayings of King Lemuel and His Mother***, the final collection. Its first verse identifies the author: "The words of King Lemuel, the oracle which his mother taught him" (Proverbs 31:1 NASB). It's unclear whether the queen mother authored just verses 2-9 or from 2 to the end of the chapter. In verses 2-9 she teaches her royal son how to rule wisely. King Lemuel wasn't a king of Judah or Israel, and we know nothing else about him and his mother. The inspiring poem in verses 10-31 form the epilogue to the book of Proverbs. Its theme is the noble wife, and it displays wisdom in practical action.

Since chapter 31 consists of just two poems, we'll examine it verse by verse, as we did the prologue.

🗨 Take a moment to pray for insight as you read God's Word.

2.  ♥ Read chapters 29–31 in Proverbs. (a) What stood out to you in your reading? Why? (b) How can you apply that insight to your life this week?

## Welcome to the Neighborhood

This chapter is all about relationships: neighbors, friends, and family. Let's start with being a good neighbor.

> **3.** Fill in the blanks from these Proverbs verses.
>
> ¹⁴:²¹ It is a sin to_____ one's neighbor,
> but blessed is the one who is_____ to the needy.
>
> ²⁵:¹⁷ Seldom set foot in your neighbor's_____—
> too much of you and they will_____ you.
>
> ²⁷:¹⁰ Do not forsake your _____
> or a _____ of your family,
> and do not go to your _____ house
> when disaster strikes you—better a _____
> nearby than a_____ far away.

In ancient times, *one's neighbor* lived in the same village, so everyone knew which family might be needy (unlike today's big cities, which have panhandlers no one knows). Verse 25:17 means don't wear out your welcome. The final verse cautions us to preserve friendships and remember that someone *nearby* may help more than family *far away*.

> **4.** ♥ What are ways you try to care for neighbors?

This lesson discussed ways to love our neighbors as ourselves. It also introduced the final two collections in the book of Proverbs. Our next lesson will show us the blessings of good friends and how to find them. We'll also examine the sorrows, joys, and responsibilities of family.

## The Little Details
### For Budding Poets

In the book of Psalms, a **thanksgiving song** gives thanks for answered prayer. It's a form of **praise psalm**. It typically has four elements.

*1) Preliminary Praise:* They usually begin with the psalmist's intention to praise God for something.

*2) Divine Description:* They describe God's attributes, often with more praise.

*3) Dilemma and Deliverance:* They report what was wrong and how God fixed it.

*4) Praise Proclamation:* They praise the Lord for the answer to prayer.[3]

While the song begins with preliminary praise, the other elements can be in any order. If you'd like to write a thanksgiving song, first write sentence prayers for each of the above elements. Then form them into poetic lines (see chapter 7 for details on poetic lines and Psalm 30 for an example).

To learn more about thanksgiving songs, see our book *Discovering Hope in the Psalms.*

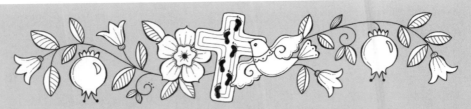

# Pam's Simply Beautiful Wisdom

*The wisest of women builds her house.*

Proverbs 14:1 ESV

*Action, not just intention, brings accomplishment.*

Greg and Julie Gorman[4]

People sometimes ask me, "How did you write and publish more than 55 books, speak almost every week, run a ministry, keep a vibrant marriage, raise three great kids, build a wonderful friendship circle, and keep your home in order?" Honestly, I was inspired long ago by the Proverbs 31 woman. While I recognize this description of a godly woman was penned as a tribute and likely covered her accomplishments throughout her lifetime, one *vital* trait consistently popped off the page as I studied the passage: She didn't just hope, dream, wish, or plan—the girl took *action!*

You've been studying Proverbs 31 in this chapter. Read it again and make note of all the verbs in this famous passage. This excellent wife does her husband good; seeks wool and flax; works with willing hands; brings food; rises while it's still night; provides food for her household; buys a field; dresses herself and her household; makes her arms strong; puts her hand to spindle and distaff; opens hands to the poor and needy; makes bedcoverings, linen garments, and sashes (and runs an "Etsy" store); laughs at the future; teaches kindness; and over all "looks well to the ways of her household and does not eat the bread of idleness" (verse 27 ESV).

For sure!

## The Result

And what is the positive outcome of her proactive action plan?

> Her children rise up and call her blessed;
> her husband also, and he praises her:
> "Many women have done excellently,
> but you surpass them all."
> Charm is deceitful, and beauty is vain,
> but a woman who fears the LORD is to be praised.
> Give her of the fruit of her hands,
> and let her works praise her in the gates (Proverbs 31:28-31 ESV).

In summary...

- Her kids rave about their awesome mom.
- Her husband proclaims her strength, value, talent, and character.
- She's held up as a role model of virtue and godliness, a woman to be praised by people.
- Best yet, her *own works*, those *accomplished tasks*, and the *character developed* in the pursuit provide an extra dose of praise.[5]

Inspired by her diligent action, I thought, *How can I replicate this hardworking woman's get-it-done style?* This was my catalyst to create a "To Do" planning sheet based on the verbs of my life. What do I need to create, buy, mail, plan, pray? Whom do I need to call or message? And so on. Eventually, I turned my planning sheet into the *Get It Done,*

*Girl! Maximizing Your Moments Action Planner* so other women can take action too. Here is a simple acrostic to help you plan your next A.C.T.I.O.N. steps in your spiritual growth:

- **A**sk God: What area of gaining wisdom does God want you to study next?

- **C**lear the "Must Dos": In the next 90 days, what are the major priorities God is calling you to address? Make space on your time schedule to whittle away at those assignments.

- **T**ackle Tough Tasks: Has God been prompting you to address an area, but you want to avoid it or procrastinate? Who can you call in for counsel or accountability?

- **I**nvest in the Future: When my coauthor Jean completes her study of a book of the Bible, she marks that accomplishment by drawing a flower next to it in the Bible's table of contents. She then decides what next book to study. The goal is to work her way through the entire Bible. What book of the Bible is the Lord directing you to next?

- **O**rganize Space and Personal Life: Think about your Sacred Selah Space, a place where you enjoy having your quiet times. Do you have one? Create a space ready for your time with God: Add a basket with various Bible versions; art supplies like colored pens, pencils, and stickers; an inspiring journal; a pillow with a quote; a coffee mug or water bottle displaying a Bible verse.

- **N**urture Those I Love: Is there a relationship God is asking you to invest in—in your marriage or with a child, grandchild, sibling, mentee, or mentor?[6]

Print off the "Sunday Selah" Reflection sheet in the extras for this study and take time each week to pray through your life. Then *take action* and discover your Proverbs-blessed life.

*Pam*

## Experiencing Scripture Creatively (Optional)

If you have extra time, consider these suggestions for creatively engaging with verses from this week's reading. The appendix has more ideas.

- Cut out a bookmark you think would bless a friend or relative from the back of the book. Color it and give it as a gift.

- Follow Karla's instructions at the end of this chapter for meditating on who you are in Christ.

- Form your answer to question 33 into a thanksgiving song, which typically has four parts (see sidebar). Here's an example:

  *A psalm of Jean praising God for help.*
  Praise the Lord for helping us find the lost gift certificate!
  　　It disappeared during dinner.
  We prayed to God for help, and we found it!
  　　Praise God, who gives wisdom and insight to those who ask.

## Day 2

# Friends and Family

"Can you take care of my kids?" Marcus asked over the phone (not his real name). He and his wife were dear to us.

He'd been drug free since he became a Christian a few years before, but one day old friends tricked him into taking cocaine, and he was instantly addicted again. When his wife was hospitalized and he realized his addiction left him unable to care for his 18-month-old daughter and 6-month-old son alone, he checked into drug rehab. But his relative who'd originally agreed to care for his kids had a crisis and needed to back out.

*How will I juggle full-time work and part-time school?* I thought. If I didn't take them, though, he'd have to leave rehab.

"Yes," I said. Soon I had a yellow playpen in the living room and two little ones in my arms. The scent of baby powder lingered in the air. I called Clay and let him know what to expect when he returned from a business trip. Both children slept through the night (thankfully!). I dropped my classes shortly after.

Friends jumped in to help. They answered questions about diaper rash, diarrhea, and day care. They escorted us to kid-friendly restaurants and laughed at our foibles as we tried to feed two kids and ourselves while retrieving hot dog slices and pureed green beans from the floor.

The babes returned home not long after their mom was discharged, but they came back to us when she needed more recovery. When they returned to her permanently, we were sad to see them go but delighted they were in a loving home.

Later, when we took in foster children, family and friends were there for us again. Clay's parents and some friends became certified for babysitting foster children so they could help when we both had to work.

Today we'll discover the perils of bad friends, the blessings of good friends, and the sorrows and joys of family.

## The Blessings of Good Friends

Proverbs 27 describes three blessings of a good friendship.

> 5.  Fill in the blanks from Proverbs 27.
>
>     27:6 _____ from a friend can be trusted, but an enemy multiplies _____ .
>
>     27:9 Perfume and incense bring _____ to the heart, and the _____ of a friend springs from their _____ advice.
>
>     27:17 As iron _____ iron, so one person _____ another.

Proverbs 27 describes three blessings of a good friendship.

A true *friend* will correct us even when it hurts, while an *enemy* pretends affection (as Judas did when he kissed Jesus to betray him[7]). *Advice* from dear friends is a gift. Running thoughts and ideas by *another* improves and hones our thinking. Conflict handled rightly between friends rubs the sharp edges off each one, just as a rock tumbler polishes sharp edges until a rock shines. David wrote, "Let a righteous man strike me—it is a kindness; let him rebuke me—it is oil for my head; let my head not refuse it" (Psalm 141:5 ESV).

> **6.** In these ESV Proverbs verses, underline the kind of friend and sibling we can be.
>
> 17:17   A friend loves at all times,
>       and a brother is born for adversity.
> 18:24   A man of many companions may come to ruin,
>       but there is a friend who sticks closer than a brother.

*A friend who loves at all times* is invaluable. Verse 18:24 is difficult to translate, but it means one reliable *friend* is better than *many* unreliable *companions*.

## The Roadblocks to Finding Faithful Friends

Though most of us desire faithful friends, they're not as common as we'd like.

> **7.** In the Proverbs verses below, box descriptions of people. Wavy-underline what the kind of friend you don't want is like.
>
> 20:6   Many claim to have unfailing love
>       but a faithful person who can find?
> 25:19   Like a broken tooth or a lame foot
>       is reliance on the unfaithful in a time of trouble.

*Many* lack the *love* they *claim* to have. Relying *on the unfaithful* is both painful and useless.

Another obstacle is that being on either end of the wealth spectrum affects who wants to befriend you.

> **8.** Compare how one's wealth or poverty affects relationships (Proverbs 19:4, 6-7).
>
> | The Wealthy | The Poor |
> | --- | --- |
> | | |

While these verses describe *what* happens, they don't claim this is what *should* happen.

## The Considerations When Choosing Friends

So how does one find faithful friends like those who helped me and avoid harmful ones like Marcus's former friends who wanted him back on drugs? Knowing the traits of each helps us not only seek a faithful friend but also to be one.

> **9.** List those with whom we should make friends and those with whom we shouldn't (Proverbs 12:26; 13:20; 14:7; 22:24-25).
>
> | Make Friends with These | Don't Make Friends with These |
> | --- | --- |
> | | |

Though most of us desire faithful friends, they're not as common as we'd like.

Verse 12:26 can be translated that the *righteous* either choose friends carefully (NIV, NKJV) or are a guide to neighbors (ESV, NASB).

> **10.** ♥ What trait did you read about that's most important to you in a friend? Why?

## The Sorrows and Joys of Family

While we choose friends, we inherit family. That means family get-togethers can be fun or frustrating, hilarious or heartbreaking, or all four at once.

> **11.** To the left of each family member below, write the letter of the description that goes with it (Proverbs 11:29; 17:2, 6; 27:8). Verse 17:6 has two family members, the others one. Each family member has one unique description.
>
> | Family Member | Description |
> | --- | --- |
> | Disgraceful children | A. Are a crown to the elderly |
> | Grandchildren | B. Are like birds who flee nests |
> | Parents | C. Are the pride of their children |
> | Those who bring ruin on a family | D. Inherit wind |
> | Those who flee home | E. Will serve a prudent servant |

To *inherit only wind* is to lose one's inheritance and thus need to become an indentured *servant*. In ancient times, a person could adopt a *servant* into the *family* who would then *share the inheritance* that a *disgraceful son* had lost. The *aged* are proud of their grandchildren, and (with the notable exception of many teens) *children* are proud of their *parents*. The one who *flees* (or strays) *from home* loses security.

> **12.** ♥ What is your favorite thing about family?

### The Honor Due Aging Parents

For many, the empty nest years become a time of caring for parents with declining health. Pam and her husband, Bill, sold their home and bought a boat to live on so they could be close enough to care for Bill's parents. When my father-in-law grew confused over finances in his nineties, he asked me to pay his bills. Later, he gave power of attorney for his care to Clay, and we managed all his affairs with help from Clay's sister and brother-in-law and his father's kind neighbors. He wanted to stay in his home, so we hired caregivers to cook his meals and drive him to the grocery store, plant nursery, and church. His friends took him golfing weekly.

As parents age, we have duties toward them.

> **13.** In the Proverbs verses below, wavy-underline how we should *not* treat parents.
>
> 19:26    Whoever robs their father and drives out their mother
>                is a child who brings shame and disgrace.

Family get-togethers can be fun or frustrating, hilarious or heartbreaking, or all four at once.

> 20:20 If someone curses their father or mother,
> their lamp will be snuffed out in pitch darkness.
> 28:24 Whoever robs their father or mother
> and says, "It's not wrong,"
> is partner to one who destroys.
> 30:17 The eye that mocks a father,
> that scorns an aged mother,
> will be pecked out by the ravens of the valley,
> will be eaten by the vultures.

The *child* who *robs* and *drives out* parents describes an adult who takes over his parents' holdings and ejects them. The law cursed the one who *curses* parents.[8] The one who *robs* parents and says it's *not wrong* is justifying the deed because the property would eventually be inherited (for example, if we had used my father-in-law's money for our personal benefit instead of for his care). *The eye that mocks* parents deserves to *be pecked out by the ravens*.

Helping elderly parents breaks our hearts when Mom suffers from Alzheimer's. It challenges our creativity when Dad insists on driving after losing his driver's license. But it brings us joy to hear from those they've blessed who now want to bless them. Family reminds us "a generation goes, and a generation comes" (Ecclesiastes 1:4 ESV). This in turn encourages us to take hold of Colossians 3:1-4 (ESV):

> If then you have been raised with Christ, seek the things that are above, where Christ is, seated at the right hand of God. Set your minds on things that are above, not on things that are on earth. For you have died, and your life is hidden with Christ in God. When Christ who is your life appears, then you also will appear with him in glory.

In this lesson, we looked at the blessings of good friends and how to find them. We also pondered the responsibilities, sorrows, and joys of family. In our next lesson, we'll discover how the noble woman builds a home.

## Day 3

# Building a Home

"Do you know why I always used to ask for candy before dinner?" Olivia asked. For many months after we started seeing the girls, Olivia had whined, pouted, begged, and cajoled before every meal. Finally, she stopped. In time, the two girls moved in with us as foster daughters.

"No, Olivia," I replied. "Why?"

"Because you said it wasn't good for me, but all my other foster parents said it wasn't good for me and then gave in when I bugged them enough. That's how I knew they didn't love me, and I wanted to know if you did."

Wow. Keeping our actions consistent with our words gives children security.

Helping elderly parents breaks our hearts when Mom suffers from Alzheimer's. It challenges our creativity when Dad insists on driving after losing his driver's license.

## The Little Details
### David A. Hubbard on Proverbs 22:6:

This proverb states an accurate principle; it does not offer an absolute promise. Good training almost always brings beneficial results; bad habits almost inevitably spell trouble for those who have acquired them and for those around them. In pastoral ministry we may use this verse to encourage Christian parents whose young people are going through stages of carelessness or rebellion. We ought not to use it to guarantee an automatic return to obedience and faith. Much of the time that will happen through faithful prayer and steady love. Tragically, there are exceptions; they call for special sensitivity toward the despair and disillusionment of disappointed parents.[9]

## Raising Little Ones

As you've surely noticed, Proverbs has much to say about raising children. That's what we'll turn to next. In the following verses, "rod" is a symbol of any type of discipline.

**14.** To the left of each Proverbs verse or passage cited below, write the letter of the reason it gives for disciplining children. Each verse has one unique match.

| Verse | Reason to Discipline Children |
|---|---|
| 13:24 | A. Discipline drives out folly |
| 19:18 | B. Discipline gives children hope |
| 22:15 | C. Discipline saves children's lives |
| 23:13-14 | D. Discipline shows love |

Parental *love* wants the best for children, while *hate* emphasizes that leaving children to their own ways will have disastrous effects later. Many temptations can lead to *death*, such as poor diet, substance abuse, smoking, stealing, and reckless behaviors. *Folly* well describes the selfishness and self-will with which all are born. Parents *discipline* children to *save them from* an early *death* due to foolish behavior.

**15.** Fill in what parents of disciplined and undisciplined children find (Proverbs 29:15, 17).

| Parents of Disciplined Kids Find | Parents of Undisciplined Kids Find |
|---|---|
| | |

From public temper tantrums to failing grades to an eventual failure to launch, *undisciplined* children embarrass parents.

### Train Up a Child?

"Train up a child in the way he should go and he won't depart from it," said my 20-something single coleader to a mom who'd asked for prayer for her rebellious teenage son. Ouch. I quickly said, "You know, people interpret that verse differently, and it doesn't mean parents of rebellious kids aren't good parents." When I called the mom later, she said, "If you hadn't said something, I would never have come back."

**16.** ♥ What are ways you've heard Proverbs 22:6 (ESV, below) interpreted?

> 22:6 Train up a child in the way he should go;
> even when he is old he will not depart from it.

☐ A promise that if you raise children correctly, they will never stray from faith and will be loving, near-perfect adults

☐ A promise that if children accept Jesus but later abandon faith, they will return to faith when old

☐ A general truism that training children according to their gifts and abilities has a lasting effect

☐ A general truism that training children to walk wisely has a lasting effect

I've heard all of these, and you may have too. But the proverb is not about faith in Jesus, for it was written before Jesus's time. It isn't a promise about faith in general either, for Josiah was the most righteous king in all of Israel and Judah, zealously establishing God's ways, but his sons were wicked.[10] Additionally, proverbs are general truisms, not promises. While the third option is popular, the last is the clearest reading and fits well with other proverbs that tell parents to train their children to walk wisely (see two sidebars). In other words, the proverb encourages parents that their perseverance has lasting effects.

It's important, however, to remember that some children foolishly refuse training. Many proverbs lament this. So if you have a rebellious child, don't beat yourself up. Acknowledge any mistakes to God, accept his grace, and pray constantly for your straying loved one.

## The Sorrows and Joys of Parenting

As foster parents, we experienced many joys but also many heartaches. One evening after a particularly difficult day, Clay went for a walk to pray among the wooden skeletons of a housing tract being built on the hill above us. He prayed, *Lord, what if these girls never come to know you?* He immediately sensed an answer: *Then you will know the fellowship of my suffering* (Philippians 3:10).

When Clay returned and told me the story, I thought, *How does Jesus feel when people reject him or choose wrong ways? Probably something similar to what we're feeling now.* After that, whenever the girls brought us sorrow, that verse comforted me. Parenting brings its share of sorrows, but by it we know the fellowship of Jesus's sufferings.

> **17.** In the Proverbs verses below, box the people with their descriptors. Underline what wise offspring bring their parents. Wavy-underline what the foolish bring.
>
> 10:1   A wise son brings joy to his father,
>         but a foolish son brings grief to his mother.
>
> 15:20   A wise son brings joy to his father,
>         but a foolish man despises his mother.
>
> 17:21   To have a fool for a child brings grief;
>         there is no joy for the parent of a godless fool.
>
> 17:25   A foolish son brings grief to his father
>         and bitterness to the mother who bore him.
>
> 28:7   A discerning son heeds instruction,
>         but a companion of gluttons disgraces his father.
>
> 29:3   A man who loves wisdom brings joy to his father,
>         but a companion of prostitutes squanders his wealth.

These passages refer to children who are teens and older. Their message: A *fool* who has rejected discipline or was undisciplined *brings grief* to the family.

### What Brings Parents Joy

But parenting also brings joy.

> **18.** In the Proverbs verses below, fill in the blanks with traits that bring parents joy to see in their children.
>
> 23:15   My son, if your heart is _____ ,
>       then my heart will be_____ indeed;

## The Little Details
### Allen P. Ross on Proverbs 22:6:

In recent years it has become popular to interpret this verse to mean that the training should be according to the child's way. The view is not new; over a thousand years ago Saadia suggested that one should train the child in accordance with his ability and potential. The wise parent will discern the natural bent of the individual child and train it accordingly... Training in accordance with a child's natural bent may be a practical and useful idea, but it is not likely what this proverb has in mind.

In the book of Proverbs there are only two "ways" a child can go: the way of the wise and the righteous, or the way of the fool and the wicked. Moreover, it is difficult to explain why a natural bent needs training. Ralbag, in fact, offered a satirical interpretation: "Train the child according to his evil inclinations (let him have his will) and he will continue in his evil way throughout life."[11]

## The Little Details
### Joy Over Spiritual Children

*3 John 4 (ESV):* I have no greater joy than to hear that my children are walking in the truth.

*1 Thessalonians 2:19-20 (ESV):* For what is our hope or joy or crown of boasting before our Lord Jesus at his coming? Is it not you? For you are our glory and joy.

*1 Thessalonians 3:8-10 (ESV):* For now we live, if you are standing fast in the Lord. For what thanksgiving can we return to God for you, for all the joy that we feel for your sake before our God, as we pray most earnestly night and day that we may see you face to face and supply what is lacking in your faith?

16 my inmost being will _____
when your lips speak what is _____ .

23:22 _____ to your father, who gave you life,
and _____ your mother when she is old.

23 Buy the _____ and do not sell it—
_____ as well.

24 The father of a _____ child has great joy;
a man who fathers a _____ son rejoices in him.

25 May your father and mother _____ ;
may she who gave you birth be _____

27:11 Be _____ , my son, and bring joy to my heart!
then I can answer anyone who treats me with _____ .

A *heart* that is *wise* lives rightly, and speech that *is right* is honest. Parents rejoice in offspring who get *truth, wisdom, instruction,* and *insight.* Parents and teachers face criticism about teaching methods that a *wise* offspring or pupil can dispel.

### Setting the Tone

We can do much to set the tone in our homes. Kind speech, apologies when we're wrong, respecting our spouses, and not disparaging our spouses are essential.

### Don't Be This Woman

**19.** What is a quarrelsome wife like (Proverbs 19:13; 27:15-16)?

Family members with whom we live affect our well-being, whether it's a *foolish child* or a *quarrelsome* wife. The latter is a constant irritant that a husband can't restrain.

**20.** To the far left of each better situation below, found in the Proverbs verses cited, write the letter of the situation that's worse. Each better situation matches one unique worse situation.

| | Verse | Better Situation | | Worse Situation |
|---|---|---|---|---|
| | 17:1 | Eating a dry crust in peace and quiet | A. | Feasting with strife |
| | 21:9 or 25:24 | Living on a corner of the roof | B. | Living with a quarrelsome and nagging wife |
| | 21:19 | Living in a desert | C. | Sharing a house with a quarrelsome wife |

Meals shouldn't be times of *strife.* The *quarrelsome wife* nags, complains, brings up old failures, and argues over all decisions. The *corner of the roof* is likely a small guest room built on a roof, such as the one the Shunammite woman built for Elisha.[12] (Solitude is better than being with such a person, so both men and women should choose their spouse wisely and cultivate kindness and respect at home.)

*Be This Woman*

What kind of woman should we strive to be, then?

21. To the left of each type of wife below, write the letter of the description that matches it (Proverbs 12:4; 14:1). Each verse has two wives. Each wife has one unique match.

| Type of Wife | Description |
|---|---|
| Disgraceful | A. Builds her house |
| Foolish | B. Is her husband's crown |
| Noble | C. Is like decay in a husband's bones |
| Wise | D. Tears her house down |

*Noble* can also be translated *excellent* and is "a many-splendored word that begins by meaning 'strength' and then branches out to include 'ability,' 'merit,' and 'reputation.'"[13] *Decay in his bones* means this wife's flaws destroy her husband's strength and happiness. The *wise woman* embodies all we've read in Proverbs about wisdom, while the *foolish one* embraces folly to the detriment of her family.

22. ♥ What's one way you try to set the tone in your home with family or friends?

In this lesson, we looked at how to build a godly home. We read advice on raising children, parenting, and setting a good tone in our homes. In the next lesson, we'll discover how a noble woman builds her house.

## *Day 4*

## The Noble Woman

My mom often called me into the kitchen to help her cook, and she taught me many fundamentals. Once I mastered white sauce, she handed over all sauce-making to me.

I wanted to pass on basic life skills to each of our three foster girls, so we had them alternate cooking with me and cleaning with Clay. I sent them out to my backyard herb garden, telling them to smell each plant and pick whichever they thought would go best with the night's veggies. Giving them that task gave them ownership of how meals turned out and made them more likely to enjoy the vegetables that night.

That and ensuring we always had ice cream and fruit juice popsicles for any child who finished her dinner encouraged them to try lots of foods. Indeed, only once did Olivia not finish a meal and so went without dessert.

23. ♥ Which household tasks did someone teach you? Which have you passed on to someone younger than you?

Proverbs 31 begins with King Lemuel's mother passing on life skills to him.

## The Little Details
### *Ruth, a Noble Woman*

In some Hebrew Bibles, the book of Ruth immediately follows Proverbs 31, where it provides a vivid example of another noble woman, this time a penniless widow.

As the story begins, Ruth is a widowed Moabite caring for her Jewish mother-in-law, Naomi, after Naomi loses her husband and both sons. Ruth goes with Naomi to Naomi's former town in Judah, saying, "Your people will be my people and your God my God" (Ruth 1:16).

One way the law of Moses provided for the poor was instructing farmers not to harvest to the end of their fields. Instead, they were to leave grain for the poor to glean. Ruth takes on the demanding work. As she toils, she catches the eye of the landowner, Boaz. He makes sure she has plenty of food to take back to Naomi.

The law also provided for male relatives to "redeem" childless widows by marrying them, buying the deceased's property, and giving the widow an heir to inherit the property. Naomi's relative Boaz redeems Ruth saying, "All the people of my town know that you are a woman of noble character" (3:11).

## A Mother's Wise Words

Proverbs 31 begins with King Lemuel's mother passing on life skills to him. The chapter consists of two poems, the first of which teaches him his responsibilities as king. Many of the values in this poem apply to every leadership position.

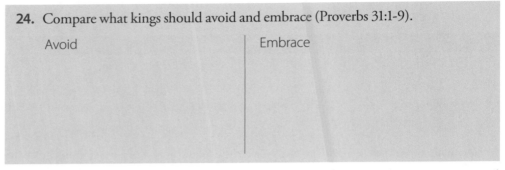

24. Compare what kings should avoid and embrace (Proverbs 31:1-9).

| Avoid | Embrace |
|---|---|
|  |  |

With power comes privileges, so the queen mother warns her son to beware women and wine. The *women* she means are *those who ruin kings*, not a godly wife. She teaches him not to *drink wine* or *crave beer* while holding court lest he *deprive* the *oppressed of their rights.* She commends giving wine and beer, though, to those who suffer physical and mental *anguish.* (I got a dental crown recently, and I thanked God for the anesthetic that kept the procedure mostly painless!) Finally, this mom reminds Lemuel of his duty as king to help those without a voice, the *destitute*, and the *poor and needy.*

While we may never rule a country, from this mother's words we can take that we should pursue justice over pleasure, avoid intoxicating substances while making important decisions, and help those in need.

## A Portrait of a Noble Wife

Now we come to the inspiring final poem of Proverbs. Here we see wisdom embodied in a noble wife. Whether or not we're married, the poem helps us see wisdom in action. While Lady Wisdom and Woman Folly in the prologue called to youths in the streets, the noble wife in the epilogue busily builds her house.

It's unclear whether Lemuel's mother taught him this poem too. If she did, she may have wanted to help him select a suitable wife. Or she may have hoped to guide her future daughter-in-law. But its inclusion in Proverbs has inspired generations of women to embrace the noble task of building a godly home. It's also an example of industriousness for all men and women.

Proverbs 31:10-31 is an acrostic poem, meaning the first poetic line starts with the first letter of the Hebrew alphabet, the second poetic line with the second letter, and so on through the end of the alphabet. It's like saying everything from A to Z is here. Acrostics made poetry easier to memorize.

### *Her Worth*

The poem begins by describing how valuable a noble woman is to a home.

25. Read Proverbs 31:10-12. (a) What is the noble wife worth (10)? (b) What does her husband have in her (11)? (c) What does she bring him (12)?

Gem-quality *rubies* are rarer than diamonds. She has earned her husband's *full confidence*, especially in her handling of money where he *lacks nothing of value*. Verse 12 is a great goal to have for all relationships but especially for spouses.

### Her Actions

The noble wife is not the idle gossiper we read about in chapter 9. Rather, she fills her time with profitable pursuits. As you read all she accomplishes, though, keep in mind that this household has servants to help with the work.

> 26. ♥ Read Proverbs 31:13-27. (a) Which of her tasks (spinning, gathering and providing food, gardening, earning, trading, weaving, helping, sewing, creating products to sell, teaching, running a large household) do you most enjoy doing yourself? (b) What is her character like (20, 25-27)? (c) Which of her attributes would you like to imitate more?

She spins *wool and flax* with a *distaff* and a *spindle* to make woolen and *linen* yarns suitable for winter and summer clothes. She shops for *food*. She doesn't wait for servants to feed her in bed but instead rises early and *provides food* for family and *servants*. What's more, *she plants a vineyard*, which could bring both nourishment and income. Her *trading* (or merchandise) *is profitable*, and she can work into the *night*.

The noble wife's generosity pours out to *the poor* and *needy*. She has *clothed* her family appropriately for the seasons (the word usually translated *scarlet* could be translated "two cloaks" or "double garment"[14]). She makes *bed coverings* and dresses well (*purple* suggests wealth). *Her husband* is a leader in the community, implying her skills contribute to the respect he garners. She's a seamstress as well, sewing *linen garments* and *sashes* not just for her family but also to sell.

But this women is *clothed* not just with fine clothing but *with strength and dignity* so that she does not fear *the days to come*. To her family, servants, and community, her words are wise and kind (*faithful instruction* is literally "law of kindness"[15]). She supervises *her household* and does not partake *of idleness*.

> 27. ♥ Which aspect of the noble wife most inspires you? Why?

In this lesson, we discovered how to be a noble woman. We read a wise mother's advice to her son and encountered a portrait of a noble wife. Our next lesson reveals how others praise the noble woman and how that relates to our spiritual lives.

----------------------------

The noble wife is not the idle gossiper we read about in chapter 9. Rather, she fills her time with profitable pursuits.

----------------------------

## In Praise of the Noble Woman

This industrious and godly woman we started to read about in the last lesson garners much praise.

> **28.** Read Proverbs 31:28-29. (a) Who praises the noble wife (28)? (b) What is their praise (29)?

The poem next explains the reasons for what it does and doesn't praise.

> **29.** Fill in the blanks from Proverbs 31:30.
>
> Charm is _____ .
> Beauty is _____ .
> A woman who fears the LORD is _____ .

External goodness or looks can be fake or fading, but internal godliness is truly worth praising. That she *fears the Lord* links back to Proverbs 1:7 in the prologue: "The fear of the Lord is the beginning of knowledge."

> **30.** Read Proverbs 31:31. (a) For what should the noble wife be honored? (b) What brings her praise?

The noble wife's actions merit *honor*, and her actions *bring her praise*. She is not a mere appendage of her husband but does good in her own right.

The Bible describes Christians as the bride of Christ (Revelation 21:2). This final verse of Proverbs is a type of what is to come when Jesus returns: "He will bring to light what is hidden in darkness and will expose the motives of the heart. At that time each will receive their praise from God" (1 Corinthians 4:5).

Indeed, here are Jesus's words to us: "Look, I am coming soon! My reward is with me, and I will give to each person according to what they have done" (Revelation 22:12). Just as the noble wife's works brought her husband's praise, so will our works bring us our heavenly Husband's praise.

In this lesson, we saw that a woman who fears the Lord is to be praised. We also discovered that this foreshadows the praise we'll receive when Jesus returns and we meet him as his bride.

---

External goodness or looks can be fake or fading, but internal godliness is truly worth praising.

---

## Wisdom's Worth

**31.** ❤ In what way did you apply wisdom from Proverbs to your life this week?

In this chapter, we looked at how to love neighbors, the blessings of good friends, the sorrows and joys of family, how to build a home, and how to be a noble woman.

We've now come to the end of our journey together. In this creative devotional study experience, we've discovered how to pursue wisdom and embrace sexual purity. We've seen why godly wisdom surpasses worldly wisdom, learned how the simple can grow wise, and figured out what godly character looks like. We've found the keys to strength in adversity and wisdom in finances. We pondered wisdom in all aspects of life and considered how to speak healing words. Now we've explored how to use wisdom to improve our relationships.

**32.** ❤ Glance back at your last answer in each chapter. Explain how Proverbs has helped you grow in wisdom the most.

**33.** ❤ Write a prayer thanking God for answering a request about community, friends, or family, or for how you've grown in wisdom. *Optional:* Form it into a praise psalm (see instructions at the end of Day 1).

### *Wisdom Worship*

Find a quiet place and prepare your heart for grateful worship.

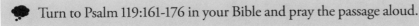 Turn to Psalm 119:161-176 in your Bible and pray the passage aloud.

May the Lord bless you with abundant wisdom in every area of your life.

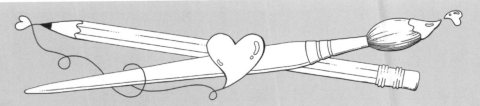

## Karla's Creative Connection

*Charm is deceptive, and beauty is fleeting; but a woman who fears the LORD is to be praised.*

Proverbs 31:30

I still remember sitting in front of the mirror, sucking in my round cheeks, giving my 13-year-old self the illusion of a thinner face with high cheekbones. Oh, to be like my older sister. She was the pretty one. I was the homely, pathetic one—or at least that's what my mother told me. She obviously didn't know or understand how her words and actions would take root in my young heart and impact how I saw myself and believed others saw me.

We live in a world that places the utmost value on our outer appearance—a culture where being beautiful and charming gets the compliments, wins awards, and earns magazine covers. So we buy the clothes and the anti-aging creams. We apply the makeup and color our hair. We go to great lengths to make ourselves beautiful. But this week's key verse reminds us of a truth we already know: Beauty is fleeting. Clothes go out of style. Our skin still wrinkles and sags. Makeup washes off, and our hair still grows gray. No matter how much time and money we spend on making ourselves look good, our outward beauty will fade and never truly satisfy our soul.

The true beauty we long for comes from within and is ultimately found in our relationship with the Lord. That's why this week's verse goes on to say, "A woman who fears the LORD is to be praised." To fear the Lord is to know him, love him, and trust him with your life. It's also about knowing who you are in him—created in his image, chosen to be his child, and beautiful in his eyes.

I was still a new believer when I read 1 Samuel 16:7: "People look at the outward appearance, but the LORD looks at the heart." I could imagine God was smiling when he looked at my heart, because I had asked Jesus to come into my life and make his home there. As I continued to study the Bible, the truths of how God sees me and who he says I am began to replace the lies I grew up with. My life was forever changed.

If you need to replace some lies you've been believing about yourself, spend some creative quiet time with God this week. Pray and ask the Lord to help you see yourself through his eyes and not your own. Look up Bible verses about who you are in Christ and meditate on them. And then rejoice in the knowledge that when God looks into your heart, he sees Jesus and the inner beauty that comes from knowing and walking with him—a beauty that will never fade.

*Karla*

# Appendix

## Creative Ideas

Engage with Scripture through the arts! Visit DiscoveringTheBibleSeries.com for info on items marked .

### Visual Arts Options

- Find techniques for expressing Scripture with art in Karla's Creative Connection offerings.
- Color the bookmarks at the start of each chapter and the full-page illustrations at the end of each chapter.
- Write a verse in calligraphy.
- Create an art journal: sketch, paint, and affix photos and words from magazines.
- ▆ Overlay a verse on top of a photograph.
- Create a diorama, sculpture, or piece of jewelry.
- Create fabric art using cross-stitch, embroidery, or appliqué.
- ▆ Scan a bookmark, use photo editing software to color it, and then print it on printable fabric to use as is or to embroider.
- Create greeting cards or T-shirts to encourage others.
- ▆ In a journaling Bible, choose one Proverbs verse to illuminate in the wide margin.

### Performing Arts Options

- ▆ Find a musical version of a Proverbs passage to play or sing.
- Act out a Proverbs passage as you read or recite it aloud to music (spoken Word poetry).
- Write music and lyrics based on a Proverbs passage.

### Literary Arts Options

- Form a Proverbs passage's message into a poem of any type you like.
- Write an encouraging letter to someone based on a Proverbs verse.

### Culinary Arts Options

- Celebrate a Christian holiday with a feast where you talk about the meaning of the holiday.
- Celebrate answered prayer with a meal where you publicly give God thanks.

### Sharing Options

- Share your creations with your small group.
- ▆ Post recordings, writings, and pictures in the Facebook group "Discovering Wisdom in Proverbs."
- Also share on Facebook, Instagram, and Twitter with #DiscoveringWisdomInProverbs.

# Notes

## Chapter 1—Proverbs 1:1–3:35: The First Step to Wisdom

1. Aesop, "The Fox & the Grapes," https://read.gov/aesop/005.html (accessed 9/27/22).

2. Aesop, "The Hare & the Tortoise," https://read.gov/aesop/025.html (accessed 9/27/22).

3. Matthew 15:6.

4. Mary Oliver, *A Poetry Handbook: A Prose Guide to Understanding and Writing Poetry* (New York: Harcourt, 1994), 37, 59.

5. Adapted from D.A. Carson, ed., *NIV Zondervan Study Bible* (Grand Rapids: Zondervan, 2015), 1,193.

6. Word studies through Bible Hub Lexicon.

7. Adapted from Pam Farrel, *7 Simple Skills for Every Woman* (Eugene: Harvest House, 2015), 76-77.

8. Farrel, *7 Simple Skills for Every Woman*, 77.

9. Mary A. Kassian, *The Right Kind of Confident: The Remarkable Grit of a God-Fearing Woman* (Nashville: Thomas Nelson, 2021), 70.

10. Luke 12:5; 1 Peter 2:16-17.

11. C.S. Lewis, *The Lion, the Witch and the Wardrobe*, first Collier Books ed. (New York: Collier Books, 1970), 76.

12. Luke 1:50; Acts 10:35.

13. Bruce K. Waltke, *The Book of Proverbs*, ed. Robert L. Hubbard, Jr.. The New International Commentary on the Old Testament, 2 vols (Grand Rapids: Eerdmans, 2004-2005), 1:63.

14. Duane A. Garrett, *Proverbs, Ecclesiastes, Song of Songs,* New American Commentary (Nashville: Broadman & Holman Publishers, 1993), 14:70.

15. Deuteronomy 18:10; Leviticus 20:2.

16. Leviticus 27:1-8.

17. Warren Baker and Eugene E. Carpenter in *The Complete Word Study Dictionary: Old Testament* (Chattanooga: AMG Publishers, 2003), s.v. 113 *'ādôn*, 136 *ădōnāy*, 430 *ĕlōhiym*, 3,068 *yhōwāh*, 3,069 *yhōwih*.

18. Leviticus 20:10; Deuteronomy 22:22.

19. Revelation 20:11–21:4.

20. Ephesians 4:26.

21. Mark Twain's letter to his wife, Olivia Clemens, 7/17/1889.

22. Leviticus 23:9-14.

23. Leviticus 23:15-22.

24. Acts 2:1-4.

25. Leviticus 23:9-14.

26. Allen P. Ross, *The Expositor's Bible Commentary: Proverbs – Isaiah*, eds. Tremper Longman III and David E. Garland (Grand Rapids: Zondervan, 2008), 6:32.

## Chapter 2—Proverbs 4:1–6:35: Sexual Sanity

1. I've changed names and some details.

2. D. Partner, "Paul, the Apostle (Saul of Tarsus)," in *Who's Who in Christian History*, ed. J.D. Douglas and Philip W. Comfort (Wheaton: Tyndale House, 1992), 536.

3. Carson, *Study Bible*, s.v. "Matthew 5:31."

4. Adapted from Farrel, *Simple Skills*, 117.

5. Adapted from Pam and Bill Farrel, *Red-Hot Romance Tips for Women* (Eugene: Harvest House, 2014), 55.

6. *7 Simple Skills for Every Woman* seminar by Pam Farrel.

7. Adapted from Bill and Pam Farrel, *Love to Love You: Creating Romantic Moments Together* (Eugene: Harvest House, 1997), 12-13.

8. "Let Me Be Your Mirror" song by Boomer and Lisa Rieff (written for Bill and Pam's 25th wedding anniversary). "Mirror" song written by Rebecca Friedlander after hearing Bill and Pam's love story.

9. The last four chapters of 2 Samuel are arranged topically, not chronologically, so 2 Samuel 21:15-17 may explain his lingering behind in 2 Samuel 11. As to David's age, he was 30 when he became king (2 Samuel 5:4) and his son Amnon was born during the seven years he ruled in Hebron (2 Samuel 3:2). Not long after David's adultery was exposed, Amnon raped his sister. If Amnon was 20, David was between 50 and 56.

10. 2 Samuel 18:33.

11. Hillary Morgan Ferrer with Amy Davison, *Mama Bear Apologetics Guide to Sexuality* (Eugene: Harvest House, 2021), 150-51.

12. 2 Samuel 11:3 compared with 23:34.

13. David A. Hubbard, *The Preacher's Commentary: Proverbs*, gen. ed. Lloyd J. Ogilvie (Nashville: Thomas Nelson, 1989), 15:94.

14. C.S. Lewis, *The Screwtape Letters* (New York: Macmillan, 1961), 49.

15. Waltke, 1:335.

16. Waltke, 1:331-32.

17. Parent PLUS loans are not based on a family's ability to pay. If parents receive a forbearance, the interest that accrues is added to the principal balance. Tara Siegel Bernard, "A Federal College Loan Program Can Trap Parents in Debt," *New York Times*, updated 9/10/2021, https://www.nytimes.com/2021/06/06/your-money/parent-plus-loans-debt.html#:~:text=A%20Federal%20College%20Loan%20Program%20Can%20Trap%20Parents,PLUS%20loans%20to%20finance%20their%20daughters%E2%80%99%20college%20educations (accessed 10/12/2022); https://nytimes.com/2021/06/08/business/they-wanted-to-help-their-college-age-children-but-wound-up-buried-in-debt.html (accessed 11/15/21).

18. "What's the 'Billy Graham Rule'?" Billy Graham Evangelistic Association, https://billygraham.org/story/the-modesto-manifesto-a-declaration-of-biblical-integrity/ (accessed 5/17/22).

19. Wendy Wang, "Who Cheats More? The Demographics of Infidelity in America," Institute for Family Studies, 1/10/18, ifstudies.org/blog/who-cheats-more-the-demographics-of-cheating-in-america (accessed 5/19/22).

20. Darlene Schacht, *Messy Beautiful Love: Hope and Redemption for Real-Life Marriages* (Nashville: Thomas Nelson, 2014), 6, Kindle.

## Chapter 3—Proverbs 7:1–9:18: Three Calls

1. Homer, *The Odyssey*, trans. Emily Wilson (New York: W. W. Norton & Company, 2018), 302-3, Kindle.

2. Homer, *The Odyssey*, 307.

3. Ross, *Proverbs*, 91.

4. Adapted from Farrel, *7 Simple Skills*, 68-71.

5. Homer, 307.

6. Waltke, 1:371.

7. Waltke, 1:377.

8. If "dark of night" (verse 9) means new moon, then her husband will be gone for two weeks until the full moon (verse 20). Night travel was best during full moons.

9. Waltke, 1:379.

10. Clay Jones, *Immortal: How the Fear of Death Drives Us and What We Can Do About It* (Eugene: Harvest House, 2020), 197–98.

11. Padraic Colum, *The Golden Fleece: And the Heroes Who Lived Before Achilles* (Mineola: Dover Publications, 2018), 16, Kindle.

12. Colum, *The Golden Fleece*, 156-57.

13. Jones, *Immortal*, 198.

14. Waltke, 1:398.

15. Kassian, 73.

16. Ross, *Proverbs*, 96.

17. Waltke, 1:409.

18. Waltke, 1:416.

19. Waltke, 1:423.

20. Allen P. Ross, *A Commentary on the Psalms,* 3 vols. (Grand Rapids: Kregel, 2011–2016), 1:185.

21. Waltke, 1:429.

22. Ross, *Proverbs*, 103.

23. Waltke, 1:433.

24. Waltke, 1:434.

25. Ross, *Proverbs*, 103.

26. Ross, *Proverbs*, 105.

27. Kassian, 93-94.

28. Ross, *Proverbs*, 107.

29. Waltke, 1:446.

30. Ross, *Psalms*, 1:267n22.

31. Ross, *Proverbs*, 108.

32. Merriam-Webster.com, https://www.merriam-webster.com/dictionary, s.v. "sacred" (accessed 10/12/22).

## Chapter 4—Proverbs 10:1–12:28: The Wise, the Simple, and the Fool

1. Adapted from Farrel, *7 Simple Skills*, 110.

2. Adapted from Farrel, *7 Simple Skills*, 105-7.

3. Revelation 21:21.

4. "Adolescent Drug Overdose Deaths Rose Exponentially for the First Time in History Due to the COVID Pandemic," UCLA Health, 4/12/22, https://www.uclahealth.org/news/adolescent-drug-overdose-deaths-rose-exponentially-first (accessed 7/16/2022).

5. Ross, *Proverbs*, 180.

6. Waltke, 2:352.

7. Hubbard, 15:144.

8. Hubbard, 15:202.

9. Hubbard, 15:369.

10. Hubbard, 15:293.

11. Ross, *Proverbs*, 145.

12. Revelation 20:14-15.

13. Genesis 3:22-24.

14. Exodus 26:31, 33.

15. Matthew 27:51.

16. Revelation 21:1.

17. Revelation 21:27.

18. Revelation 21:18-21.

## Chapter 5—Proverbs 13:1–15:33: Walk This Way!

1. Ross, *Psalms*, 1:185-86.

2. Ross, *Psalms*, 1:193-94.

3. Romans 3:20.

4. Psalm 94:12; John 14:21; Philippians 2:13; Hebrews 12:11; 1 John 3:10.

5. Philippians 1:6.

6. Numbers 16:32; Romans 2:5.

7. Hubbard, 15:145.

8. Shepherd's Press blog, "Apples of Gold, Settings of Silver." Published July 13, 2020, https://www.shepherdpress.com/apples-of-gold-settings-of-silver/.

9. Adapted from *The Marriage Code* by Bill and Pam Farrel, (Eugene: Harvest House, 2009), 216-17.

10. Adapted from *Red-Hot Romance Tips for Women* by Bill and Pam Farrel (Eugene: Harvest House, 2014), 27.

11. Those who think all people (including themselves) are basically good often don't understand why Jesus had to die. That eventually can lead to loss of faith.

12. Clay Jones, "Original Sin: Its Importance and Fairness," *Christian Research Journal* 34:6 (2011). A copy of the article can be found here: http://www.equip.org/article/original-sin-its-importance-and-fairness/#christian-books-3.

13. Ross, *Proverbs*, 151.

14. Ross, *Proverbs,* 151.

15. Matthew 6:14; 18:33; Luke 6:35.

16. Ross, *Proverbs*, 139.

17. Hubbard, 15:299.

18. Revelation 20:11-15.

19. Thaddeus J. Williams, *Confronting Injustice Without Compromising Truth: 12 Questions Christians Should Ask About Social Justice* (Grand Rapids: Zondervan Academic, 2020), 70, Kindle.

20. Hubbard, 15:455.

21. Ross, *Proverbs*, 122.

22. Ross, *Proverbs*, 127.

23. Hubbard, 15:337-38.

24. George M. Schwab, "The Book of Proverbs," in *Cornerstone Biblical Commentary, Vol 7: The Book of Psalms, The Book of Proverbs* (Carol Stream: Tyndale House Publishers, 2009), 587.

25. Williams, 63.

26. Kassian, 150-51.

27. Ross, *Proverbs*, 122.

28. Jones, *Immortal*, 204.

29. Revelation 21:4, 27; 22:2.

## Chapter 6—Proverbs 16:1–18:24: The Keys to Strength in Adversity

1. Hubbard, 15:202.

2. Adapted from Pam Farrel, *Becoming a Brave New Woman* (Eugene: Harvest House, 2012), 57-58.

3. Williams, 45.

4. Ross, *Proverbs*, 144-45.

5. Hubbard, 15:244-45.

6. Hubbard, 15:204.

7. Ross, *Proverbs*, 118.

8. Kassian, 155.

9. Ross, *Proverbs*, 192.

10. Williams, 45-46.

11. Hubbard, 15:208-9.

12. Ross, *Proverbs*, 163.

13. Ross, *Proverbs*, 140.

14. Hubbard, 15:245.

15. As quoted in the U.S. Navy's *Chips Ahoy* magazine (July 1986), Source: https://quotepark.com/quotes/1899187-grace-hopper-its-easier-to-ask-forgiveness-than-it-is-to-get-p/ (accessed 6/13/22).

16. Nathan Isaacs, "Urim and Thummim," in *The International Standard Bible Encyclopedia*, ed. James Orr et al. (Chicago: The Howard-Severance Company, 1915), s.v. "Urim and Thummim."

17. Ross, *Proverbs*, 145.

18. Millard J. Erickson, *Introducing Christian Doctrine*, ed. L. Arnold Hustad (Grand Rapids: Baker, 1992), 85-86.

19. Erickson, 85.

20. Williams, 119-20.

21. Williams, 44-5. Quotes Romans 3:23.

22. Waltke, 1:105.

23. Ross, *Proverbs*, 208.

## Chapter 7—Proverbs 19:1–22:16: Money Matters

1. Hubbard, 15:255.

2. Adapted from a blog post by Bill and Pam Farrel on *Love-Wise* Dec 2017 (and in column by Bill and Pam Farrel in *Just Between Us Magazine*), https://www.love-wise.com/his-and-hers-financial-styles-from-just-between-us-ministry-magazine/. Longer versions of *Financial Personalities* appear in *The Marriage Code*, by Pam and Bill Farrel (Eugene: Harvest House, 2009), 151-62.

3. Natasha Crain, *Faithfully Different: Regaining Biblical Clarity in a Secular Culture* (Eugene: Harvest House, 2022), 52.

4. Merriam-Webster.com, https://www.merriam-webster.com/dictionary, s.v. "security" (accessed 2/16/22).

5. Merriam-Webster.com, s.v. "surety" (accessed 2/16/22).

6. Donna Rosato, "How Much Should Parents Borrow for Their Kid's College?," *Consumer Reports*, https://www.consumerreports.org/paying-for-college/how-much-should-parents-borrow-for-their-kids-college/ (accessed 5/17/19).

7. The word translated *hastily* in 13:11 could be translated "dishonest" (NIV) (Ross, *Proverbs*, 128). Verse 20:21 translates a different word *hastily*, one that can mean "obtain by greed." But there's a textual issue that causes some translators to read a similar Hebrew word that simply means "to be in haste." Warren Baker and Eugene E. Carpenter, in *The Complete Word Study Dictionary: Old Testament* (Chattanooga: AMG Publishers, 2003), s.v. "973."

8. Michelle Crouch, "13 Things Lotto Winners Won't Tell You: Life After Winning the Lottery," *Reader's Digest*, 1/4/2022, https://www.rd.com/list/13-things-lottery-winners/ (accessed 8/17/2022).

9. Currently, I use Quicken Home & Business.

10. Ross, *Psalms*, 3:557.

## Chapter 8—Proverbs 22:17–25:14: Assorted Words to the Wise

1. Hillary Morgan Ferrer, ed., *Mama Bear Apologetics: Empowering Your Kids to Challenge Cultural Lies* (Eugene: Harvest House, 2019), 50.

2. Ferrer, *Empowering*, 50.

3. Ferrer, *Empowering*, 53.

4. Carson, *Study Bible*, s.v. "Proverbs 24:23-34."

5. 1 Kings 4:32.

6. Adapted from Farrel, *7 Simple Skills*, 76, 81, 84-85.

7. During the divided kingdom, Israel had 20 rulers to Judah's 11.

8. J.I. Marais, "Heart," in *The International Standard Bible Encyclopedia*, ed. James Orr et al. (Chicago: The Howard-Severance Company, 1915), 1,351.

9. John Wesley, *An Earnest Appeal to Men of Reason and Religion*, as quoted in *The Works of the Rev. John Wesley*, vol. 8, (New York: J. J. Harper, 1827), 191. Emphasis in original.

10. "It" and "anxiety" (or "depression") are feminine, while "heart" is masculine. Hubbard, 15:227.

11. Ross, *Proverbs*, 219-20.

12. Ross, *Psalms*, 1:267n22.

13. Unknown, *Times of London*, October 9, 1858, as quoted in Arthur

Schopenhauer, *Parerga and Paralipomena: Short Philosophical Essays*, vol. 2, trans. E.F.J. Payne (Oxford: Clarendon, 1974), 216.

14. Ross, *Proverbs*, 209.

15. Hubbard, 15:207.

16. Ross, *Proverbs*, 118.

17. Waltke, 2:465n89.

18. See 2 Peter 2:12 and Jude 10.

19. Waltke, 2:469.

20. For example, Matthew 2:15 says Jesus fulfills "what the Lord had said through the prophet: 'Out of Egypt I called my son.'" Matthew quotes Hosea 11:1, which reads, "When Israel was a child, I loved him, and out of Egypt I called my son." In another example, Hebrews 11:1 applies 2 Samuel 7:14 to Jesus, which was initially about Solomon: "I will be to him a father, and he shall be to me a son."

21. Waltke, 2:473.

22. Waltke, 2:473-74.

## Chapter 9—Proverbs 25:15–28:28: Words That Harm and Words That Heal

1. Adapted from a story in *The Marriage Code* by Bill and Pam Farrel (Eugene: Harvest House, 2009), 242-43.

2. Adapted from a story in *A Couple's Journey with God*, by Bill and Pam Farrel (Eugene: Harvest House, 2012), 233.

3. Burt Helm, "Pizzagate Nearly Destroyed My Restaurant. Then My Customers Helped Me Fight Back," *Inc.*, 7/2017, https://www.inc.com/magazine/201707/burt-helm/how-i-did-it-james-alefantis-comet-ping-pong.html, (accessed 3/23/2022). For more on this, see Josh Mitchell and Daniel Nasaw, "Man Arrested With Gun at Comet Ping Pong, Washington Eatery Subject of Fake News Hoax," *Wall Street Journal*, 12/4/16, https://www.wsj.com/articles/BL-WB-66873 (accessed 4/12/22).

4. John 8:31-32.

5. Ferrer, *Empowering*, 53-54.

6. Merriam-Webster.com, s.v. "gossip" (accessed 4/4/2022).

7. Merriam-Webster.com, s.v. "slander" (accessed 4/4/2022).

8. Proverbs 10:18.

9. For example, in 2012, then-U.S. senator Harry Reid accused U.S. presidential candidate Mitt Romney of not having paid taxes for a decade. Romney later released his previous two years of tax returns, proving Reid wrong. After the election, a reporter asked Reid why he continued to allege a falsehood. Reid replied, "Romney didn't win, did he?" Chris Cillizza, "Harry Reid lied about Mitt Romney's taxes. He's still not sorry." *The Washington Post*, 9/15/2016, https://www.washingtonpost.com/news/the-fix/wp/2016/09/15/harry-reid-lied-about-mitt-romneys-taxes-hes-still-not-sorry/ (accessed 3/24/2022).

10. 1 Timothy 5:13 (ESV).

11. Merriam-Webster.com, s.v. "argue" (accessed 3/29/2022).

12. Merriam-Webster.com, s.v. "quarrelsome" (accessed 3/29/2022).

13. Merriam-Webster.com, s.v. "ad hominem" (accessed 3/29/2022).

14. Ross, *Proverbs*, 157.

15. Hubbard, 15:276.

16. Hubbard, 15:220-21.

17. ESV.

18. Hubbard, 15:229.

## Chapter 10—Proverbs 29:1–31:31: Neighbors, Friends, and Family

1. "5 Ways Men Can Support Pregnancy Centers," https://www.caringnetwork.com/news/5-ways-men-can-support-pregnancy-centers#:~:text=How%20Can%20Men%20Support%20Pregnancy%20Centers

%3F%201%20Start,Become%20known%20as%20an%20advocate%20for%20life.%20.

2. Waltke, 2:456n10.

3. Adapted from Pam Farrel, Jean E. Jones, and Karla Dornacher, *Discovering Hope in the Psalms: A Creative Bible Study Experience* (Eugene: Harvest House, 2017), 192.

4. From live mentoring call with Gorman Leadership: *Married for a Purpose*, https://www.gormanleadership.com/.

5. Adapted from *Get It Done, Girl!: Maximize Your Moments Action Planner* by Pam Farrel (Oxnard, CA: Love-Wise Publishing, 2019), 8.

6. Adapted from Pam Farrel, *Get It Done, Girl* (Oxnard, CA: Love-Wise Publishers, 2019), 10-14.

7. Matthew 26:48-49.

8. Exodus 21:17 said they should be put to death. However, Ross notes that "in practice this curse may have been a social punishment only, i.e., the curser of parents being considered by others as dead." Ross, *Proverbs*, 177.

9. Hubbard, 15:310.

10. 2 Kings 23:25, 31-37.

11. Ross, *Proverbs*, 189. Quoting Ralbag, as cited in Julius Hillel Greenstone, *Proverbs: With Commentary*, (United States: Jewish Publication Society of America, 1950), 234.

12. 2 Kings 4:10.

13. Hubbard, 15:438.

14. Ross, *Proverbs*, 249.

15. Ross, *Proverbs*, 250.

## Acknowledgments

### All of Us

To our *Discovering Jesus in the Old Testament, Discovering Hope in the Psalms, Discovering Joy in Philippians*, and *Discovering Good News in John* readers, thank you for being our traveling companions on this creative devotional study journey. Without you, this project would never have come to fruition. To Hope Lyda, our editor, we are grateful for your patience, insights, and encouragement. To Bob Hawkins, Kathleen Kerr, Kari Duffy, and the rest of the Harvest House team, thank you for taking on this project and embracing the vision. To Jean Kavich Bloom, our copy editor, we're blessed by your keen eye and fine attention to detail. Janelle Coury, thank you for the gorgeous interior. To our endorsers, VIP influencers, and launch team, thanks for investing your gift of time in these Bible studies.

### Pam Farrel

A heartfelt thank you to my amazing husband, Bill—for balancing caregiving your parents, coaching people and teaming for our Love-Wise ministry, and being my sounding board, resident theologian, and in-house tech wonder! To Robin and Penny, thanks for being my Aaron and Hur. Your prayers carry me. To Jan, thank you for being a wonderful mix of creative wonder, techie whiz, fabulous assistant, and gracious friend. To our Love-Wise Membership Community, thanks for being the wind beneath our wings. To all the precious women who have been in my *Discovering the Bible* Zoom face-to-face Bible studies—you are life givers to me. To Jean, your rich Bible teaching helps me become a better believer. To Karla, your art inspires my soul and is a sanity-saver in these days of negative headlines. To Jesus, thank you for being the great "I Am." All I'll ever need is met in who you are!

### Jean E. Jones

To Clay, thank you for reading the manuscript, offering insights, taking over chores so I can write, and being a wonderful and amazing husband. To Angie Wright, Jean Strand, Virginia Thompson, and Shawna Stevens, you timed the lessons and gave valuable feedback. Thank you! To Pam Farrel, thank you for your inspiring devotionals, marketing enthusiasm, and lasting friendship. Your smile warms my heart. To Karla Dornacher, your art continues to inspire and amaze me, and I'm grateful you're part of this team. To our Lord Jesus Christ, thank you for revealing wisdom in the pages of Proverbs that has helped me grow in you. Thank you for dying and rising that we might have eternal life with you. To all our readers, thank you for your kind support, without which these books wouldn't exist.

### Karla Dornacher

Thank you first and foremost to Jesus. You have been my best friend, comforter, and encourager through the last two years of learning to live a widow's life. Without you, I would not have been able to do any of this. Thank you! To my family, your faith in me has been extraordinary, and your love and kindness have been beyond measure. You are more than I deserve. To my online community, you have no idea how much you mean to me. Your love and support blow me away. And to my coauthors, Jean and Pam, your patience with me and your passion for God's Word humbles me and encourages me to never give up. Thank you!

## Pam Farrel

Pam Farrel is an international speaker and author or coauthor of more than 50 books, including *7 Simple Skills for Every Woman* and the bestselling *Men Are Like Waffles, Women Are Like Spaghetti* (more than 350,000 copies sold). Pam has loved studying and teaching the Bible for over 40 years and is wife to Bill Farrel. Together they enrich relationships through their ministry, Love-Wise. She and her husband enjoy the beach near their home, living on a live-aboard boat, and often making family memories with their three sons, three daughters-in-law, and seven grandchildren.

Love-Wise.com | Twitter: @pamfarrel |Facebook: billandpamfarrel & Creative Biblical Expressions

## Jean E. Jones

Jean E. Jones started teaching the Bible in high school and has served on women's ministry leadership teams for 20 years. She enjoys writing Bible study guides that help people put God's words into actions. With Pam and Karla, she's written five volumes in the Discovering the Bible series of creative devotional experiences, including *Discovering Good News in John*. Jean has written for Crosswalk.com, *Today's Christian Woman,* and *Home Life*. She is a member of Women in Apologetics. Her husband, Dr. Clay Jones, is a visiting scholar at Talbot School of Theology.

JeanEJones.net | Twitter: @JeanEstherJones | Facebook: JeanEJonesAuthor | YouTube: JeanEJones

## Karla Dornacher

Karla Dornacher is a storyteller at heart with a passion to inspire and encourage other women through her art and creativity. She has written and illustrated more than 20 books, licensed her art for use on numerous gift and home decor products, and self-published several Christian coloring books for adults. Karla also offers a variety of Scripture art prints and digital ministry resources online through her website and Etsy shop. Karla is presently learning to embrace her new life as a widow after 50 years of marriage to her late husband, Michael, and is looking forward to whatever God has planned for her in the days ahead.

karladornacher.com | Facebook: karladornacher

WHOEVER IS PATIENT HAS GREAT UNDERSTANDING, BUT ONE WHO IS QUICK-TEMPERED DISPLAYS FOLLY. PROVERBS 14:29

WHOEVER LOVES DISCIPLINE LOVES KNOWLEDGE, BUT WHOEVER HATES CORRECTION IS STUPID. PROVERBS 12:1

PROVERBS 12:1
TRUST AND OBEY
CORRECTION
DISCIPLINE
WISDOM

THE FEAR OF THE LORD IS THE BEGINNING OF WISDOM, AND KNOWLEDGE OF THE HOLY ONE IS UNDERSTANDING. PROVERBS 9:10

FOR YOUR WAYS ARE IN FULL VIEW OF THE LORD, AND HE EXAMINES ALL YOUR PATHS. PROVERBS 5:21

TRUST IN THE LORD WITH ALL YOUR HEART AND LEAN NOT ON YOUR OWN UNDERSTANDING; IN ALL YOUR WAYS SUBMIT TO HIM, AND HE WILL MAKE YOUR PATHS STRAIGHT. PROVERBS 3:5-6